NO FEAR SHAKESPEARE

NO FEAR SHAKESPEARE

Antony and Cleopatra
As You Like It
The Comedy of Errors
Hamlet
Henry IV, Parts One and Two
Henry V
Julius Caesar
King Lear
Macbeth
The Merchant of Venice
A Midsummer Night's Dream
Much Ado About Nothing
Othello
Richard III
Romeo and Juliet
Sonnets
The Taming of the Shrew
The Tempest
Twelfth Night

NO FEAR SHAKESPEARE

HAMLET

SPARK NOTES

Spark Publishing
A Division of Barnes & Noble, Inc.
120 Fifth Avenue
New York, NY 10011
www.sparknotes.com

Please submit all comments and questions or report errors to www.sparknotes.com/errors

Library of Congress Cataloging-in-Publication Data

Shakespeare, William, 1564–1616.
  Hamlet / edited by John Crowther.
    p. cm.—(No fear Shakespeare)
  Summary: Presents the original text of Shakespeare's play side by side with a modern version, with marginal notes and explanations and full descriptions of each character.
  ISBN: 1-58663-844-0 (pbk.) ISBN: 1-41140-042-9 (hc.)
1. Hamlet (Legendary character)—Drama. 2. Murder victims' families—Drama. 3. Fathers—Death—Drama. 4. Princes—Drama. 5. Revenge—Drama. 6. Denmark—Drama. [1. Shakespeare, William, 1564–1616. Hamlet. 2. Plays. 3. English literature—History and criticism.]
I. Crowther, John (John C.) II. Title.
PR2807 .A25 2003
822.3'3—dc21
                        2003004283

Printed and bound in the United States of America

50 49

There's matter in these sighs, these profound heaves.
You must translate: 'tis fit we understand them.

(Hamlet, 4.1.1–2)

FEAR NOT.

Have you ever found yourself looking at a Shakespeare play, then down at the footnotes, then back at the play, and still not understanding? You know what the individual words mean, but they don't add up. SparkNotes' *No Fear Shakespeare* will help you break through all that. Put the pieces together with our easy-to-read translations. Soon you'll be reading Shakespeare's own words fearlessly—and actually enjoying it.

No Fear Shakespeare puts Shakespeare's language side-by-side with a facing-page translation into modern English—the kind of English people actually speak today. When Shakespeare's words make your head spin, our translation will help you sort out what's happening, who's saying what, and why.

HAMLET

Characters ix

ACT ONE

Scene 1 2
Scene 2 18
Scene 3 40
Scene 4 50
Scene 5 60

ACT TWO

Scene 1 76
Scene 2 86

ACT THREE

Scene 1 134
Scene 2 150
Scene 3 186
Scene 4 194

ACT FOUR

Scene 1 212
Scene 2 216
Scene 3 220
Scene 4 228
Scene 5 234
Scene 6 254
Scene 7 258

ACT FIVE

Scene 1 274
Scene 2 300

CHARACTERS

Hamlet—The prince of Denmark, and a student at the University of Wittenberg. At the beginning of the play, Hamlet's father, King Hamlet, has recently died, and his mother, Queen Gertrude, has married the new king, Hamlet's uncle Claudius. Hamlet is melancholy, bitter, and cynical, full of hatred for his uncle and disgust at his mother for marrying him. When the ghost of Hamlet's father appears and claims to have been murdered by Claudius, Hamlet becomes obsessed with avenging his father's death but keeps thinking of reasons why he should wait before killing Claudius—then chastizes himself for failing to act boldly. Hamlet is a character of contradictions. He admires characters like Fortinbras and the Player King, who behave passionately and even violently for no good reason, but is himself thoughtful, reflective, and philosophical. At times Hamlet is indecisive and hesitant, but at other times he is prone to rash and impulsive acts of violence.

Claudius—The king of Denmark, Hamlet's uncle. The villain of the play, Claudius is a calculating, ambitious politician, adept at manipulating others for his own ends and willing to execute, assassinate, or murder to stay in power. He doesn't understand Hamlet or Hamlet's motives, but he is quick to perceive Hamlet as a threat and take decisive action against him. Claudius does occasionally show signs of remorse and human feeling—his affection for Gertrude, for instance, seems sincere.

Gertrude—The queen of Denmark, Hamlet's mother, recently married to Claudius. We never get to observe Gertrude on her own, so we know much more about how Hamlet feels about her than about how she sees herself. She seems clearly to love Hamlet, but Hamlet sees her as a weak, even depraved, woman motivated wholly by lust. Hamlet has such strong feelings about her sex life that he becomes momentarily distracted from his revenge quest, urging her toward a life of chastity.

Polonius—The Lord Chamberlain of Claudius's court, and the father of Laertes and Ophelia. Polonius has good intentions, but he tends to be somewhat conniving and underhanded. He frequently leaps to the wrong conclusions, and his speeches are comically pompous and long-winded. He is completely incapable of figuring out what Hamlet is up to.

Horatio—Hamlet's close friend, who studied with the prince at the University of Wittenberg. Hamlet trusts Horatio above any of the other characters, valuing him for his even temper and equanimity—qualities that Hamlet seems to despise in himself. Horatio is loyal and helpful to Hamlet throughout the play. After Hamlet's death, Horatio remains alive to tell Hamlet's story.

Ophelia—Polonius's daughter, a beautiful young woman with whom Hamlet has been in love. A sweet and innocent young girl, Ophelia dutifully strives to obey her father and her brother, Laertes, allowing Polonius to use her in his scheme to spy on Hamlet. When her father dies, her sanity unravels, and in her madness she paints a scathing picture of young men as sexually exploitative and unfaithful, and her mad speeches about flowers conceal implied condemnations of Claudius and Gertrude.

Laertes—Polonius's son and Ophelia's brother, a young man who spends much of the play in France. Passionate and quick to action, Laertes is a foil for the reflective and agonized Hamlet.

Fortinbras—The young prince of Norway, whose father the king (also named Fortinbras) was killed by Hamlet's father (also named Hamlet). Now Fortinbras wishes to attack Denmark to avenge his father's honor, making him another foil for Prince Hamlet. Hamlet admires Fortinbras for his willingness to fight for no good reason.

The Ghost—The specter of Hamlet's recently deceased father. The ghost, who claims to have been murdered by Claudius, calls upon Hamlet to avenge him. However, it is not entirely certain whether the ghost is what it appears to be. Hamlet speculates that the ghost might be a devil sent to deceive him and tempt him into murder, and the question of what the ghost is or where it comes from is never definitively resolved.

Rosencrantz and **Guildenstern**—Two slightly bumbling courtiers, former friends of Hamlet from Wittenberg, who are summoned by Claudius and Gertrude to discover the cause of Hamlet's strange behavior.

Osric—The foolish courtier who summons Hamlet to his duel with Laertes. His speeches are pretentious and difficult to understand.

Voltimand and **Cornelius**—Courtiers whom Claudius sends to Norway to persuade the king to prevent Fortinbras from attacking.

Marcellus and **Barnardo**—The officers who first see the ghost walking the ramparts of Elsinore and who summon Horatio to witness it. Marcellus is present when Hamlet first encounters the ghost.

Francisco—A soldier and guardsman at Elsinore.

Reynaldo—Polonius's servant, sent to France by Polonius to check up on and spy on Laertes.

HAMLET

ACT ONE
SCENE 1

Enter BARNARDO *and* FRANCISCO, *two sentinels*

BARNARDO
Who's there?

FRANCISCO
Nay, answer me. Stand and unfold yourself.

BARNARDO
Long live the king!

FRANCISCO
                    Barnardo?

BARNARDO
                                        He.

FRANCISCO
You come most carefully upon your hour.

BARNARDO
5   'Tis now struck twelve. Get thee to bed, Francisco.

FRANCISCO
For this relief much thanks. 'Tis bitter cold,
And I am sick at heart.

BARNARDO
                              Have you had quiet guard?

FRANCISCO
Not a mouse stirring.

BARNARDO
                              Well, good night.
If you do meet Horatio and Marcellus,
10   The rivals of my watch, bid them make haste.

FRANCISCO
I think I hear them.—Stand, ho! Who's there?

Enter HORATIO *and* MARCELLUS

ACT ONE
SCENE 1

BARNARDO *and* FRANCISCO, *two watchmen, enter.*

BARNARDO
Who's there?

FRANCISCO
No, who are *you?* Stop and identify yourself.

BARNARDO
Long live the king!

FRANCISCO
Is that Barnardo?

BARNARDO
Yes, it's me.

FRANCISCO
You've come right on time.

BARNARDO
The clock's just striking twelve. Go home to bed, Francisco.

FRANCISCO
Thanks for letting me go. It's bitterly cold out, and I'm depressed.

BARNARDO
Has it been a quiet night?

FRANCISCO
I haven't even heard a mouse squeak.

BARNARDO
Well, good night. If you happen to see Horatio and Marcellus, who are supposed to stand guard with me tonight, tell them to hurry.

FRANCISCO
I think I hear them. —Stop! Who's there?

MARCELLUS *and* HORATIO *enter.*

HORATIO
                                        Friends to this ground.

MARCELLUS
And liegemen to the Dane.

FRANCISCO
                                        Give you good night.

MARCELLUS
O, farewell, honest soldier. Who hath relieved you?

FRANCISCO
Barnardo has my place. Give you good night.
                                        Exit FRANCISCO

MARCELLUS
15   Holla, Barnardo.

BARNARDO
Say what, is Horatio there?

HORATIO
A piece of him.

BARNARDO
Welcome, Horatio.—Welcome, good Marcellus.

MARCELLUS
What, has this thing appeared again tonight?

BARNARDO
20   I have seen nothing.

MARCELLUS
Horatio says 'tis but our fantasy
And will not let belief take hold of him
Touching this dreaded sight twice seen of us.
Therefore I have entreated him along
25   With us to watch the minutes of this night,
That if again this apparition come
He may approve our eyes and speak to it.

HORATIO
Tush, tush, 'twill not appear.

HORATIO

Friends of this country.

MARCELLUS

And servants of the Danish king.

FRANCISCO

Good night to you both.

MARCELLUS

Good-bye. Who's taken over the watch for you?

FRANCISCO

Barnardo's taken my place. Good night.

FRANCISCO *exits.*

MARCELLUS

Hello, Barnardo.

BARNARDO

Hello. Is Horatio here too?

HORATIO

More or less.

BARNARDO

Welcome, Horatio. Welcome, Marcellus.

MARCELLUS

So, tell us, did you see that thing again tonight?

BARNARDO

I haven't seen anything.

MARCELLUS

Horatio says we're imagining it, and won't let himself
believe anything about this horrible thing that we've
seen twice now. That's why I've begged him to come
on our shift tonight, so that if the ghost appears he can
see what we see and speak to it.

HORATIO

Oh, nonsense. It's not going to appear.

BARNARDO
                       Sit down a while
And let us once again assail your ears,
30   That are so fortified against our story,
What we have two nights seen.

HORATIO
                        Well, sit we down,
And let us hear Barnardo speak of this.

BARNARDO
Last night of all,
When yond same star that's westward from the pole
35   Had made his course t' illume that part of heaven
Where now it burns, Marcellus and myself,
The bell then beating one—

Enter **GHOST**

MARCELLUS
Peace, break thee off. Look where it comes again!

BARNARDO
In the same figure like the king that's dead.

MARCELLUS
40   *(to* **HORATIO***)* Thou art a scholar. Speak to it, Horatio.

BARNARDO
Looks it not like the king? Mark it, Horatio.

HORATIO
Most like. It harrows me with fear and wonder.

BARNARDO
It would be spoke to.

MARCELLUS
               Question it, Horatio.

HORATIO
What art thou that usurp'st this time of night
45   Together with that fair and warlike form
In which the majesty of buried Denmark
Did sometimes march? By heaven, I charge thee, speak.

BARNARDO

Sit down for a while, and we'll tell you again the story you don't want to believe, about what we've seen two nights now.

HORATIO

Well, let's sit down and listen to Barnardo tell us.

BARNARDO

Last night, when that star to the west of the North Star had traveled across the night sky to that point where it's shining now, at one o'clock, Marcellus and I—

The GHOST *enters.*

MARCELLUS

Quiet, shut up! It's come again.

BARNARDO

Looking just like the dead king.

MARCELLUS

(to HORATIO*)* You're well-educated, Horatio. Say something to it.

BARNARDO

Doesn't he look like the king, Horatio?

HORATIO

Very much so. It's terrifying.

BARNARDO

It wants us to speak to it.

MARCELLUS

Ask it something, Horatio.

HORATIO

What are you, that you walk out so late at night, looking like the dead king of Denmark when he dressed for battle? By God, I order you to speak.

MARCELLUS
It is offended.

BARNARDO
See, it stalks away.

HORATIO
Stay! Speak, speak! I charge thee, speak!

Exit GHOST

MARCELLUS
50   'Tis gone and will not answer.

BARNARDO
How now, Horatio? You tremble and look pale.
Is not this something more than fantasy?
What think you on 't?

HORATIO
Before my God, I might not this believe
55   Without the sensible and true avouch
Of mine own eyes.

MARCELLUS
Is it not like the king?

HORATIO
As thou art to thyself.
Such was the very armour he had on
60   When he the ambitious Norway combated.
So frowned he once when, in an angry parle,
He smote the sledded Polacks on the ice.
'Tis strange.

MARCELLUS
Thus twice before, and jump at this dead hour,
65   With martial stalk hath he gone by our watch.

HORATIO
In what particular thought to work I know not,
But in the gross and scope of mine opinion
This bodes some strange eruption to our state.

MARCELLUS

> It looks like you've offended it.

BARNARDO

> Look, it's going away.

HORATIO

> Stay! Speak! Speak! I order you, speak!

> *The* GHOST *exits.*

MARCELLUS

> It's gone. It won't answer now.

BARNARDO

> What's going on, Horatio? You're pale and trembling. You agree now that we're not imagining this, don't you? What do you think about it?

HORATIO

> I swear to God, if I hadn't seen this with my own eyes I'd never believe it.

MARCELLUS

> Doesn't it look like the king?

HORATIO

> Yes, as much as you look like yourself. The king was wearing exactly this armor when he fought the king of Norway. And the ghost frowned just like the king did once when he attacked the Poles, traveling on the ice in sleds. It's weird.

MARCELLUS

> It's happened like this twice before, always at this exact time. He stalks by us at our post like a warrior.

HORATIO

> I don't know exactly how to explain this, but I have a general feeling this means bad news for our country.

MARCELLUS
Good now, sit down and tell me, he that knows,
70 Why this same strict and most observant watch
So nightly toils the subject of the land,
And why such daily cast of brazen cannon
And foreign mart for implements of war,
Why such impress of shipwrights, whose sore task
75 Does not divide the Sunday from the week.
What might be toward, that this sweaty haste
Doth make the night joint laborer with the day?
Who is 't that can inform me?

HORATIO
                          That can I.
At least, the whisper goes so: our last king,
80 Whose image even but now appeared to us,
Was, as you know, by Fortinbras of Norway,
Thereto pricked on by a most emulate pride,
Dared to the combat; in which our valiant Hamlet
(For so this side of our known world esteemed him)
85 Did slay this Fortinbras, who by a sealed compact
Well ratified by law and heraldry,
Did forfeit, with his life, all those his lands
Which he stood seized of to the conqueror,
Against the which a moiety competent
90 Was gagèd by our king, which had returned
To the inheritance of Fortinbras
Had he been vanquisher, as, by the same covenant
And carriage of the article designed,
His fell to Hamlet. Now, sir, young Fortinbras,
95 Of unimprovèd mettle hot and full,
Hath in the skirts of Norway here and there
Sharked up a list of lawless resolutes,
For food and diet, to some enterprise
That hath a stomach in 't, which is no other—
100 As it doth well appear unto our state—
But to recover of us, by strong hand

MARCELLUS

All right, let's sit down and discuss that question. Somebody tell me why this strict schedule of guards has been imposed, and why so many bronze cannons are being manufactured in Denmark, and so many weapons bought from abroad, and why the shipbuilders are so busy they don't even rest on Sunday. Is something about to happen that warrants working this night and day? Who can explain this to me?

HORATIO

I can. Or at least I can describe the rumors. As you know, our late king, whom we just now saw as a ghost, was the great rival of Fortinbras, king of Norway. Fortinbras dared him to battle. In that fight, our courageous Hamlet (or at least that's how we thought of him) killed old King Fortinbras, who—on the basis of a valid legal document—surrendered all his territories, along with his life, to his conqueror. If our king had lost, he would have had to do the same. But now old Fortinbras's young son, also called Fortinbras— he is bold, but unproven—has gathered a bunch of thugs from the lawless outskirts of the country. For some food, they're eager to take on the tough enterprise of securing the lands the elder Fortinbras lost.

And terms compulsatory, those foresaid lands
So by his father lost. And this, I take it,
Is the main motive of our preparations,
105   The source of this our watch, and the chief head
Of this posthaste and rummage in the land.

BARNARDO
I think it be no other but e'en so.
Well may it sort that this portentous figure
Comes armèd through our watch so like the king
110   That was and is the question of these wars.

HORATIO
A mote it is to trouble the mind's eye.
In the most high and palmy state of Rome,
A little ere the mightiest Julius fell,
The graves stood tenantless and the sheeted dead
115   Did squeak and gibber in the Roman streets
As stars with trains of fire and dews of blood,
Disasters in the sun, and the moist star
Upon whose influence Neptune's empire stands
Was sick almost to doomsday with eclipse.
120   And even the like precurse of feared events,
As harbingers preceding still the fates
And prologue to the omen coming on,
Have heaven and earth together demonstrated
Unto our climatures and countrymen.

Enter GHOST

125   But soft, behold! Lo, where it comes again.
I'll cross it though it blast me.—Stay, illusion!

GHOST *spreads his arms*

If thou hast any sound or use of voice,
Speak to me.

As far as I understand, that's why we're posted here tonight and why there's such a commotion in Denmark lately.

BARNARDO

I think that's exactly right—that explains why the ghost of the late king would haunt us now, since he caused these wars.

HORATIO

The ghost is definitely something to worry about. In the high and mighty Roman Empire, just before the emperor Julius Caesar was assassinated, corpses rose out of their graves and ran through the streets of Rome speaking gibberish. There were shooting stars, and blood mixed in with the morning dew, and threatening signs on the face of the sun. The moon, which controls the tides of the sea, was so eclipsed it almost went completely out. And we've had similar omens of terrible things to come, as if heaven and earth have joined together to warn us what's going to happen.

The GHOST *enters.*

Wait, look! It has come again. I'll meet it if it's the last thing I do. —Stay here, you hallucination!

The GHOST *spreads his arms.*

If you have a voice or can make sounds, speak to me.

If there be any good thing to be done
130 That may to thee do ease and grace to me,
Speak to me.
If thou art privy to thy country's fate,
Which happily foreknowing may avoid,
Oh, speak!
135 Or if thou hast uphoarded in thy life
Extorted treasure in the womb of earth,
For which, they say, you spirits oft walk in death,
Speak of it. Stay and speak!

The cock crows

—Stop it, Marcellus.

MARCELLUS
Shall I strike at it with my partisan?

HORATIO
140 Do, if it will not stand.

BARNARDO
'Tis here.

HORATIO
'Tis here.

Exit GHOST

MARCELLUS
'Tis gone.
We do it wrong, being so majestical,
To offer it the show of violence,
For it is, as the air, invulnerable,
145 And our vain blows malicious mockery.

BARNARDO
It was about to speak when the cock crew.

If there's any good deed I can do that will bring you peace and me honor, speak to me. If you have some secret knowledge of your country's sad fate—which might be avoided if we knew about it—then, please, speak. Or if you've got some buried treasure somewhere, which they say often makes ghosts restless, then tell us about it. Stay and speak!

A rooster crows.

Keep it from leaving, Marcellus.

MARCELLUS

Should I strike it with my spear?

HORATIO

Yes, if it doesn't stand still.

BARNARDO

It's over here.

HORATIO

There it is.

The **GHOST** *exits.*

MARCELLUS

It's gone. We were wrong to threaten it with violence, since it looks so much like a king. Besides, we can't hurt it anymore than we can hurt the air. Our attack was stupid, futile, and wicked.

BARNARDO

It was about to say something when the rooster crowed.

HORATIO

And then it started like a guilty thing
Upon a fearful summons. I have heard
The cock, that is the trumpet to the morn,
150   Doth with his lofty and shrill-sounding throat
Awake the god of day, and, at his warning,
Whether in sea or fire, in earth or air,
Th' extravagant and erring spirit hies
To his confine, and of the truth herein
155   This present object made probation.

MARCELLUS

It faded on the crowing of the cock.
Some say that ever 'gainst that season comes
Wherein our Saviour's birth is celebrated,
The bird of dawning singeth all night long.
160   And then, they say, no spirit dare stir abroad.
The nights are wholesome. Then no planets strike,
No fairy takes, nor witch hath power to charm,
So hallowed and so gracious is that time.

HORATIO

So have I heard and do in part believe it.
165   But look, the morn, in russet mantle clad,
Walks o'er the dew of yon high eastward hill.
Break we our watch up, and by my advice,
Let us impart what we have seen tonight
Unto young Hamlet, for, upon my life,
170   This spirit, dumb to us, will speak to him.
Do you consent we shall acquaint him with it,
As needful in our loves, fitting our duty?

MARCELLUS

Let's do 't, I pray, and I this morning know
Where we shall find him most conveniently.

Exeunt

HORATIO

And then it acted startled, like a guilty person caught by the law. I've heard that the rooster awakens the god of day with its trumpetlike crowing, and makes all wandering ghosts, wherever they are, hurry back to their hiding places. We've just seen proof of that.

MARCELLUS

Yes, it faded away when the rooster crowed. Some people say that just before Christmas the rooster crows all night long, so that no ghost dares go wandering, and the night is safe. The planets have no sway over us, fairies' spells don't work, and witches can't bewitch us. That's how holy that night is.

HORATIO

Yes, I've heard the same thing and sort of believe it. But look, morning is breaking beyond that hill in the east, turning the sky red. Let's interrupt our watch and go tell young Hamlet what we've seen tonight. I'm sure this ghost that's so silent with us will speak to him. Don't you agree that we owe it to him to tell him about this, out of duty and love?

MARCELLUS

Let's do it. I know where we'll find him this morning.

They exit.

ACT 1, SCENE 2

Enter CLAUDIUS, *king of Denmark;* GERTRUDE *the queen;*
HAMLET; POLONIUS; *his son* LAERTES; *and his daughter*
OPHELIA; LORDS *attendant*

CLAUDIUS
Though yet of Hamlet our dear brother's death
The memory be green, and that it us befitted
To bear our hearts in grief and our whole kingdom
To be contracted in one brow of woe,
5   Yet so far hath discretion fought with nature
That we with wisest sorrow think on him
Together with remembrance of ourselves.
Therefore our sometime sister, now our queen,
Th' imperial jointress to this warlike state,
10   Have we—as 'twere with a defeated joy,
With an auspicious and a dropping eye,
With mirth in funeral and with dirge in marriage,
In equal scale weighing delight and dole—
Taken to wife. Nor have we herein barred
15   Your better wisdoms, which have freely gone
With this affair along. For all, our thanks.
Now follows that you know. Young Fortinbras,
Holding a weak supposal of our worth
Or thinking by our late dear brother's death
20   Our state to be disjoint and out of frame,
Colleaguèd with the dream of his advantage,
He hath not failed to pester us with message
Importing the surrender of those lands
Lost by his father, with all bonds of law,
25   To our most valiant brother. So much for him.

Enter VOLTEMAND *and* CORNELIUS

Now for ourself and for this time of meeting

ACT 1, SCENE 2

CLAUDIUS, *the king of Denmark, enters, along with* GERTRUDE *the queen,* HAMLET, POLONIUS, POLONIUS'S *son* LAERTES *and daughter* OPHELIA, *and* LORDS *who wait on the king.*

CLAUDIUS

Although I still have fresh memories of my brother the elder Hamlet's death, and though it was proper to mourn him throughout our kingdom, life still goes on—I think it's wise to mourn him while also thinking about my own well being. Therefore, I've married my former sister-in-law, the queen, with mixed feelings of happiness and sadness. I know that in marrying Gertrude I'm only doing what all of you have wisely advised all along—for which I thank you. Now, down to business. You all know what's happening. Young Fortinbras, underestimating my strength or imagining that the death of the king has thrown my country into turmoil, dreams of getting the better of me, and never stops pestering me with demands that I surrender the territory his father lost to the elder Hamlet, my dead brother-in-law. So much for Fortinbras.

VOLTEMAND *and* CORNELIUS *enter.*

Now, here's what needs to be done.

Thus much the business is: we have here writ
To Norway, uncle of young Fortinbras—
Who, impotent and bedrid, scarcely hears
30   Of this his nephew's purpose—to suppress
His further gait herein, in that the levies,
The lists, and full proportions are all made
Out of his subject; and we here dispatch
You, good Cornelius, and you, Voltemand,
35   For bearers of this greeting to old Norway,
Giving to you no further personal power
To business with the king more than the scope
Of these dilated articles allow. *(gives them a paper)*
Farewell, and let your haste commend your duty.

CORNELIUS, VOLTEMAND
40   In that and all things will we show our duty.

CLAUDIUS
We doubt it nothing. Heartily farewell.

Exeunt **VOLTEMAND** *and* **CORNELIUS**

And now, Laertes, what's the news with you?
You told us of some suit. What is 't, Laertes?
You cannot speak of reason to the Dane
45   And lose your voice. What wouldst thou beg, Laertes,
That shall not be my offer, not thy asking?
The head is not more native to the heart,
The hand more instrumental to the mouth,
Than is the throne of Denmark to thy father.
50   What wouldst thou have, Laertes?

LAERTES
My dread lord,
Your leave and favor to return to France,
From whence though willingly I came to Denmark
To show my duty in your coronation,
Yet now, I must confess, that duty done,
55   My thoughts and wishes bend again toward France
And bow them to your gracious leave and pardon.

I've written to Fortinbras's uncle, the present head of Norway, an old bedridden man who knows next to nothing about his nephew's plans. I've told the uncle to stop those plans, which he has the power to do, since all the troops assembled by young Fortinbras are Norwegian, and thus under the uncle's control. I'm giving the job of delivering this letter to you, good Cornelius, and you, Voltemand. Your business in Norway will be limited to this task. *(he gives them a paper)* Now good-bye. Show your loyalty by leaving quickly, rather than with elaborate speeches.

CORNELIUS, VOLTEMAND

We'll do our duty to you in that and everything else.

CLAUDIUS

I have no doubt you will. Good-bye.

CORNELIUS *and* **VOLTEMAND** *exit.*

And now, Laertes, what do you have to tell me? You have a favor you to ask of me. What is it, Laertes? You'll never waste your words when talking to the king of Denmark. What could you ever ask for that I wouldn't give you? Your father and the Danish throne are as close as the mind and the heart, or the hand and the mouth. What would you like, Laertes?

LAERTES

My lord, I want your permission to go back to France, which I left to come to Denmark for your coronation. I confess, my thoughts are on France, now that my duty is done. Please, let me go.

CLAUDIUS
> Have you your father's leave? What says Polonius?

POLONIUS
> He hath, my lord, wrung from me my slow leave
> By laborsome petition, and at last
> 60 Upon his will I sealed my hard consent.
> I do beseech you, give him leave to go.

CLAUDIUS
> Take thy fair hour, Laertes. Time be thine,
> And thy best graces spend it at thy will.—
> But now, my cousin Hamlet, and my son—

HAMLET
> 65 *(aside)* A little more than kin and less than kind.

CLAUDIUS
> How is it that the clouds still hang on you?

HAMLET
> Not so, my lord. I am too much i' the sun.

GERTRUDE
> Good Hamlet, cast thy nighted color off,
> And let thine eye look like a friend on Denmark.
> 70 Do not forever with thy vailèd lids
> Seek for thy noble father in the dust.
> Thou know'st 'tis common. All that lives must die,
> Passing through nature to eternity.

HAMLET
> Ay, madam, it is common.

GERTRUDE
>   If it be,
> 75 Why seems it so particular with thee?

CLAUDIUS

Do you have your father's permission? What does Polonius say?

POLONIUS

My son has worn me down by asking me so many times. In the end I grudgingly consented. I beg you, let him go.

CLAUDIUS

In that case, leave when you like, Laertes, and spend your time however you wish. I hereby grant your request, and hope you have a good time. And now, Hamlet, my nephew and my son—

HAMLET

(speaking so no one else can hear) Too many family ties there for me.

CLAUDIUS

Why are you still so gloomy, with a cloud hanging over you?

HAMLET

It's not true, sir. Your son is out in the sun.

GERTRUDE

My dear Hamlet, stop wearing these black clothes, and be friendly to the king. You can't spend your whole life with your eyes to the ground remembering your noble father. It happens all the time, what lives must die eventually, passing to eternity.

HAMLET

Yes, mother, it happens all the time.

GERTRUDE

So why does it seem so particular to you?

HAMLET
"Seems," madam? Nay, it is. I know not "seems."
'Tis not alone my inky cloak, good mother,
Nor customary suits of solemn black,
Nor windy suspiration of forced breath,
80 No, nor the fruitful river in the eye,
Nor the dejected 'havior of the visage,
Together with all forms, moods, shapes of grief,
That can denote me truly. These indeed "seem,"
For they are actions that a man might play.
85 But I have that within which passeth show,
These but the trappings and the suits of woe.

CLAUDIUS
'Tis sweet and commendable in your nature, Hamlet,
To give these mourning duties to your father.
But you must know your father lost a father,
90 That father lost, lost his, and the survivor bound
In filial obligation for some term
To do obsequious sorrow. But to persever
In obstinate condolement is a course
Of impious stubbornness. 'Tis unmanly grief.
95 It shows a will most incorrect to heaven,
A heart unfortified, a mind impatient,
An understanding simple and unschooled.
For what we know must be and is as common
As any the most vulgar thing to sense,
100 Why should we in our peevish opposition
Take it to heart? Fie! 'Tis a fault to heaven,
A fault against the dead, a fault to nature,
To reason most absurd, whose common theme
Is death of fathers, and who still hath cried,
105 From the first corse till he that died today,
"This must be so." We pray you, throw to earth
This unprevailing woe, and think of us
As of a father. For let the world take note,
You are the most immediate to our throne,

HAMLET

"Seem," mother? No, it *is*. I don't know what you mean by "seem." Neither my black clothes, my dear mother, nor my heavy sighs, nor my weeping, nor my downcast eyes, nor any other display of grief can show what I really feel. It's true that all these things "seem" like grief, since a person could use them to fake grief if he wanted to. But I've got more real grief inside me that you could ever see on the surface. These clothes are just a hint of it.

CLAUDIUS

Hamlet, you are so sweet and such a good son to mourn your father like this. But you have to remember, that your father lost his father, who lost his father before him, and every time, each son has had to mourn his father for a certain period. But overdoing it is just stubborn. It's not manly. It's not what God wants, and it betrays a vulnerable heart and an ignorant and weak mind. Since we know that everyone must die sooner or later, why should we take it to heart? You're committing a crime against heaven, against the dead, and against nature. And it's irration-al, since the truth is that all fathers must die. Please give up this useless mourning of yours and start thinking of me as your new father.

110 And with no less nobility of love
Than that which dearest father bears his son
Do I impart toward you. For your intent
In going back to school in Wittenberg,
It is most retrograde to our desire.
115 And we beseech you, bend you to remain
Here in the cheer and comfort of our eye,
Our chiefest courtier, cousin, and our son.

GERTRUDE
Let not thy mother lose her prayers, Hamlet.
I pray thee, stay with us. Go not to Wittenberg.

HAMLET
120 I shall in all my best obey you, madam.

CLAUDIUS
Why, 'tis a loving and a fair reply.
Be as ourself in Denmark.—Madam, come.
This gentle and unforced accord of Hamlet
Sits smiling to my heart, in grace whereof
125 No jocund health that Denmark drinks today
But the great cannon to the clouds shall tell,
And the king's rouse the heavens shall bruit again,
Respeaking earthly thunder. Come away.
Flourish. Exeunt all but HAMLET

HAMLET
Oh, that this too, too sullied flesh would melt,
130 Thaw, and resolve itself into a dew,
Or that the Everlasting had not fixed
His canon 'gainst self-slaughter! O God, God!
How weary, stale, flat, and unprofitable
Seem to me all the uses of this world!
135 Fie on 't, ah fie! 'Tis an unweeded garden
That grows to seed. Things rank and gross in nature
Possess it merely. That it should come to this.
But two months dead—nay, not so much, not two.
So excellent a king, that was to this
140 Hyperion to a satyr. So loving to my mother

Because everyone knows that you are the man closest to this throne, and I love you just as much as any father loves his son. And your plans for going back to Wittenberg are not what I want. I'm asking you now to stay here in my company as the number-one member of my court, my nephew and now my son too.

GERTRUDE

Please answer my prayers, Hamlet, and stay with us. Don't go back to Wittenberg.

HAMLET

I'll obey you as well as I can, ma'am.

CLAUDIUS

That's the right answer—it shows your love. Stay in Denmark like us.—My dear wife, come. Hamlet's agreeing to stay makes me happy, and every merry toast I'll drink today will be heard as far as the clouds overhead. My drinking will be echoed in the heavens. Let's go.

Trumpets play. Everyone except HAMLET *exits.*

HAMLET

Ah, I wish my dirty flesh could melt away into a vapor, or that God had not made a law against suicide. Oh God, God! How tired, stale, and pointless life is to me. Damn it! It's like a garden that no one's taking care of, and that's growing wild. Only nasty weeds grow in it now. I can't believe it's come to this. My father's only been dead for two months—no, not even two. Such an excellent king, as superior to my uncle as a god is to a beast, and so loving toward my mother that he kept the wind from blowing too hard on her face.

That he might not beteem the winds of heaven
Visit her face too roughly.—Heaven and earth,
Must I remember? Why, she would hang on him
As if increase of appetite had grown
145   By what it fed on, and yet, within a month—
Let me not think on 't. Frailty, thy name is woman!—
A little month, or ere those shoes were old
With which she followed my poor father's body,
Like Niobe, all tears. Why she, even she—
150   O God, a beast that wants discourse of reason
Would have mourned longer!—married with my uncle,
My father's brother, but no more like my father
Than I to Hercules. Within a month,
Ere yet the salt of most unrighteous tears
155   Had left the flushing in her gallèd eyes,
She married. O most wicked speed, to post
With such dexterity to incestuous sheets!
It is not nor it cannot come to good,
But break, my heart, for I must hold my tongue.

Enter HORATIO, MARCELLUS, *and* BARNARDO

HORATIO
160   Hail to your lordship.

HAMLET
                        I am glad to see you well.—
Horatio? Or I do forget myself?

HORATIO
The same, my lord, and your poor servant ever.

HAMLET
Sir, my good friend, I'll change that name with you.
And what make you from Wittenberg, Horatio?—
165   Marcellus!

MARCELLUS
                My good lord.

Oh God, do I have to remember that? She would hang on to him, and the more she was with him the more she wanted to be with him; she couldn't get enough of him. Yet even so, within a month of my father's death (I don't even want to think about it. Oh women! You are so weak!), even before she had broken in the shoes she wore to his funeral, crying like crazy—even an animal would have mourned its mate longer than she did!—there she was marrying my uncle, my father's brother, who's about as much like my father as I'm like Hercules. Less than a month after my father's death, even before the tears on her cheeks had dried, she remarried. Oh, so quick to jump into a bed of incest! That's not good, and no good can come of it either. But my heart must break in silence, since I can't mention my feelings aloud.

HORATIO, MARCELLUS, *and* BARNARDO *enter.*

HORATIO

Hello, sir.

HAMLET

Nice to see you again, Horatio—that is your name, right?

HORATIO

That's me, sir. Still your respectful servant.

HAMLET

Not my servant, but my friend. I'll change that name for you. But what are you doing so far from Wittenberg, Horatio? —Oh, Marcellus?

MARCELLUS

Hello, sir.

HAMLET
> *(to* MARCELLUS*)* I am very glad to see you.—*(to* BARNARDO*)*
> Good even, sir.
> *(to* HORATIO*)* —But what, in faith, make you from
> Wittenberg?

HORATIO
> A truant disposition, good my lord.

HAMLET
> I would not hear your enemy say so,
170 > Nor shall you do mine ear that violence,
> To make it truster of your own report
> Against yourself. I know you are no truant.
> But what is your affair in Elsinore?
> We'll teach you to drink deep ere you depart.

HORATIO
175 > My lord, I came to see your father's funeral.

HAMLET
> I pray thee, do not mock me, fellow student.
> I think it was to see my mother's wedding.

HORATIO
> Indeed, my lord, it followed hard upon.

HAMLET
> Thrift, thrift, Horatio! The funeral baked meats
180 > Did coldly furnish forth the marriage tables.
> Would I had met my dearest foe in heaven
> Or ever I had seen that day, Horatio.
> My father—methinks I see my father.

HORATIO
> Where, my lord?

HAMLET
>   In my mind's eye, Horatio.

HORATIO
185 > I saw him once. He was a goodly king.

HAMLET
> He was a man. Take him for all in all.
> I shall not look upon his like again.

HAMLET

(to MARCELLUS*)* So nice to see you.—*(to* BARNARDO*)* Hello, sir.*(to* HORATIO*)*—But what are you doing away from Wittenberg, Horatio?

HORATIO

I felt like skipping school, sir.

HAMLET

I wouldn't allow your enemies to say that, and I won't believe it from you. I know you'd never skip school. What are you doing here in Elsinore? I'll teach you to drink hard by the time you leave.

HORATIO

Sir, we came to see your father's funeral.

HAMLET

Please, don't make fun of me. I think you came to see my mother's wedding instead.

HORATIO

Well, sir, it's true it came soon after.

HAMLET

It was all about saving a few bucks, Horatio. The leftovers from the funeral dinner made a convenient wedding banquet. Oh, I'd rather have met my fiercest enemy in heaven, Horatio, than have lived through that terrible day! My father—I think I see my father.

HORATIO

Where, sir?

HAMLET

In my imagination, Horatio.

HORATIO

I saw him once. He was an admirable king.

HAMLET

He was a great human being. He was perfect in everything. I'll never see the likes of him again.

HORATIO
My lord, I think I saw him yesternight.

HAMLET
Saw who?

HORATIO
190 My lord, the king your father.

HAMLET
The king my father?!

HORATIO
Season your admiration for a while
With an attent ear, till I may deliver,
Upon the witness of these gentlemen,
195 This marvel to you.

HAMLET
For God's love, let me hear.

HORATIO
Two nights together had these gentlemen,
Marcellus and Barnardo, on their watch,
In the dead waste and middle of the night,
Been thus encountered: a figure like your father,
200 Armed at point exactly, cap-à-pie,
Appears before them and with solemn march
Goes slow and stately by them. Thrice he walked
By their oppressed and fear-surprisèd eyes
Within his truncheon's length, whilst they, distilled
205 Almost to jelly with the act of fear,
Stand dumb and speak not to him. This to me
In dreadful secrecy impart they did,
And I with them the third night kept the watch,
Where—as they had delivered, both in time,
210 Form of the thing, each word made true and good—
The apparition comes. I knew your father.
These hands are not more like.

HAMLET
But where was this?

HORATIO

Sir, I think I saw him last night.

HAMLET

Saw who?

HORATIO

Your father, sir. The dead king.

HAMLET

The king my father?!

HORATIO

Don't get too excited yet, sir. Just listen carefully while I tell you the amazing thing I saw, with these gentlemen as witnesses.

HAMLET

For God's sake, let me hear it.

HORATIO

After midnight, for two nights running, these two guards, Marcellus and Barnardo, saw a figure that looked very much like your father, in full armor from head to toe. It just appeared before them and marched past them with slow dignity three times, a staff's distance from their amazed eyes, while they turned, quaking with fear and too shocked to speak. They told me all about this, so on the third night I agreed to come stand guard with them, to see for myself. It happened again, just as they had described. I knew your father. This ghost looked as much like him as my two hands are like each other.

HAMLET

But where did this happen?

MARCELLUS
My lord, upon the platform where we watch.

HAMLET
Did you not speak to it?

HORATIO
My lord, I did,
215 But answer made it none. Yet once methought
It lifted up its head and did address
Itself to motion, like as it would speak.
But even then the morning cock crew loud,
And at the sound it shrunk in haste away
220 And vanished from our sight.

HAMLET
'Tis very strange.

HORATIO
As I do live, my honored lord, 'tis true.
And we did think it writ down in our duty
To let you know of it.

HAMLET
Indeed, indeed, sirs, but this troubles me.
225 Hold you the watch tonight?

MARCELLUS, BARNARDO
We do, my lord.

HAMLET
Armed, say you?

MARCELLUS, BARNARDO
Armed, my lord.

HAMLET
From top to toe?

MARCELLUS, BARNARDO
My lord, from head to foot.

HAMLET
Then saw you not his face?

HORATIO
Oh yes, my lord. He wore his beaver up.

MARCELLUS

On the platform where we stand guard, sir.

HAMLET

Didn't you talk to it?

HORATIO

I did, sir, but it didn't answer me. It raised its head once as if it was about to speak, but just then the rooster started crowing, and the ghost vanished from sight.

HAMLET

That's very strange.

HORATIO

I swear to God it's true, sir. We thought you ought to know about it.

HAMLET

Yes, I should know, but it disturbs me. Are you on duty again tonight?

MARCELLUS, BARNARDO

Yes, sir.

HAMLET

It was armed, you say?

MARCELLUS, BARNARDO

Armed, sir.

HAMLET

From head to toe?

MARCELLUS, BARNARDO

Yes, from top to bottom, sir.

HAMLET

So you couldn't see his face, then?

HORATIO

Oh, yes, we could, sir. He had his helmet visor up.

HAMLET
>What, looked he frowningly?

HORATIO
>   A countenance more

230 In sorrow than in anger.

HAMLET
>   Pale or red?

HORATIO
>Nay, very pale.

HAMLET
>   And fixed his eyes upon you?

HORATIO
>Most constantly.

HAMLET
>I would I had been there.

HORATIO
>It would have much amazed you.

HAMLET
235 Very like. Stayed it long?

HORATIO
>While one with moderate haste might tell a hundred.

MARCELLUS, BARNARDO
>Longer, longer.

HORATIO
>Not when I saw 't.

HAMLET
>His beard was grizzled, no?

HORATIO
240 It was, as I have seen it in his life,
>A sable silvered.

HAMLET
>   I will watch tonight. Perchance
>'Twill walk again.

HORATIO
>   I warrant it will.

HAMLET

Was he frowning?

HORATIO

He looked more sad than angry.

HAMLET

Was he pale or flushed and red-faced?

HORATIO

Very pale, sir.

HAMLET

Did he stare at you?

HORATIO

The whole time.

HAMLET

I wish I'd been there.

HORATIO

You would have been very shocked.

HAMLET

I'm sure I would have. Did it stay a long time?

HORATIO

About as long as it would take someone to count slowly to a hundred.

MARCELLUS, BARNARDO

No, longer than that.

HORATIO

Not the time I saw it.

HAMLET

His beard was gray, right?

HORATIO

It was just like in real life, dark brown with silver whiskers in it.

HAMLET

I'll stand guard with you tonight. Maybe it'll come again.

HORATIO

I bet it will.

HAMLET
If it assume my noble father's person,
I'll speak to it, though Hell itself should gape
245 And bid me hold my peace. I pray you all,
If you have hitherto concealed this sight,
Let it be tenable in your silence still.
And whatsoever else shall hap tonight,
Give it an understanding, but no tongue.
250 I will requite your loves. So fare you well.
Upon the platform, 'twixt eleven and twelve,
I'll visit you.

HORATIO, MARCELLUS, BARNARDO
Our duty to your honor.

HAMLET
Your loves, as mine to you. Farewell.

Exeunt all but **HAMLET**

My father's spirit in arms. All is not well.
255 I doubt some foul play. Would the night were come!
Till then sit still, my soul. Foul deeds will rise,
Though all the earth o'erwhelm them, to men's eyes.

Exit

HAMLET

> If it looks like my good father, I'll speak to it, even if Hell itself opens up and tells me to be quiet. I ask you, if you've kept this a secret, keep doing so. Whatever happens tonight, don't talk about it. I'll return the favor. So good-bye for now. I'll see you on the guards' platform between eleven and twelve tonight.

HORATIO, MARCELLUS, BARNARDO

> We'll do our duty to you, sir.

HAMLET

> Give me your love instead, as I give you mine. Good-bye.

> > *Everyone except* **HAMLET** *exits.*

> My father's ghost—armed! Something's wrong. I suspect some foul play. I wish the night were here already! Until then, I have to remain calm. Bad deeds will be revealed, no matter how people try to hide them.

> > **HAMLET** *exits.*

ACT 1, SCENE 3

Enter LAERTES *and* OPHELIA, *his sister*

LAERTES

My necessaries are embarked. Farewell.
And, sister, as the winds give benefit
And convey is assistant, do not sleep,
But let me hear from you.

OPHELIA

Do you doubt that?

LAERTES

5   For Hamlet and the trifling of his favor,
Hold it a fashion and a toy in blood,
A violet in the youth of primy nature,
Forward, not permanent, sweet, not lasting,
The perfume and suppliance of a minute.
10   No more.

OPHELIA

No more but so?

LAERTES

Think it no more.
For nature, crescent, does not grow alone
In thews and bulk, but, as this temple waxes,
The inward service of the mind and soul
Grows wide withal. Perhaps he loves you now,
15   And now no soil nor cautel doth besmirch
The virtue of his will, but you must fear.
His greatness weighed, his will is not his own,
For he himself is subject to his birth.
He may not, as unvalued persons do,
20   Carve for himself, for on his choice depends
The safety and health of this whole state.
And therefore must his choice be circumscribed
Unto the voice and yielding of that body
Whereof he is the head. Then if he says he loves you,

ACT 1, SCENE 3

LAERTES *and his sister* OPHELIA *enter.*

LAERTES

My belongings are on the ship already. Good-bye. And, my dear sister, as long as the winds are blowing and ships are sailing, let me hear from you—write.

OPHELIA

Do you doubt I'll write?

LAERTES

As for Hamlet and his attentions to you, just consider it a big flirtation, the temporary phase of a hot-blooded youth. It won't last. It's sweet, but his affection will fade after a minute. Not a second more.

OPHELIA

No more than a minute?

LAERTES

Try to think of it like that, anyway. When a youth grows into a man, he doesn't just get bigger in his body—his responsibilities grow too. He may love you now, and may have only the best intentions, but you have to be on your guard. Remember that he belongs to the royal family, and his intentions don't matter that much—he's a slave to his family obligations. He can't simply make personal choices for himself the way common people can, since the whole country depends on what he does. His choice has to agree with what the nation wants.

It fits your wisdom so far to believe it
25   As he in his particular act and place
May give his saying deed, which is no further
Than the main voice of Denmark goes withal.
Then weigh what loss your honor may sustain
If with too credent ear you list his songs,
30   Or lose your heart, or your chaste treasure open
To his unmastered importunity.
Fear it, Ophelia. Fear it, my dear sister,
And keep you in the rear of your affection,
Out of the shot and danger of desire.
35   The chariest maid is prodigal enough
If she unmask her beauty to the moon.
Virtue itself 'scapes not calumnious strokes.
The canker galls the infants of the spring
Too oft before their buttons be disclosed.
40   And in the morn and liquid dew of youth,
Contagious blastments are most imminent.
Be wary, then. Best safety lies in fear.
Youth to itself rebels, though none else near.

OPHELIA
I shall the effect of this good lesson keep
45   As watchman to my heart. But, good my brother,
Do not, as some ungracious pastors do,
Show me the steep and thorny way to heaven
Whiles, like a puffed and reckless libertine,
Himself the primrose path of dalliance treads
50   And recks not his own rede.

LAERTES
                        O, fear me not.

Enter POLONIUS

I stay too long. But here my father comes.
A double blessing is a double grace.
Occasion smiles upon a second leave.

So if he says he loves you, you should be wise enough to see that his words only mean as much as the state of Denmark allows them to mean. Then think about how shameful it would be for you to give in to his seductive talk and surrender your treasure chest to his greedy hands. Watch out, Ophelia. Just keep your love under control, and don't let yourself become a target of his lust. Simply exposing your beauty to the moon at night is risky enough—you don't have to expose yourself to him. Even good girls sometimes get a bad reputation. Worms ruin flowers before they blossom. Baby blooms are most susceptible to disease. So be careful. Fear will keep you safe. Young people often lose their self-control even without any help from others.

OPHELIA

I'll keep your words of wisdom close to my heart. But, my dear brother, don't be like a bad priest who fails to practice what he preaches, showing me the steep and narrow way to heaven while you frolic on the primrose path of sin.

LAERTES

Don't worry, I won't.

POLONIUS *enters.*

I've been here too long. And here comes father. What good luck, to have him bless my leaving not once but twice.

POLONIUS

55   Yet here, Laertes? Aboard, aboard, for shame!
        The wind sits in the shoulder of your sail
        And you are stayed for. There, my blessing with thee.
        And these few precepts in thy memory
        Look thou character. Give thy thoughts no tongue,
60   Nor any unproportioned thought his act.
        Be thou familiar but by no means vulgar.
        Those friends thou hast, and their adoption tried,
        Grapple them unto thy soul with hoops of steel,
        But do not dull thy palm with entertainment
65   Of each new-hatched, unfledged comrade. Beware
        Of entrance to a quarrel, but being in,
        Bear 't that th' opposèd may beware of thee.
        Give every man thy ear but few thy voice.
        Take each man's censure but reserve thy judgment.
70   Costly thy habit as thy purse can buy,
        But not expressed in fancy—rich, not gaudy,
        For the apparel oft proclaims the man,
        And they in France of the best rank and station
        Are of a most select and generous chief in that.
75   Neither a borrower nor a lender be,
        For loan oft loses both itself and friend,
        And borrowing dulls the edge of husbandry.
        This above all: to thine own self be true,
        And it must follow, as the night the day,
80   Thou canst not then be false to any man.
        Farewell. My blessing season this in thee.

LAERTES

        Most humbly do I take my leave, my lord.

POLONIUS

        The time invites you. Go. Your servants tend.

LAERTES

        Farewell, Ophelia, and remember well
85   What I have said to you.

POLONIUS

You're still here? Shame on you—get on board! The wind is filling your ship's sail, and they're waiting for you. Here, I give you my blessing again. And just try to remember a few rules of life. Don't say what you're thinking, and don't be too quick to act on what you think. Be friendly to people but don't overdo it. Once you've tested out your friends and found them trustworthy, hold onto them. But don't waste your time shaking hands with every new guy you meet. Don't be quick to pick a fight, but once you're in one, hold your own. Listen to many people, but talk to few. Hear everyone's opinion, but reserve your judgment. Spend all you can afford on clothes, but make sure they're quality, not flashy, since clothes make the man—which is doubly true in France. Don't borrow money and don't lend it, since when you lend to a friend, you often lose the friendship as well as the money, and borrowing turns a person into a spendthrift. And, above all, be true to yourself. Then you won't be false to anybody else. Good-bye, son. I hope my blessing will help you absorb what I've said.

LAERTES

I humbly say good-bye to you, father.

POLONIUS

Now go, the time is right. Your servants are waiting.

LAERTES

Good-bye, Ophelia. Remember what I've told you.

OPHELIA
'Tis in my memory locked,
And you yourself shall keep the key of it.

LAERTES
Farewell.

Exit LAERTES

POLONIUS
What is 't, Ophelia, he hath said to you?

OPHELIA
So please you, something touching the Lord Hamlet.

POLONIUS
90 Marry, well bethought.
'Tis told me he hath very oft of late
Given private time to you, and you yourself
Have of your audience been most free and bounteous.
If it be so as so 'tis put on me—
95 And that in way of caution—I must tell you,
You do not understand yourself so clearly
As it behooves my daughter and your honor.
What is between you? Give me up the truth.

OPHELIA
He hath, my lord, of late made many tenders
100 Of his affection to me.

POLONIUS
Affection! Pooh, you speak like a green girl,
Unsifted in such perilous circumstance.
Do you believe his "tenders," as you call them?

OPHELIA
I do not know, my lord, what I should think.

POLONIUS
105 Marry, I'll teach you. Think yourself a baby
That you have ta'en these tenders for true pay,
Which are not sterling. Tender yourself more dearly,
Or—not to crack the wind of the poor phrase,
Running it thus—you'll tender me a fool.

OPHELIA

It's locked away in my memory, and you've got the key.

LAERTES

Good-bye.

LAERTES *exits.*

POLONIUS

What did he tell you, Ophelia?

LAERTES

Something about Hamlet.

POLONIUS

A good thing he did, by God. I've heard Hamlet's been spending a lot of time alone with you recently, and you've made yourself quite available to him. If things are the way people tell me they are—and they're only telling me this to warn me—then I have to say, you're not conducting yourself with the self-restraint a daughter of mine should show. What's going on between you two? Tell me the truth.

OPHELIA

He's offered me a lot of affection lately.

POLONIUS

"Affection!" That's nothing! You're talking like some innocent girl who doesn't understand the ways of the world. Do you believe his "offers," as you call them?

OPHELIA

I don't know what to believe, father.

POLONIUS

Then I'll tell you. Believe that you are a foolish little baby for believing these "offers" are something real. Offer yourself more respect, or—not to beat this word to death—you'll offer me the chance to be a laughing-stock.

OPHELIA

110   My lord, he hath importuned me with love
        In honorable fashion.

POLONIUS

        Ay, "fashion" you may call it. Go to, go to.

OPHELIA

        And hath given countenance to his speech, my lord,
        With almost all the holy vows of heaven.

POLONIUS

115   Ay, springes to catch woodcocks. I do know,
        When the blood burns, how prodigal the soul
        Lends the tongue vows. These blazes, daughter,
        Giving more light than heat, extinct in both
        Even in their promise as it is a-making,
120   You must not take for fire. From this time
        Be somewhat scanter of your maiden presence.
        Set your entreatments at a higher rate
        Than a command to parley. For Lord Hamlet,
        Believe so much in him that he is young,
125   And with a larger tether may he walk
        Than may be given you. In few, Ophelia,
        Do not believe his vows, for they are brokers
        Not of that dye which their investments show,
        But mere implorators of unholy suits,
130   Breathing like sanctified and pious bawds,
        The better to beguile. This is for all:
        I would not, in plain terms, from this time forth,
        Have you so slander any moment leisure,
        As to give words or talk with the Lord Hamlet.
135   Look to 't, I charge you. Come your ways.

OPHELIA

        I shall obey, my lord.

                                        Exeunt

OPHELIA

Father, he's always talked about love in an honorable fashion—

POLONIUS

Yes, "fashion" is just the word—a passing whim. Go on.

OPHELIA

And he's made the holiest vows to me, to back up what he says.

POLONIUS

These vows are just traps for stupid birds. I know when a man is on fire, he'll swear anything. But when a heart's on fire, it gives out more light than heat, and the fire will be out even before he's done making his promises. Don't mistake that for true love. From now on, spend a little less time with him and talk to him less. Make yourself a precious commodity. Remember that Hamlet is young and has a lot more freedom to fool around than you do. In short, Ophelia, don't believe his love vows, since they're like flashy pimps who wear nice clothes to lead a woman into filthy acts. To put it plainly, don't waste your time with Hamlet. Do as I say. Now come along.

OPHELIA

I'll do as you say, father.

They exit.

ACT 1, SCENE 4

Enter HAMLET, HORATIO, *and* MARCELLUS

HAMLET
>The air bites shrewdly. It is very cold.

HORATIO
>It is a nipping and an eager air.

HAMLET
>What hour now?

HORATIO
>I think it lacks of twelve.

MARCELLUS
5 No, it is struck.

HORATIO
>Indeed? I heard it not. It then draws near the season
>Wherein the spirit held his wont to walk.

A flourish of trumpets and two pieces of ordnance goes off

>What does this mean, my lord?

HAMLET
>The king doth wake tonight and takes his rouse,
10 Keeps wassail and the swaggering upspring reels,
>And, as he drains his draughts of Rhenish down,
>The kettle-drum and trumpet thus bray out
>The triumph of his pledge.

HORATIO
>Is it a custom?

HAMLET
15 Ay, marry, is 't.
>But to my mind, though I am native here
>And to the manner born, it is a custom
>More honored in the breach than the observance.
>This heavy-headed revel east and west
20 Makes us traduced and taxed of other nations.

ACT 1, SCENE 4

HAMLET, HORATIO, *and* MARCELLUS *enter.*

HAMLET

The air is biting cold.

HORATIO

Yes, it's definitely nippy.

HAMLET

What time is it?

HORATIO

A little before twelve, I think.

MARCELLUS

No, it's just after twelve; I heard the clock strike.

HORATIO

Really? I didn't hear it. So it's nearly the time when the ghost likes to appear.

Trumpets play offstage and two cannons are fired.

What does that mean, sir?

HAMLET

The king is staying up all night drinking and dancing. As he guzzles down his German wine, the musicians make a ruckus to celebrate his draining another cup.

HORATIO

Is that a tradition?

HAMLET

Yes, it is. But though I was born here and should consider that tradition part of my own heritage, I think it would be better to ignore it than practice it. Other countries criticize us for our loud partying.

They clepe us drunkards and with swinish phrase
Soil our addition. And indeed it takes
From our achievements, though performed at height,
The pith and marrow of our attribute.

25   So oft it chances in particular men
That for some vicious mole of nature in them—
As in their birth (wherein they are not guilty,
Since nature cannot choose his origin),
By the o'ergrowth of some complexion,

30   Oft breaking down the pales and forts of reason,
Or by some habit that too much o'erleavens
The form of plausive manners—that these men,
Carrying, I say, the stamp of one defect,
Being nature's livery or fortune's star,

35   Their virtues else (be they as pure as grace,
As infinite as man may undergo)
Shall in the general censure take corruption
From that particular fault. The dram of evil
Doth all the noble substance of a doubt,

40   To his own scandal.

Enter GHOST

HORATIO
Look, my lord, it comes!

HAMLET
Angels and ministers of grace defend us!
Be thou a spirit of health or goblin damned,
Bring with thee airs from heaven or blasts from hell,

45   Be thy intents wicked or charitable,
Thou comest in such a questionable shape
That I will speak to thee. I'll call thee "Hamlet,"
"King," "Father," "royal Dane." O, answer me!
Let me not burst in ignorance, but tell

50   Why thy canonized bones, hearsed in death,
Have burst their cerements; why the sepulcher,

They call us drunks and insult our noble titles. And our drunkenness does detract from our achievements, as great as they are, and lessens our reputations. It's just like what happens to certain people who have some birth defect (which they are not responsible for, since nobody chooses how he's born), or some weird habit or compulsion that changes them completely. It happens sometimes that one little defect in these people, as wonderful and talented as they may be, will make them look completely bad to other people. A tiny spot of evil casts doubt on their good qualities and ruins their reputations.

The GHOST *enters.*

HORATIO

Look, sir—here it comes!

HAMLET

Oh angels, protect us! Whether you're a good spirit or a cursed demon, whether you bring heavenly breezes or blasts of hell fire, whether your intentions are good or evil, you look so strange I want to talk to you. I'll call you "Hamlet Senior," "King," "Father," "royal Dane." Answer me! Don't drive me crazy with curiosity, but tell me why your church-buried bones have burst out of their coffin, and why your tomb,

Wherein we saw thee quietly interred,
Hath oped his ponderous and marble jaws
To cast thee up again. What may this mean,
55　That thou, dead corse, again in complete steel
Revisits thus the glimpses of the moon,
Making night hideous and we fools of nature,
So horridly to shake our disposition
With thoughts beyond the reaches of our souls?
60　Say why is this? Wherefore? What should we do?

GHOST *beckons* HAMLET

HORATIO
It beckons you to go away with it,
As if it some impartment did desire
To you alone.

MARCELLUS
　　　　　　　Look, with what courteous action
It waves you to a more removèd ground.
65　But do not go with it.

HORATIO
　　　　　　　No, by no means.

HAMLET
It will not speak. Then I will follow it.

HORATIO
Do not, my lord.

HAMLET
　　　　　　　Why, what should be the fear?
I do not set my life in a pin's fee,
And for my soul—what can it do to that,
70　Being a thing immortal as itself?
It waves me forth again. I'll follow it.

HORATIO
What if it tempt you toward the flood, my lord,
Or to the dreadful summit of the cliff
That beetles o'er his base into the sea,

where we quietly buried you, has opened up its heavy marble jaws to spit you out again. What could it mean that you have put on your armor again, you corpse, and have come back to look at the moon, making the night terrifying and stirring us humans with supernatural fears? Why? What do you want from us? What should we do?

The GHOST *motions for* HAMLET *to come with it.*

HORATIO

It wants you to go off with it, as if it wants to tell you something alone.

MARCELLUS

Look how politely it's pointing you to a place that's farther away. But don't go.

HORATIO

Definitely not.

HAMLET

It's not going to speak, so I'll follow it.

HORATIO

Don't do it, sir.

HAMLET

Why, what's the danger? I don't value my life one bit. And as for my soul, how can the ghost endanger that, since it's as immortal as the ghost is? Look, it's waving me over again. I'll follow it.

HORATIO

What if it tempts you to jump into the sea, sir? Or to the terrifying cliff that overhangs the water,

75 And there assume some other horrible form,
Which might deprive your sovereignty of reason
And draw you into madness? Think of it.
The very place puts toys of desperation,
Without more motive, into every brain
80 That looks so many fathoms to the sea
And hears it roar beneath.

HAMLET
It waves me still.
—Go on. I'll follow thee.

MARCELLUS
You shall not go, my lord.

MARCELLUS and HORATIO try to hold HAMLET back

HAMLET
Hold off your hands.

HORATIO
85 Be ruled. You shall not go.

HAMLET
My fate cries out
And makes each petty artery in this body
As hardy as the Nemean lion's nerve.
Still am I called.—Unhand me, gentlemen.
(draws his sword)
By heaven, I'll make a ghost of him that lets me.
90 I say, away!—Go on. I'll follow thee.
Exeunt GHOST and HAMLET

HORATIO
He waxes desperate with imagination.

MARCELLUS
Let's follow. 'Tis not fit thus to obey him.

HORATIO
Have after. To what issue will this come?

where it takes on some other horrible form that drives you insane. Think about it. The edge of the sea makes people feel despair even at the best of times. All they have to do is look into its depths and hear it roar far below.

HAMLET

It's still waving to me. —Go ahead, I'll follow.

MARCELLUS

You're not going, sir.

MARCELLUS and HORATIO try to hold HAMLET back.

HAMLET

Let go of me.

HORATIO

Calm down. You're not going anywhere.

HAMLET

It's my fate calling me. Every nerve in my body is now as tough as steel. The ghost is still waving me over. Let me go, gentlemen. *(he draws his sword)*
I swear, if anyone holds me back, I'll make a ghost of him! I say, get away!—Go ahead, I'll follow you.

The GHOST and HAMLET exit.

HORATIO

His imagination is making him crazy.

MARCELLUS

Let's follow them. It's not right to obey his orders to let him go alone.

HORATIO

Go ahead and follow him. But what does all this mean, where will it all end?

MARCELLUS
Something is rotten in the state of Denmark.

HORATIO
95   Heaven will direct it.

MARCELLUS
                    Nay, let's follow him.

Exeunt

MARCELLUS

It means that something is rotten in the state of Denmark.

HORATIO

If that's true, we should let God take care of it.

MARCELLUS

No, let's follow him.

They exit.

ACT 1, SCENE 5

Enter GHOST *and* HAMLET

HAMLET
Where wilt thou lead me? Speak, I'll go no further.

GHOST
Mark me.

HAMLET
I will.

GHOST
My hour is almost come
When I to sulfurous and tormenting flames
Must render up myself.

HAMLET
Alas, poor ghost!

GHOST
5   Pity me not, but lend thy serious hearing
To what I shall unfold.

HAMLET
Speak. I am bound to hear.

GHOST
So art thou to revenge when thou shalt hear.

HAMLET
What?

GHOST
I am thy father's spirit,
10   Doomed for a certain term to walk the night
And for the day confined to fast in fires,
Till the foul crimes done in my days of nature
Are burnt and purged away. But that I am forbid
To tell the secrets of my prison house,
15   I could a tale unfold whose lightest word
Would harrow up thy soul, freeze thy young blood,

ACT 1, SCENE 5

The GHOST *and* HAMLET *enter.*

HAMLET

Where are you taking me? Speak. I'm not going any farther.

GHOST

Listen to me.

HAMLET

I will.

GHOST

The hour has almost come when I have to return to the horrible flames of purgatory.

HAMLET

Ah, poor ghost!

GHOST

Don't pity me. Just listen carefully to what I have to tell you.

HAMLET

Speak. I'm ready to hear you.

GHOST

You must be ready for revenge, too, when you hear me out.

HAMLET

What?

GHOST

I'm the ghost of your father, doomed for a certain period of time to walk the earth at night, while during the day I'm trapped in the fires of purgatory until I've done penance for my past sins. If I weren't forbidden to tell you the secrets of purgatory, I could tell you stories that would slice through your soul, freeze your blood,

According to Catholic doctrine, purgatory is a place where souls go to be punished for their sins before going to heaven.

Make thy two eyes, like stars, start from their spheres,
Thy knotted and combinèd locks to part
And each particular hair to stand on end,
20   Like quills upon the fearful porpentine.
But this eternal blazon must not be
To ears of flesh and blood. List, list, O, list!
If thou didst ever thy dear father love—

HAMLET
O God!

GHOST
25   Revenge his foul and most unnatural murder.

HAMLET
Murder?

GHOST
Murder most foul, as in the best it is.
But this most foul, strange and unnatural.

HAMLET
Haste me to know 't, that I, with wings as swift
30   As meditation or the thoughts of love,
May sweep to my revenge.

GHOST
                                        I find thee apt,
And duller shouldst thou be than the fat weed
That roots itself in ease on Lethe wharf,
Wouldst thou not stir in this. Now, Hamlet, hear.
35   'Tis given out that, sleeping in my orchard,
A serpent stung me. So the whole ear of Denmark
Is by a forgèd process of my death
Rankly abused. But know, thou noble youth,
The serpent that did sting thy father's life
40   Now wears his crown.

HAMLET
O my prophetic soul! My uncle?

make your eyes jump out of their sockets, and your hair stand on end like porcupine quills. But mortals like you aren't allowed to hear this description of the afterlife. Listen, listen! If you ever loved your poor dear father—

HAMLET

Oh God!

GHOST

Take revenge for his horrible murder, that crime against nature.

HAMLET

Murder?

GHOST

His most horrible murder. Murder's always horrible, but this one was especially horrible, weird, and unnatural.

HAMLET

Hurry and tell me about it, so I can take revenge right away, faster than a person falls in love.

GHOST

Lethe was a river in the underworld of classical Greek mythology, whose waters induced forgetfulness.

I'm glad you're eager. You'd have to be as lazy as a weed on the shores of Lethe not to get riled up here. Now listen, Hamlet. Everyone was told that a poisonous snake bit me when I was sleeping in the orchard. But in fact, that's a lie that's fooled everyone in Denmark. You should know, my noble son, the real snake that stung your father is now wearing his crown.

HAMLET

I knew it! My uncle?

GHOST

Ay, that incestuous, that adulterate beast,
With witchcraft of his wit, with traitorous gifts—
O wicked wit and gifts, that have the power
45 So to seduce!—won to his shameful lust
The will of my most seeming-virtuous queen.
O Hamlet, what a falling off was there!
From me, whose love was of that dignity
That it went hand in hand even with the vow
50 I made to her in marriage, and to decline
Upon a wretch whose natural gifts were poor
To those of mine.
But virtue, as it never will be moved,
Though lewdness court it in a shape of heaven,
55 So lust, though to a radiant angel linked,
Will sate itself in a celestial bed
And prey on garbage.
But soft! Methinks I scent the morning air.
Brief let me be. Sleeping within my orchard,
60 My custom always of the afternoon,
Upon my secure hour thy uncle stole
With juice of cursed hebenon in a vial,
And in the porches of my ears did pour
The leperous distilment, whose effect
65 Holds such an enmity with blood of man
That swift as quicksilver it courses through
The natural gates and alleys of the body
And with a sudden vigor doth posset
And curd, like eager droppings into milk,
70 The thin and wholesome blood. So did it mine.
And a most instant tetter barked about,
Most lazar-like, with vile and loathsome crust
All my smooth body.
Thus was I, sleeping, by a brother's hand
75 Of life, of crown, of queen at once dispatched,
Cut off even in the blossoms of my sin,

GHOST

Yes, that incestuous, adulterous animal. With his clever words and fancy gifts, he seduced my seemingly virtuous queen, persuading her to give in to his lust. They were evil words and gifts to seduce her like that! Oh, Hamlet, how far she fell! She went from me, who loved her with the dignity and devotion that suits a legitimate marriage, to a wretch whose natural gifts were poor compared to mine. But just as you can't corrupt a truly virtuous person no matter how you try, the opposite is also true: a lustful person like her can satisfy herself in a heavenly union and then move on to garbage. But hang on, I think I smell the morning air. So let me be brief here. Your uncle snuck up to me while I was sleeping in the orchard, as I always used to do in the afternoon, and poured a vial of henbane poison into my ear—that poison that moves like quicksilver through the veins and curdles the blood, which is just what it did to me. I broke out in a scaly rash that covered my smooth body with a revolting crust. And that's how my brother robbed me of my life, my crown, and my queen all at once. He cut me off in the middle of a sinful life.

Unhouseled, disappointed, unaneled.
No reckoning made, but sent to my account
With all my imperfections on my head.
80   Oh, horrible, oh, horrible, most horrible!
If thou hast nature in thee, bear it not.
Let not the royal bed of Denmark be
A couch for luxury and damnèd incest.
But howsoever thou pursuest this act,
85   Taint not thy mind, nor let thy soul contrive
Against thy mother aught. Leave her to heaven
And to those thorns that in her bosom lodge
To prick and sting her. Fare thee well at once.
The glowworm shows the matin to be near,
90   And 'gins to pale his uneffectual fire.
Adieu, adieu, adieu. Remember me.

Exit

HAMLET
O all you host of heaven! O earth! What else?
And shall I couple hell? Oh, fie! Hold, hold, my heart,
And you, my sinews, grow not instant old,
95   But bear me stiffly up. Remember thee!
Ay, thou poor ghost, whiles memory holds a seat
In this distracted globe. Remember thee!
Yea, from the table of my memory
I'll wipe away all trivial fond records,
100   All saws of books, all forms, all pressures past
That youth and observation copied there,
And thy commandment all alone shall live
Within the book and volume of my brain,
Unmixed with baser matter. Yes, by heaven!
105   O most pernicious woman!
O villain, villain, smiling, damnèd villain!
My tables!——Meet it is I set it down
That one may smile, and smile, and be a villain.
At least I'm sure it may be so in Denmark. *(writes)*
110   So, uncle, there you are. Now to my word.

I had no chance to repent my sins or receive last rites. Oh, it's horrible, horrible, so horrible! If you are human, don't stand for it. Don't let the Danish king's bed be a nest of incest. But however you go about your revenge, don't corrupt your mind or do any harm to your mother. Leave her to God and her own guilt. Now, good-bye. The glowworm's light is beginning to fade, so morning is near. Good-bye, good-bye, good-bye. Remember me.

The GHOST *exits.*

HAMLET

Ah, all you up in heaven! And earth! What else? Shall I include hell as well? Damn it! Keep beating, my heart, and muscles, don't grow old yet—keep me standing. Remember you! Yes, you poor ghost, as long as I have any power of memory in this distracted head. Remember you! Yes, I'll wipe my mind clean of all trivial facts and memories and preserve only your commandment there. Yes, by God! Oh, you evil woman! Oh, you villain, villain, you damned, smiling villain! Where's my notebook?—It's a good idea for me to write down that one can smile and smile, and be a villain. At least it's possible in Denmark. *(he writes)* So, uncle, there you are. Now it's time to deal with the vow I made to my father.

It is "Adieu, adieu. Remember me."
I have sworn 't.

Enter HORATIO *and* MARCELLUS

HORATIO
My lord, my lord!

MARCELLUS
Lord Hamlet—

HORATIO
115   Heaven secure him!

HAMLET
So be it.

HORATIO
        Illo, ho, ho, my lord!

HAMLET
Hillo, ho, ho, boy. Come, bird, come.

MARCELLUS
How is 't, my noble lord?

HORATIO
What news, my lord?

HAMLET
120   Oh, wonderful!

HORATIO
Good my lord, tell it.

HAMLET
        No. You'll reveal it.

HORATIO
Not I, my lord, by heaven.

MARCELLUS
Nor I, my lord.

HAMLET
How say you, then? Would heart of man once think it?
125   But you'll be secret?

HORATIO, MARCELLUS
        Ay, by heaven, my lord.

He said, "Remember me." I swore I would.

MARCELLUS *and* HORATIO *enter.*

HORATIO
Sir, sir!

MARCELLUS
Lord Hamlet.—

HORATIO
Please let him be all right!

HAMLET
I'm all right.

HORATIO
Oh-ho-ho, sir!

HAMLET
Oh-ho-ho, kid! Come here.

MARCELLUS
So how did it go, sir?

HORATIO
What happened, sir?

HAMLET
It was incredible!

HORATIO
Oh, please, tell us, sir.

HAMLET
No, you'll talk.

HORATIO
I swear I won't, sir.

MARCELLUS
I won't either, sir.

HAMLET
Okay. But you promise you can keep a secret?

HORATIO, MARCELLUS
Yes, I swear.

HAMLET
> There's ne'er a villain dwelling in all Denmark
> But he's an arrant knave.

HORATIO
> There needs no ghost, my lord, come from the grave
> To tell us this.

HAMLET
>   Why, right, you are in the right.
> 130 And so, without more circumstance at all,
> I hold it fit that we shake hands and part.
> You, as your business and desire shall point you—
> For every man has business and desire,
> Such as it is—and for my own poor part,
> 135 Look you, I'll go pray.

HORATIO
> These are but wild and whirling words, my lord.

HAMLET
> I'm sorry they offend you, heartily.
> Yes faith, heartily.

HORATIO
>   There's no offense, my lord.

HAMLET
> Yes, by Saint Patrick, but there is, Horatio,
> 140 And much offense too. Touching this vision here,
> It is an honest ghost, that let me tell you.
> For your desire to know what is between us,
> O'ermaster 't as you may. And now, good friends,
> As you are friends, scholars and soldiers,
> 145 Give me one poor request.

HORATIO
>   What is 't, my lord? We will.

HAMLET
> Never make known what you have seen tonight.

HORATIO, MARCELLUS
> My lord, we will not.

HAMLET

Any villain in Denmark is going to be, well, a villain.

HORATIO

You don't need a ghost returning from the grave to tell you that, sir.

HAMLET

Yes, you're absolutely right. So, without further ado, the best thing to do now is probably just to shake hands and go our separate ways. You go and take care of your business (since everybody has some business to take care of, whatever it is worth), and I'll go and pray.

HORATIO

You're talking in such a crazy way, sir.

HAMLET

I'm sorry if I offended you; yes, very sorry.

HORATIO

Oh, don't worry about it, sir. No offense taken.

HAMLET

Ah, but there is, Horatio, there's a lot of offense. As for this ghost we just saw, he's a real one, I can tell you that much. But regarding what happened between us, don't ask—I can't tell you. And now, my friends, my courageous and educated friends, do me one small favor.

HORATIO

What is it, sir? Of course we will.

HAMLET

Don't ever tell anyone what you've seen tonight.

HORATIO, MARCELLUS

We won't, sir.

HAMLET

Nay, but swear 't.

HORATIO
In faith, my lord, not I.

MARCELLUS

Nor I, my lord, in faith.

HAMLET
Upon my sword.

MARCELLUS

We have sworn, my lord, already.

HAMLET
150   Indeed, upon my sword, indeed.

GHOST
(cries under the stage) Swear!

HAMLET
Ha, ha, boy! Sayst thou so? Art thou there, truepenny?
Come on, you hear this fellow in the cellarage.
Consent to swear.

HORATIO
155   Propose the oath, my lord.

HAMLET
Never to speak of this that you have seen.
Swear by my sword.

GHOST
(beneath)   Swear.

HAMLET
Hic et ubique? Then we'll shift our ground.
Come hither, gentlemen,
160   And lay your hands again upon my sword.
Swear by my sword
Never to speak of this that you have heard.

GHOST
(beneath) Swear by his sword.

HAMLET
Well said, old mole! Canst work i' th' earth so fast?
165   A worthy pioneer! Once more remove, good friends.

HAMLET

No, you have to swear it.

HORATIO

I swear to God I won't.

MARCELLUS

Me too, I won't, I swear to God.

HAMLET

Swear by my sword.

MARCELLUS

But we already swore, sir.

HAMLET

Yes, but swear by my sword this time.

GHOST

(calls out from under the stage) Swear!

HAMLET

Ha ha, is that what you say, kid? Are you down there, my man?—Come on, you hear this guy down in the basement. Agree to swear.

HORATIO

Tell us what to swear, sir.

HAMLET

You swear never to mention what you've seen. Swear by my sword.

GHOST

(from under the stage) Swear.

HAMLET

You're everywhere, aren't you? Maybe we should move. Come over here, gentlemen, and put your hands on my sword again. Swear by my sword you'll never mention what you've heard.

GHOST

(from under the stage) Swear by his sword.

HAMLET

You said it right, old mole. You're pretty busy down there in the dirt, aren't you? What a tunneler! Let's move again, my friends.

HORATIO

O day and night, but this is wondrous strange!

HAMLET

And therefore as a stranger give it welcome.
There are more things in heaven and earth, Horatio,
Than are dreamt of in your philosophy. But come,
170 Here, as before, never, so help you mercy,
How strange or odd soe'er I bear myself
(As I perchance hereafter shall think meet
To put an antic disposition on),
That you, at such times seeing me, never shall—
175 With arms encumbered thus, or this headshake,
Or by pronouncing of some doubtful phrase,
As "Well, well, we know," or "We could an if we would,"
Or "If we list to speak," or "There be an if they might,"
Or such ambiguous giving out—to note
180 That you know aught of me. This not to do,
So grace and mercy at your most need help you,
Swear.

GHOST

(beneath) Swear!

HAMLET

Rest, rest, perturbèd spirit!—So, gentlemen,
With all my love I do commend me to you,
185 And what so poor a man as Hamlet is
May do, to express his love and friending to you,
God willing, shall not lack. Let us go in together,
And still your fingers on your lips, I pray.
The time is out of joint. O cursèd spite,
190 That ever I was born to set it right!
Nay, come, let's go together.

Exeunt

HORATIO

My God, this is unbelievably strange.

HAMLET

Then give it a nice welcome, as you would give to any stranger. There are more things in heaven and earth, Horatio, than you've even dreamed of. But now listen to me. No matter how strangely I act (since I may find it appropriate to act a little crazy in the near future), you must never, ever let on—with a gesture of your hands or a certain expression on your face—that you know anything about what happened to me here tonight. You must never say anything like, "Ah, yes, just as we suspected," or "We could tell you a thing or two about him," or anything like that. Swear you won't.

GHOST

(from under the stage) Swear.

HAMLET

Okay, then, unhappy ghost, you can rest now. So, gentlemen, I thank you heartily and with all my love, and I'll repay you however I can some day. Let's go back to court together, but *shhh,* please. No talking about this. There is so much out of whack in these times. And damn the fact that I'm supposed to fix it! Come on, let's go.

They exit.

ACT TWO

SCENE 1

Enter POLONIUS *with his man* REYNALDO

POLONIUS
Give him this money and these notes, Reynaldo.

REYNALDO
I will, my lord.

POLONIUS
You shall do marvelous wisely, good Reynaldo,
Before you visit him, to make inquire
5 Of his behavior.

REYNALDO
My lord, I did intend it.

POLONIUS
Marry, well said, very well said. Look you, sir,
Inquire me first what Danskers are in Paris,
And how, and who, what means, and where they keep
What company at what expense; and finding
10 By this encompassment and drift of question
That they do know my son, come you more nearer
Than your particular demands will touch it.
Take you, as 'twere, some distant knowledge of him,
As thus: "I know his father and his friends,
15 And, in part, him." Do you mark this, Reynaldo?

REYNALDO
Ay, very well, my lord.

POLONIUS
"And in part him, but," you may say, "not well.
But, if 't be he I mean, he's very wild.
Addicted so and so.—" And there put on him
20 What forgeries you please. Marry, none so rank
As may dishonor him. Take heed of that.
But, sir, such wanton, wild, and usual slips

ACT TWO
SCENE 1

POLONIUS *enters with his servant* REYNALDO.

POLONIUS

Give him this money and these letters, Reynaldo.

REYNALDO

I will, sir.

POLONIUS

It would be wonderfully wise of you, my dear Reynaldo, to ask around about his behavior a little before you visit him.

REYNALDO

That's what I thought too, sir.

POLONIUS

Excellent, very good. Ask around and find out what Danish people are in Paris—who they are, where they live and how much money they have, who their friends are. And if you find out in this general sort of questioning that they happen to know my son, you'll find out much more than if you asked specific questions about him. Just tell them you vaguely know Laertes, say something like, "I'm a friend of his father and I sort of know him," or whatever. Do you get what I'm saying, Reynaldo?

REYNALDO

Yes, very well, sir.

POLONIUS

You should say, "I sort of know him, but not well. Is it the same Laertes who's a wild party animal? Isn't he the one who's always," and so on. Then just make up whatever you want—of course, nothing so bad that it would shame him. I mean make up any stories that

As are companions noted and most known
To youth and liberty.

REYNALDO

As gaming, my lord?

POLONIUS

25 Ay, or drinking, fencing, swearing,
Quarreling, drabbing—you may go so far.

REYNALDO

My lord, that would dishonor him!

POLONIUS

'Faith, no, as you may season it in the charge.
You must not put another scandal on him
30 That he is open to incontinency.
That's not my meaning. But breathe his faults so quaintly
That they may seem the taints of liberty,
The flash and outbreak of a fiery mind,
A savageness in unreclaimèd blood,
35 Of general assault.

REYNALDO

But, my good lord—

POLONIUS

Wherefore should you do this?

REYNALDO

Ay, my lord. I would know that.

POLONIUS

Marry, sir, here's my drift:
(And I believe it is a fetch of wit)
40 You, laying these slight sullies on my son
As 'twere a thing a little soiled i' th' working—
Mark you, your party in converse, him you would sound,
Having ever seen in the prenominate crimes
The youth you breathe of guilty, be assured
45 He closes with you in this consequence:
"Good sir" or so, or "Friend," or "Gentleman,"
According to the phrase or the addition
Of man and country.

sound like your average young guy, the kind of trouble they get into.

REYNALDO

Like gambling, sir?

POLONIUS

That's right, or drinking, swearing, fist-fighting, visiting prostitutes—that kind of thing.

REYNALDO

But that would ruin his reputation!

POLONIUS

Oh no, not if you say it right. I don't want you to say he's a sex fiend, that's not what I mean. Just mention his faults lightly, so they make him seem like a free spirit who's gone a little too far.

REYNALDO

But, sir—

POLONIUS

Why should you do this, you want to know?

REYNALDO

Yes, sir. I'd like to know.

POLONIUS

Well, here's what I'm thinking. (I'm quite proud of myself for coming up with this.) As you talk with someone and hint about my son's faults and little sins, you'll watch his reaction, and if he's ever seen Laertes do any of these things, it will only be natural for him to agree with you, at which point he'll call you "sir," or "my good friend," depending on who the person is, where he comes from, and so on.

REYNALDO
　　　　　　　　Very good, my lord.

POLONIUS
And then, sir, does he this, he does—What was I about to
50　　say? By the mass, I was about to say something. Where did
I leave?

REYNALDO
At "closes in the consequence," at "'friend,'
Or so" and "'gentleman.'"

POLONIUS
At "closes in the consequence." Ay, marry.
55　　He closes thus: "I know the gentleman.
I saw him yesterday"—or "t' other day,"
Or then, or then, with such or such—"and, as you say,
There was he gaming, there o'ertook in's rouse,
There falling out at tennis," or, perchance,
60　　"I saw him enter such a house of sale"—
Videlicet a brothel, or so forth. See you now,
Your bait of falsehood takes this carp of truth.
And thus do we of wisdom and of reach,
With windlasses and with assays of bias,
65　　By indirections find directions out.
So by my former lecture and advice
Shall you my son. You have me, have you not?

REYNALDO
My lord, I have.

POLONIUS
　　　　　　　　God be wi' you. Fare you well.

REYNALDO
Good my lord.

POLONIUS
70　　Observe his inclination in yourself.

REYNALDO
I shall, my lord.

REYNALDO

Yes, sir.

POLONIUS

And then he'll . . . he'll . . . wait, what was I about to say? Good God, I was about to say something. What was I saying?

REYNALDO

At, "It will be natural for him to agree with you . . . he'll call you 'sir,' 'friend,'" et cetera.

POLONIUS

"It will be natural for him to agree with you." Ah, yes, that's right. If he agrees he'll say something like this: "Yes, I know the gentleman you're referring to. I just saw him yesterday," or "the other day," or whenever it is, you know, "and there he was gambling," or "there he was, totally wasted, or fighting with somebody about a tennis match, or going into a house of ill repute"—that means a whorehouse, you know—or whatever. Make sure your little lie brings out the truth. We're doing this wisely and intelligently, indirectly, finding out things by roundabout means. That's how you'll find out what my son is up to in Paris. You get my point, don't you?

REYNALDO

Yes, I do, sir.

POLONIUS

God bless you. Have a safe trip.

REYNALDO

Thank you, sir.

POLONIUS

Don't forget to see what he's up to with your own eyes. Don't trust gossip.

REYNALDO

I will, sir.

POLONIUS
And let him ply his music.

REYNALDO
Well, my lord.

POLONIUS
Farewell.

Exit **REYNALDO**

Enter **OPHELIA**

How now, Ophelia? What's the matter?

OPHELIA
75   O my lord, my lord, I have been so affrighted!

POLONIUS
With what, i' th' name of God?

OPHELIA
My lord, as I was sewing in my closet,
Lord Hamlet, with his doublet all unbraced;
No hat upon his head; his stockings fouled,
80   Ungartered, and down-gyvèd to his ankle;
Pale as his shirt; his knees knocking each other;
And with a look so piteous in purport
As if he had been loosèd out of hell
To speak of horrors—he comes before me.

POLONIUS
85   Mad for thy love?

OPHELIA
My lord, I do not know.
But truly, I do fear it.

POLONIUS
What said he?

OPHELIA
He took me by the wrist and held me hard.
Then goes he to the length of all his arm,
And, with his other hand thus o'er his brow,
90   He falls to such perusal of my face
As he would draw it. Long stayed he so.

POLONIUS

And I hope he's studying his music like he's supposed to.

REYNALDO

Got it, sir.

POLONIUS

Good-bye.

REYNALDO exits.

OPHELIA enters.

Ophelia, what's the matter?

OPHELIA

Oh, father, father, I've just had such a scare!

POLONIUS

From what, in God's name?

OPHELIA

Father, I was up in my room sewing when Hamlet came in with no hat on his head, his shirt unbuttoned, and his stockings dirty, undone, and down around his ankles. He was pale as his undershirt, and his knees were knocking together. He looked so out of sorts, as if he'd just come back from hell. He came up to me.

POLONIUS

Is he crazy with love for you?

OPHELIA

I'm not sure, but I'm afraid he might be.

POLONIUS

What did he say?

OPHELIA

He grabbed me by the wrist and held me hard, then backed away an arm's length and just looked at me, staring at me like an artist about to paint my picture. He stayed like that a long time.

At last, a little shaking of mine arm
And thrice his head thus waving up and down,
He raised a sigh so piteous and profound
95 As it did seem to shatter all his bulk
And end his being. That done, he lets me go,
And, with his head over his shoulder turned,
He seemed to find his way without his eyes,
For out o' doors he went without their helps,
100 And to the last bended their light on me.

POLONIUS
Come, go with me. I will go seek the king.
This is the very ecstasy of love,
Whose violent property fordoes itself
And leads the will to desperate undertakings
105 As oft as any passion under heaven
That does afflict our natures. I am sorry.
What, have you given him any hard words of late?

OPHELIA
No, my good lord. But as you did command
I did repel his fetters and denied
110 His access to me.

POLONIUS
                        That hath made him mad.
I am sorry that with better heed and judgment
I had not quoted him. I feared he did but trifle
And meant to wreck thee. But beshrew my jealousy!
By heaven, it is as proper to our age
115 To cast beyond ourselves in our opinions
As it is common for the younger sort
To lack discretion. Come, go we to the king.
This must be known, which, being kept close, might move
More grief to hide than hate to utter love.
120 Come.

Exeunt

Finally, after shaking my arm a little, and jerking his head up and down three times, he sighed like it was his last breath. After that he let me go. He left the room with his head turned back on me, finding his way out without looking, since his eyes were on me the whole time.

POLONIUS

Come with me. I'll go tell the king about this. This is definitely love-craziness. Love is such a violent emotion that it makes people self-destruct, as much as any strong emotion. I'm so sorry. Did you tell him anything that might have hurt his feelings lately?

OPHELIA

No, father, but I did what you told me to do and sent back his letters and wouldn't let him visit me.

POLONIUS

That's what made him crazy. I regret not observing him more closely before I told you to do that. I thought he was just toying with you and meant to ruin your reputation. Damn my suspicious thoughts! It's as common for us old people to assume we know more than we do as for young people to be too wild and crazy. Come on, let's go see the king. We've got to discuss this matter, which could cause more trouble if we keep it secret than if we discuss it openly.

They exit.

ACT 2, SCENE 2

Flourish. Enter King CLAUDIUS *and Queen* GERTRUDE, ROSENCRANTZ *and* GUILDENSTERN, *and attendants*

CLAUDIUS
　　　　Welcome, dear Rosencrantz and Guildenstern.
　　　　Moreover that we much did long to see you,
　　　　The need we have to use you did provoke
　　　　Our hasty sending. Something have you heard
5　　　　Of Hamlet's "transformation"—so call it
　　　　Since nor th' exterior nor the inward man
　　　　Resembles that it was. What it should be,
　　　　More than his father's death, that thus hath put him
　　　　So much from th' understanding of himself,
10　　　　I cannot dream of. I entreat you both
　　　　That, being of so young days brought up with him
　　　　And since so neighbored to his youth and 'havior,
　　　　That you vouchsafe your rest here in our court
　　　　Some little time so by your companies
15　　　　To draw him on to pleasures and to gather,
　　　　So much as from occasion you may glean,
　　　　Whether aught, to us unknown, afflicts him thus
　　　　That, opened, lies within our remedy.

GERTRUDE
　　　　Good gentlemen, he hath much talked of you.
20　　　　And sure I am two men there are not living
　　　　To whom he more adheres. If it will please you
　　　　To show us so much gentry and good will
　　　　As to expend your time with us awhile
　　　　For the supply and profit of our hope,
25　　　　Your visitation shall receive such thanks
　　　　As fits a king's remembrance.

ACT 2, SCENE 2

Trumpets play. CLAUDIUS *and* GERTRUDE *enter with*
ROSENCRANTZ, GUILDENSTERN, *and attendants.*

CLAUDIUS

Welcome, dear Rosencrantz and Guildenstern. I've
wanted to see you for a long time now, but I sent for
you so hastily because I need your help right away.
You've probably heard about the "change" that's
come over Hamlet—that's the only word for it, since
inside and out he's different from what he was before.
I can't imagine what's made him so unlike himself,
other than his father's death. Since you both grew up
with him and are so familiar with his personality and
behavior, I'm asking you to stay a while at court and
spend some time with him. See if you can get Hamlet
to have some fun, and find out if there's anything in
particular that's bothering him, so we can set about
trying to fix it.

GERTRUDE

Gentlemen, Hamlet's talked a lot about you, and I
know there are no two men alive he's fonder of. If
you'll be so good as to spend some time with us and
help us out, you'll be thanked on a royal scale.

ROSENCRANTZ
                                        Both your majesties
         Might, by the sovereign power you have of us,
         Put your dread pleasures more into command
         Than to entreaty.

GUILDENSTERN
                                        But we both obey
30   And here give up ourselves, in the full bent,
         To lay our service freely at your feet
         To be commanded.

CLAUDIUS
         Thanks, Rosencrantz and gentle Guildenstern.

GERTRUDE
         Thanks, Guildenstern and gentle Rosencrantz.
35   And I beseech you instantly to visit
         My too much changèd son. Go, some of you,
         And bring these gentlemen where Hamlet is.

GUILDENSTERN
         Heavens make our presence and our practices
         Pleasant and helpful to him!

GERTRUDE
                                        Ay, amen!

Exeunt ROSENCRANTZ *and* GUILDENSTERN,
                                escorted by attendants

Enter POLONIUS

POLONIUS
40   Th' ambassadors from Norway, my good lord,
         Are joyfully returned.

CLAUDIUS
         Thou still hast been the father of good news.

POLONIUS
         Have I, my lord? I assure my good liege,
         I hold my duty as I hold my soul,
45   Both to my God and to my gracious king.
         And I do think—or else this brain of mine
         Hunts not the trail of policy so sure

ROSENCRANTZ

> Both you and the king might have ordered us to execute your command, instead of asking us so politely.

GUILDENSTERN

> But we'll obey. Our services are entirely at your command.

CLAUDIUS

> Thanks, Rosencrantz and worthy Guildenstern.

GERTRUDE

> Thanks, Guildenstern and worthy Rosencrantz.
> I beg you to pay a visit right away to my son, who's changed too much. Servants, take these gentlemen to see Hamlet.

GUILDENSTERN

> I hope to God we can make him happy and do him some good!

GERTRUDE

> Amen to that!

> > ROSENCRANTZ *and* GUILDENSTERN *exit,*
> > *escorted by attendants.*

> POLONIUS *enters.*

POLONIUS

> The ambassadors are back from Norway, sir.

CLAUDIUS

> Once again you bring good news.

POLONIUS

> Do I, sir? I assure your majesty I'm only doing my duty both to my God and my good king. And I believe—unless this brain of mine is not so politically cunning

As it hath used to do—that I have found
The very cause of Hamlet's lunacy.

CLAUDIUS

50   Oh, speak of that. That do I long to hear.

POLONIUS

Give first admittance to th' ambassadors.
My news shall be the fruit to that great feast.

CLAUDIUS

Thyself do grace to them, and bring them in.

Exit POLONIUS

He tells me, my dear Gertrude, he hath found
55   The head and source of all your son's distemper.

GERTRUDE

I doubt it is no other but the main:
His father's death and our o'erhasty marriage.

Enter POLONIUS *with ambassadors* VOLTEMAND *and*
CORNELIUS

CLAUDIUS

Well, we shall sift him.—Welcome, my good friends!
Say, Voltemand, what from our brother Norway?

VOLTEMAND

60   Most fair return of greetings and desires.
Upon our first, he sent out to suppress
His nephew's levies, which to him appeared
To be a preparation 'gainst the Polack,
But, better looked into, he truly found
65   It was against your highness. Whereat grieved—
That so his sickness, age, and impotence
Was falsely borne in hand—sends out arrests
On Fortinbras, which he, in brief, obeys,
Receives rebuke from Norway, and in fine
70   Makes vow before his uncle never more
To give th' assay of arms against your majesty.

as it used to be—that I've found out why Hamlet's gone crazy.

CLAUDIUS

Tell me! I want very much to find out.

POLONIUS

All right, but first let the ambassadors speak. Then you can hear my news, as dessert.

CLAUDIUS

Then be so kind as to show them in.

POLONIUS exits.

Gertrude, he says he's found out the reason for your son's insanity.

GERTRUDE

I doubt it's anything but the obvious reason: his father's dying and our quick marriage.

POLONIUS enters with the ambassadors
VOLTEMAND and CORNELIUS.

CLAUDIUS

Well, we'll get to the bottom of it. Welcome, my good friends. Tell me, Voltemand, what's the news from the king of Norway?

VOLTEMAND

Greetings to you too, your Highness. As soon as we raised the matter, the king sent out messengers to stop his nephew's war preparations, which he originally thought were directed against Poland but learned on closer examination were directed against you. He was very upset that Fortinbras had taken advantage of his being old and sick to deceive him, and he ordered Fortinbras's arrest. Fortinbras swore never to threaten Denmark again.

Whereon old Norway, overcome with joy,
Gives him three thousand crowns in annual fee
And his commission to employ those soldiers,
75 So levied as before, against the Polack,
With an entreaty, herein further shown,
That it might please you to give quiet pass
Through your dominions for this enterprise,
On such regards of safety and allowance
80 As therein are set down. *(gives* CLAUDIUS *a document)*

CLAUDIUS
                              It likes us well,
And at our more considered time we'll read,
Answer, and think upon this business.
Meantime we thank you for your well-took labor.
Go to your rest. At night we'll feast together.
85 Most welcome home!
                              Exeunt VOLTEMAND *and* CORNELIUS

POLONIUS
This business is well ended.
My liege and madam, to expostulate
What majesty should be, what duty is,
Why day is day, night night, and time is time,
90 Were nothing but to waste night, day, and time.
Therefore, since brevity is the soul of wit
And tediousness the limbs and outward flourishes,
I will be brief: your noble son is mad.
Mad call I it, for, to define true madness,
95 What is 't but to be nothing else but mad?
But let that go.

GERTRUDE
More matter, with less art.

POLONIUS
Madam, I swear I use no art at all.
That he is mad, 'tis true. Tis true, 'tis pity,
100 And pity 'tis 'tis true—a foolish figure,
But farewell it, for I will use no art.

The old king was so overjoyed by this promise that he gave young Fortinbras an annual income of three thousand crowns and permission to lead his soldiers into Poland, asking you officially in this letter to allow his troops to pass through your kingdom on their way to Poland. He's assuring you of your safety. *(he gives* CLAUDIUS *a document)*

A crown is a kind of gold coin.

CLAUDIUS

I like this news, and when I have time I'll read this and think about how to reply. Meanwhile, thank you for your efforts. Go relax now. Tonight we'll have dinner. Welcome back!

VOLTEMAND *and* CORNELIUS *exit.*

POLONIUS

Well, that turned out well in the end. Sir and madam, to make grand speeches about what majesty is, what service is, or why day is day, night is night, and time is time is just a waste of a lot of day, night, and time. Therefore, since the essence of wisdom is not talking too much, I'll get right to the point here. Your son is crazy. "Crazy" I'm calling it, since how can you say what craziness is except to say that it's craziness? But that's another story.

GERTRUDE

Please, stick to the point.

POLONIUS

Madam, I'm doing nothing but sticking to the point. It's true he's crazy, and it's a shame it's true, and it's truly a shame he's crazy—but now I sound foolish, so I'll get right to the point.

Mad let us grant him then. And now remains
That we find out the cause of this effect,
Or rather say, the cause of this defect,
105　For this effect defective comes by cause.
Thus it remains, and the remainder thus. Perpend.
I have a daughter—have while she is mine—
Who in her duty and obedience, mark,
Hath given me this. Now gather and surmise.
110　*(reads a letter) "To the celestial and my soul's idol, the most
beautified Ophelia"*—That's an ill phrase, a vile phrase.
"Beautified" is a vile phrase. But you shall hear. Thus:
(reads the letter) "In her excellent white bosom, these," etc.—

GERTRUDE
Came this from Hamlet to her?

POLONIUS
115　Good madam, stay a while. I will be faithful.
(reads the letter)
　　　"Doubt thou the stars are fire,
　　　Doubt that the sun doth move,
　　　Doubt truth to be a liar,
　　　But never doubt I love.
120　　O dear Ophelia, I am ill at these numbers. I have not
art to reckon my groans, but that I love thee best, oh,
most best, believe it. Adieu.
　　　Thine evermore, most dear lady,
　　　whilst this machine is to him,
　　　　　　　　　　　　　Hamlet."
125　This in obedience hath my daughter shown me,
And more above, hath his solicitings,
As they fell out by time, by means, and place,
All given to mine ear.

CLAUDIUS
But how hath she received his love?

Now, if we agree Hamlet's crazy, then the next step is to figure out the cause of this effect of craziness, or I suppose I should say the cause of this defect, since this defective effect is caused by something. This is what we must do, and that's exactly what needs to be done. Think about it. I have a daughter (I have her until she gets married) who's given me this letter, considering it her duty. Listen and think about this: "To the heavenly idol of my soul, the most beautified Ophelia"— By the way, "beautified" sounds bad, it sounds awful, it sounds crude, it's a terrible use of the word. But I'll go on: "In her excellent white bosom," et cetera, et cetera—you don't need to hear all this stuff . . .

GERTRUDE

Hamlet wrote this letter to Ophelia?

POLONIUS

Madam, please be patient. I'll read it to you.
> *"You may wonder if the stars are fire,*
> *You may wonder if the sun moves across the sky.*
> *You may wonder if the truth is a liar,*
> *But never wonder if I love.*

Oh, Ophelia, I'm bad at poetry. I can't put my feelings into verse, but please believe I love you best, oh, best of all. Believe it.
> *Yours forever, my dearest one,*
> *as long as I live—still chugging along,*
> > > *Hamlet."*

Dutifully and obediently my daughter showed me this letter, and more like it. She's told me all about how Hamlet has been courting her—all the details of where, and what he said, and when.

CLAUDIUS

And how did she react to all this?

POLONIUS
130   What do you think of me?

CLAUDIUS
    As of a man faithful and honorable.

POLONIUS
    I would fain prove so. But what might you think,
    When I had seen this hot love on the wing—
    As I perceived it, I must tell you that,
135   Before my daughter told me—what might you,
    Or my dear majesty your queen here, think,
    If I had played the desk or table-book,
    Or given my heart a winking, mute and dumb,
    Or looked upon this love with idle sight?
140   What might you think? No, I went round to work,
    And my young mistress thus I did bespeak:
    "Lord Hamlet is a prince out of thy star.
    This must not be." And then I prescripts gave her,
    That she should lock herself from his resort,
145   Admit no messengers, receive no tokens.
    Which done, she took the fruits of my advice;
    And he, repelled—a short tale to make—
    Fell into a sadness, then into a fast,
    Thence to a watch, thence into a weakness,
150   Thence to a lightness, and, by this declension,
    Into the madness wherein now he raves
    And all we mourn for.

CLAUDIUS
    (to GERTRUDE*)* Do you think 'tis this?

GERTRUDE
                     It may be, very like.

POLONIUS
    Hath there been such a time—I would fain know that—
155   That I have positively said, "'Tis so,"
    When it proved otherwise?

CLAUDIUS
                    Not that I know.

POLONIUS

Sir, what is your opinion of me?

CLAUDIUS

I know you are loyal and honorable.

POLONIUS

I would like to prove to you that I am. But what would you have thought of me if I had kept quiet when I found out about this hot little love (which I noticed even before my daughter told me about it)? My dear queen, what would you have thought of me if I had turned a blind eye to what was happening between Hamlet and my daughter? No, I had to do something. And so I said to my daughter: "Lord Hamlet is a prince, he's out of your league. You have to end this." And then I gave her orders to stay away from him, and not to accept any messages or little gifts from him. She did what I said. When she rejected Hamlet, he became sad, and stopped eating, stopped sleeping, got weak, got dizzy, and as a result lost his mind. And that's why he's crazy now, and all of us feel sorry for him.

CLAUDIUS

(to GERTRUDE*)* Do you think that's why Hamlet's crazy?

GERTRUDE

It may be, it certainly may be.

POLONIUS

Has there ever been a time—I'd really like to know—when I've definitely said something was true, and it turned out not to be true?

CLAUDIUS

Not that I know of.

POLONIUS
(points to his head and shoulders)
Take this from this if this be otherwise.
If circumstances lead me, I will find
Where truth is hid, though it were hid indeed
160   Within the center.

CLAUDIUS
                    How may we try it further?

POLONIUS
You know sometimes he walks four hours together
Here in the lobby.

GERTRUDE
                 So he does indeed.

POLONIUS
At such a time I'll loose my daughter to him.
(to CLAUDIUS*)* Be you and I behind an arras then,
165   Mark the encounter. If he love her not
And be not from his reason fall'n thereon,
Let me be no assistant for a state
But keep a farm and carters.

CLAUDIUS
                    We will try it.

Enter HAMLET, *reading on a book*

GERTRUDE
But look where sadly the poor wretch comes reading.

POLONIUS
170   Away, I do beseech you, both away.
I'll board him presently. O, give me leave.
               Exeunt CLAUDIUS *and* GERTRUDE
How does my good Lord Hamlet?

HAMLET
Well, God-'a'-mercy.

POLONIUS

> *(pointing to his head and shoulders)* Chop my head off if I'm wrong. I'll follow the clues and uncover the truth, even if it's at the very center of the earth.

CLAUDIUS

> What can we do to find out if it's true?

POLONIUS

> Well, you know he sometimes walks here in the lobby for four hours at a time.

GERTRUDE

> Yes, he does.

POLONIUS

> When he's there next time, I'll send my daughter to see him. *(to* CLAUDIUS*)* You and I will hide behind the arras and watch what happens. If it turns out that Hamlet's not in love after all, and hasn't gone mad from love, then you can fire me from my court job and I'll go work on a farm.

An arras is a hanging wall-tapestry.

CLAUDIUS

> We'll try what you suggest.

> HAMLET *enters, reading a book.*

GERTRUDE

> Look how sadly he's coming in, reading his book.

POLONIUS

> Please go away, both of you. I'll speak to him now. Oh, please let me.

> CLAUDIUS *and* GERTRUDE *exit.*

> How are you, Hamlet?

HAMLET

> Fine, thank you.

POLONIUS
Do you know me, my lord?

HAMLET
175   Excellent well. You are a fishmonger.

POLONIUS
Not I, my lord.

HAMLET
Then I would you were so honest a man.

POLONIUS
Honest, my lord?

HAMLET
Ay, sir. To be honest, as this world goes, is to be one man
180   picked out of ten thousand.

POLONIUS
That's very true, my lord.

HAMLET
For if the sun breed maggots in a dead dog, being a good
kissing carrion— Have you a daughter?

POLONIUS
I have, my lord.

HAMLET
185   Let her not walk i' th' sun. Conception is a blessing, but, as
your daughter may conceive—Friend, look to 't.

POLONIUS
(aside) How say you by that? Still harping on my daughter.
Yet he knew me not at first. He said I was a fishmonger. He
is far gone, far gone. And truly in my youth I suffered much
190   extremity for love, very near this. I'll speak to him again.—
(to **HAMLET***)* What do you read, my lord?

HAMLET
Words, words, words.

POLONIUS
What is the matter, my lord?

POLONIUS

Do you know who I am?

HAMLET

Of course. You sell fish.

POLONIUS

No, not me, sir.

HAMLET

In that case I wish you were as good a man as a fish seller.

POLONIUS

Good, sir?

HAMLET

Yes, sir. Only one man in ten thousand is good in this world.

POLONIUS

That's definitely true, my lord.

HAMLET

Since if the sun breeds maggots on a dead dog, kissing the corpse—by the way, do you have a daughter?

POLONIUS

I do indeed, my lord.

HAMLET

Then by all means never let her walk in public. Procreation is a good thing, but if your daughter gets pregnant . . . look out, friend.

POLONIUS

(to himself) Now, what does he mean by that? Still harping on my daughter. But he didn't recognize me at first. He mistook me for a fish seller. He's far gone. But when I was young I went crazy for love too, almost as bad as this. I'll talk to him again.—*(to* **HAMLET***)* What are you reading, your highness?

HAMLET

A lot of words.

POLONIUS

And what is the subject?

HAMLET

Between who?

POLONIUS

195   I mean, the matter that you read, my lord.

HAMLET

Slanders, sir. For the satirical rogue says here that old men
have gray beards, that their faces are wrinkled, their eyes
purging thick amber and plum-tree gum, and that they
have a plentiful lack of wit, together with most weak
200   hams—all which, sir, though I most powerfully and
potently believe, yet I hold it not honesty to have it thus set
down; for yourself, sir, should be old as I am, if like a crab
you could go backward.

POLONIUS

(aside) Though this be madness, yet there is method in 't.—
205   *(to* **HAMLET***)* Will you walk out of the air, my lord?

HAMLET

Into my grave.

POLONIUS

Indeed, that is out of the air. *(aside)* How pregnant
sometimes his replies are. A happiness that often madness
hits on, which reason and sanity could not so prosperously
210   be delivered of. I will leave him and suddenly contrive the
means of meeting between him and my daughter.—*(to*
HAMLET*)* My honorable lord, I will most humbly take my
leave of you.

HAMLET

You cannot, sir, take from me any thing that I will more
215   willingly part withal—except my life, except my life, except
my life.

POLONIUS

Fare you well, my lord.

HAMLET

(aside) These tedious old fools!

Enter ROSENCRANTZ *and* GUILDENSTERN

HAMLET

Between whom?

POLONIUS

I mean, what do the words say?

HAMLET

Oh, just lies, sir. The sly writer says here that old men have gray beards, their faces are wrinkled, their eyes full of gunk, and that they have no wisdom and weak thighs. Of course I believe it all, but I don't think it's good manners to write it down, since you yourself, sir, would grow as old as I am, if you could only travel backward like a crab.

POLONIUS

(to himself) There's a method to his madness. *(to* **HAMLET***)* Will you step outside, my lord?

HAMLET

Into my grave.

POLONIUS

Well, that's certainly out of this world, all right. *(to himself)* His answers are so full of meaning sometimes! He has a way with words, as crazy people often do, and that sane people don't have a talent for. I'll leave him now and arrange a meeting between him and my daughter. *(to* **HAMLET***)* My lord, I'll take my leave of you now.

"take my leave" = say good-bye

HAMLET

You can't take anything from me that I care less about—except my life, except my life, except my life.

POLONIUS

Good-bye, my lord.

HAMLET

(to himself) These boring old fools!

ROSENCRANTZ *and* **GUILDENSTERN** *enter.*

POLONIUS
You go to seek the Lord Hamlet. There he is.

ROSENCRANTZ
220   God save you, sir!

Exit **POLONIUS**

GUILDENSTERN
My honored lord!

ROSENCRANTZ
My most dear lord!

HAMLET
My excellent good friends! How dost thou, Guildenstern?
Ah, Rosencrantz! Good lads, how do you both?

ROSENCRANTZ
225   As the indifferent children of the earth.

GUILDENSTERN
Happy, in that we are not overhappy.
On Fortune's cap we are not the very button.

HAMLET
Nor the soles of her shoes?

ROSENCRANTZ
Neither, my lord.

HAMLET
230   Then you live about her waist, or in the middle of her
favors?

GUILDENSTERN
Faith, her privates we.

HAMLET
In the secret parts of Fortune? Oh, most true. She
is a strumpet. What news?

ROSENCRANTZ
235   None, my lord, but that the world's grown honest.

POLONIUS

You're looking for Lord Hamlet. He's right over there.

ROSENCRANTZ

Thank you, sir.

POLONIUS *exits.*

GUILDENSTERN

My lord!

ROSENCRANTZ

My dear sir!

HAMLET

Ah, my good old friends! How are you, Guildenstern? And Rosencrantz! Boys, how are you both doing?

ROSENCRANTZ

Oh, as well as anybody.

GUILDENSTERN

Happy that we're not too happy, lucky in being not too lucky. We're not exactly at the top of our luck.

HAMLET

But you're not down and out, either, are you?

ROSENCRANTZ

No, we're just somewhere in the middle, my lord.

HAMLET

So you're around Lady Luck's waist?

GUILDENSTERN

Yes, we're the privates in her army.

HAMLET

Ha, ha, so you've gotten into her private parts? Of course—Lady Luck is such a slut. Anyway, what's up?

ROSENCRANTZ

Not much, my lord. Just that the world's become honest.

HAMLET
> Then is doomsday near. But your news is not true. Let me question more in particular. What have you, my good friends, deserved at the hands of fortune that she sends you to prison hither?

GUILDENSTERN
240 > Prison, my lord?

HAMLET
> Denmark's a prison.

ROSENCRANTZ
> Then is the world one.

HAMLET
> A goodly one, in which there are many confines, wards, and dungeons, Denmark being one o' th' worst.

ROSENCRANTZ
245 > We think not so, my lord.

HAMLET
> Why, then, 'tis none to you, for there is nothing either good or bad, but thinking makes it so. To me it is a prison.

ROSENCRANTZ
> Why then, your ambition makes it one. 'Tis too narrow for your mind.

HAMLET
250 > O God, I could be bounded in a nutshell and count myself a king of infinite space, were it not that I have bad dreams.

GUILDENSTERN
> Which dreams indeed are ambition, for the very substance of the ambitious is merely the shadow of a dream.

HAMLET
> A dream itself is but a shadow.

ROSENCRANTZ
255 > Truly, and I hold ambition of so airy and light a quality that it is but a shadow's shadow.

HAMLET

In that case, the end of the world is approaching. But you're wrong. Let me ask you a particular question. What crimes have you committed to be sent here to this prison?

GUILDENSTERN

Prison, my lord?

HAMLET

Denmark's a prison.

ROSENCRANTZ

Then I guess the whole world is one.

HAMLET

Yes, quite a large one, with many cells and dungeons, Denmark being one of the worst.

ROSENCRANTZ

We don't think so, my lord.

HAMLET

Well, then it isn't one to you, since nothing is really good or bad in itself—it's all what a person thinks about it. And to me, Denmark is a prison.

ROSENCRANTZ

That must be because you're so ambitious. It's too small for your large mind.

HAMLET

Small? No, I could live in a walnut shell and feel like the king of the universe. The real problem is that I have bad dreams.

GUILDENSTERN

Dreams are a sign of ambition, since ambition is nothing more than the shadow of a dream.

HAMLET

But a dream itself is just a shadow.

ROSENCRANTZ

Exactly. In fact, I consider ambition to be so light and airy that it's only the shadow of a shadow.

HAMLET

Then are our beggars bodies, and our monarchs and outstretched heroes the beggars' shadows. Shall we to th' court? For by my fay, I cannot reason.

ROSENCRANTZ, GUILDENSTERN

260   We'll wait upon you.

HAMLET

No such matter. I will not sort you with the rest of my servants, for, to speak to you like an honest man, I am most dreadfully attended. But in the beaten way of friendship, what make you at Elsinore?

ROSENCRANTZ

265   To visit you, my lord, no other occasion.

HAMLET

Beggar that I am, I am even poor in thanks; but I thank you, and sure, dear friends, my thanks are too dear a halfpenny. Were you not sent for? Is it your own inclining? Is it a free visitation? Come, come, deal justly with me. Come, come.

270   Nay, speak.

GUILDENSTERN

What should we say, my lord?

HAMLET

Why, any thing, but to th' purpose. You were sent for, and there is a kind of confession in your looks which your modesties have not craft enough to color. I know the good

275   king and queen have sent for you.

ROSENCRANTZ

To what end, my lord?

HAMLET

That you must teach me. But let me conjure you, by the rights of our fellowship, by the consonancy of our youth, by the obligation of our ever-preserved love, and by what

280   more dear a better proposer could charge you withal: be even and direct with me whether you were sent for or no.

ROSENCRANTZ

(to GUILDENSTERN*)* What say you?

HAMLET

Then I guess beggars are the ones with bodies, while ambitious kings and heroes are just the shadows of beggars. Should we go inside? I seem to be losing my mind a bit.

ROSENCRANTZ, GUILDENSTERN

We're at your service, whatever you say.

HAMLET

No, no, I won't class you with my servants, since—to be frank with you—my servants are terrible. But tell me as my friends, what are you doing here at Elsinore?

ROSENCRANTZ

Visiting you, my lord. There's no other reason.

HAMLET

Well, then, I thank you, though I'm such a beggar that even my thanks are not worth much. Did someone tell you to visit me? Or was it just your whim, on your own initiative? Come on, tell me the truth.

GUILDENSTERN

What should we say, my lord?

HAMLET

Anything you like, as long as it answers my question. You were sent for. You've got a guilty look on your faces, which you're too honest to disguise. I know the king and queen sent for you.

ROSENCRANTZ

Why would they do that, my lord?

HAMLET

That's what I want you to tell me. Let me remind you of our old friendship, our youth spent together, the duties of our love for each other, and whatever else will make you answer me straight.

ROSENCRANTZ

(to GUILDENSTERN*)* What do you think?

HAMLET
> *(aside)* Nay, then, I have an eye of you—If you love me, hold
> not off.

GUILDENSTERN
> My lord, we were sent for.

HAMLET
285 > I will tell you why. So shall my anticipation prevent your
> discovery, and your secrecy to the king and queen moult no
> feather. I have of late—but wherefore I know not—lost all
> my mirth, forgone all custom of exercises, and indeed it
> goes so heavily with my disposition that this goodly frame,
290 > the earth, seems to me a sterile promontory; this most
> excellent canopy, the air—look you, this brave o'erhanging
> firmament, this majestical roof fretted with golden fire—
> why, it appears no other thing to me than a foul and
> pestilent congregation of vapors. What a piece of work is a
300 > man! How noble in reason, how infinite in faculty! In form
> and moving how express and admirable! In action how like
> an angel, in apprehension how like a god! The beauty of the
> world. The paragon of animals. And yet, to me, what is this
> quintessence of dust? Man delights not me. No, nor woman
305 > neither, though by your smiling you seem to say so.

ROSENCRANTZ
> My lord, there was no such stuff in my thoughts.

HAMLET
> Why did you laugh then, when I said "man delights not
> me"?

ROSENCRANTZ
> To think, my lord, if you delight not in man, what Lenten
310 > entertainment the players shall receive from you. We coted
> them on the way, and hither are they coming to offer you
> service.

HAMLET

(to himself) I've got my eye on you. *(to* GUILDENSTERN*)* If you care about me, you'll be honest with me.

GUILDENSTERN

My lord, we were sent for.

HAMLET

I'll tell you why—so you won't have to tell *me* and give away any secrets you have with the king and queen. Recently, though I don't know why, I've lost all sense of fun, stopped exercising—the whole world feels sterile and empty. This beautiful canopy we call the sky—this majestic roof decorated with golden sunlight—why, it's nothing more to me than disease-filled air. What a perfect invention a human is, how noble in his capacity to reason, how unlimited in thinking, how admirable in his shape and movement, how angelic in action, how godlike in understanding! There's nothing more beautiful. We surpass all other animals. And yet to me, what are we but dust? Men don't interest me. No—women neither, but you're smiling, so you must think they do.

ROSENCRANTZ

My lord, I wasn't thinking anything like that.

HAMLET

So why did you laugh when I said that men don't interest me?

ROSENCRANTZ

I was just thinking that if people don't interest you, you'll be pretty bored by the actors on their way here. We crossed paths with a drama company just a while ago, and they're coming to entertain you.

HAMLET

> He that plays the king shall be welcome. His majesty shall
> have tribute of me. The adventurous knight shall use his
315   foil and target, the lover shall not sigh gratis, the humorous
> man shall end his part in peace, the clown shall make those
> laugh whose lungs are tickle o' th' sear, and the lady shall
> say her mind freely, or the blank verse shall halt for 't. What
> players are they?

ROSENCRANTZ

320   Even those you were wont to take delight in, the tragedians
> of the city.

HAMLET

> How chances it they travel? Their residence, both in
> reputation and profit, was better both ways.

ROSENCRANTZ

> I think their inhibition comes by the means of the late
325   innovation.

HAMLET

> Do they hold the same estimation they did when I was in the
> city? Are they so followed?

ROSENCRANTZ

> No, indeed are they not.

HAMLET

> How comes it? Do they grow rusty?

ROSENCRANTZ

330   Nay, their endeavor keeps in the wonted pace. But there is,
> sir, an eyrie of children, little eyases, that cry out on the top
> of question and are most tyrannically clapped for 't. These
> are now the fashion, and so berattle the common stages—so
> they call them—that many wearing rapiers are afraid of
335   goose quills and dare scarce come thither.

HAMLET

> The one who plays the part of the king will be particularly welcome. I'll treat him like a real king. The adventurous knight will wave around his sword and shield, the lover will be rewarded for his sighs, the crazy character can rant all he wants, the clown will make everybody laugh, and the lady character can say whatever's on her mind, or I'll stop the play. Which troupe is it?

ROSENCRANTZ

> The tragic actors from the city, the ones you used to enjoy so much.

HAMLET

> What are they doing on the road? They made more money and got more attention in the city.

ROSENCRANTZ

> But things have changed there, and it's easier for them on the road now.

HAMLET

> Are they as popular as they used to be when I lived in the city? Do they attract big audiences?

ROSENCRANTZ

> No, not like before.

HAMLET

> Why? Are they getting rusty?

ROSENCRANTZ

> No, they're busy and as excellent as ever. The problem is that they have to compete with a group of children who yell out their lines and receive outrageous applause for it. These child actors are now in fashion, and they've so overtaken the public theaters that society types hardly come at all, they're so afraid of being mocked by the playwrights who write for the boys.

HAMLET

What, are they children? Who maintains 'em? How are they escoted? Will they pursue the quality no longer than they can sing? Will they not say afterwards, if they should grow themselves to common players (as it is most like if 340 their means are no better), their writers do them wrong to make them exclaim against their own succession?

ROSENCRANTZ

Faith, there has been much to do on both sides, and the nation holds it no sin to tar them to controversy. There was, for a while, no money bid for argument unless the poet and 345 the player went to cuffs in the question.

HAMLET

Is 't possible?

GUILDENSTERN

Oh, there has been much throwing about of brains.

HAMLET

Do the boys carry it away?

ROSENCRANTZ

Ay, that they do, my lord. Hercules and his load too.

HAMLET

350 It is not very strange. For my uncle is King of Denmark, and those that would make mouths at him while my father lived give twenty, forty, fifty, a hundred ducats apiece for his picture in little. 'Sblood, there is something in this more than natural, if philosophy could find it out.

Flourish for the PLAYERS *within*

GUILDENSTERN

355 There are the players.

HAMLET

What, you mean kid actors? Who takes care of them? Who pays their way? Will they stop working when their voices mature? Aren't the playwrights hurting them by making them upstage adult actors, which they are going to grow up and become? (Unless, of course, they have trust funds.)

ROSENCRANTZ

There's been a whole debate on the topic. For a while, no play was sold to the theaters without a big fight between the children's playwright and the actors playing adult roles.

HAMLET

Are you kidding?

GUILDENSTERN

Oh, there's been a lot of quarreling.

HAMLET

And the boys are winning so far?

ROSENCRANTZ

Yes, they are, my lord—little boys are carrying the whole theater on their backs, like Hercules carried the world.

HAMLET

Actually, it's not so unusual when you think about it. My uncle is king of Denmark, and the same people who made fun of him while my father was still alive are now rushing to pay twenty, forty, fifty, a hundred ducats apiece for miniature portraits of him. There's something downright unnatural about it, if a philosopher stopped to think about it.

Trumpets play offstage, announcing the arrival of the PLAYERS.

players = actors

GUILDENSTERN

The actors are here.

HAMLET

Gentlemen, you are welcome to Elsinore. Your hands, come then. Th' appurtenance of welcome is fashion and ceremony. Let me comply with you in this garb—lest my extent to the players, which, I tell you, must show fairly

360 outwards, should more appear like entertainment than yours. You are welcome. But my uncle-father and aunt-mother are deceived.

GUILDENSTERN

In what, my dear lord?

HAMLET

I am but mad north-north-west. When the wind is southerly,

365 I know a hawk from a handsaw.

Enter POLONIUS

POLONIUS

Well be with you, gentlemen.

HAMLET

Hark you, Guildenstern, and you too—at each ear a hearer. *(indicates* POLONIUS*)* That great baby you see there is not yet out of his swaddling-clouts.

ROSENCRANTZ

370 Happily he's the second time come to them, for they say an old man is twice a child.

HAMLET

(aside to ROSENCRANTZ *and* GUILDENSTERN*)* I will prophesy he comes to tell me of the players. Mark it. *(to* POLONIUS*)*— You say right, sir. O' Monday morning, 'twas so indeed.

POLONIUS

375 My lord, I have news to tell you.

HAMLET

My lord, I have news to tell you. When Roscius was an actor in Rome—

POLONIUS

The actors are come hither, my lord.

HAMLET

Gentlemen, welcome to Elsinore. Don't be shy—shake hands with me. If I'm going to welcome you I have to go through all these polite customs, don't I? And if we don't shake hands, when I act all nice to the players it will seem like I'm happier to see them than you. You are very welcome here. But still, my uncle-father and aunt-mother have got the wrong idea.

GUILDENSTERN

In what sense, my lord?

HAMLET

I'm only crazy sometimes. At other times, I know what's what.

POLONIUS *enters.*

POLONIUS

Gentlemen, I hope you are well.

HAMLET

Listen, Guildenstern, and you too, Rosencrantz—listen as close as you can! *(he gestures toward* POLONIUS*)* This big baby is still in diapers.

ROSENCRANTZ

Yes, the second time around, since, as they say, old people become children again.

HAMLET

I bet he's coming to tell me about the actors; just watch. *(pretending to have a different conversation)* You're right, sir, that happened on Monday morning.

POLONIUS

My lord, I have news for you.

HAMLET

My lord, I have news for you. When Roscius was an actor in ancient Rome —

POLONIUS

The actors have arrived, my lord.

HAMLET
Buzz, buzz.

POLONIUS
380   Upon my honor—

HAMLET
Then came each actor on his ass—

POLONIUS
The best actors in the world, either for tragedy, comedy, history, pastoral, pastoral-comical, historical-pastoral, tragical-historical, tragical-comical-historical-pastoral, scene individable, or poem unlimited. Seneca cannot be too heavy, nor Plautus too light. For the law of writ and the liberty, these are the only men.

HAMLET
O Jephthah, judge of Israel, what a treasure hadst thou!

POLONIUS
What a treasure had he, my lord?

HAMLET
390   Why,

> One fair daughter and no more,
> The which he lovèd passing well.

POLONIUS
(aside) Still on my daughter.

HAMLET
Am I not i' th' right, old Jephthah?

POLONIUS
395   If you call me Jephthah, my lord, I have a daughter that I love passing well.

HAMLET

Yawn, snore.

POLONIUS

I swear—

HAMLET

—each actor arrived on his ass.

POLONIUS

Shakespeare is making fun of the way his contemporaries classified drama.

They are the best actors in the world, either for tragedy, comedy, history, pastoral, pastoral-comical, historical-pastoral, tragical-historical, tragical-comical-historical, one-act plays, or long poems. The tragic playwright Seneca is not too heavy for them to handle nor is the comic writer Plautus too light. For formal plays or freer dramas, these are the best actors around.

HAMLET

In the Bible, Jephthah unwittingly sacrifices his daughter by making a vow too hastily. The lines below in italics are lyrics from a popular song about Jepthah. Hamlet sings them.

Oh, Jephthah, judge of ancient Israel, what a treasure you had!

POLONIUS

What treasure did he have, my lord?

HAMLET

Well, *(sings)*
> *One fine daughter, and no more,*
> *Whom he loved more than anything—.*

POLONIUS

(to himself) Still talking about my daughter, I see.

HAMLET

Aren't I right, Jephthah, old man?

POLONIUS

If you're calling me Jephthah, my lord, I do have a daughter I love more than anything, yes.

HAMLET
Nay, that follows not.

POLONIUS
What follows, then, my lord?

HAMLET
Why,

400 *As by lot, God wot,*
and then, you know,
It came to pass, as most like it was—
The first row of the pious chanson will show you more, for
look where my abridgement comes.

Enter the PLAYERS

405 You are welcome, masters, welcome, all!—I am glad to see
thee well.—Welcome, good friends.—O old friend? Why,
thy face is valenced since I saw thee last. Comest thou to
beard me in Denmark?—What, my young lady and
mistress! By 'r Lady, your ladyship is nearer to heaven than
410 when I saw you last, by the altitude of a chopine. Pray God,
your voice, like a piece of uncurrent gold, be not cracked
within the ring.—Masters, you are all welcome. We'll e'en
to 't like French falconers, fly at any thing we see. We'll have
a speech straight. Come, give us a taste of your quality.
415 Come, a passionate speech.

FIRST PLAYER
What speech, my good lord?

HAMLET
I heard thee speak me a speech once, but it was never acted.
Or, if it was, not above once, for the play, I remember,
pleased not the million. 'Twas caviary to the general. But it
420 was—as I received it, and others, whose judgments in such
matters cried in the top of mine—an excellent play, well

HAMLET

No, that's not logical.

POLONIUS

What is logical, then, my lord?

HAMLET

Why,

>   As if by chance, God knows,

and then, you know,

>   It happened, as you'd expect—

If you want to know more, you can refer to the popular song, because now I have to stop.

The PLAYERS enter.

Welcome, welcome to all of you. *(he turns to one of the actors)*—Oh, you, I'm glad to see you. *(turns back to all of them)*—Welcome, my good friends. *(turns to another actor)*—Oh, it's you! You've grown a beard since I saw you last. Are you going to put a beard on me too? *(turns to an actor dressed as a woman)*—Well hello, my young lady friend. You've grown as much as the height of a pair of platform shoes at least! I hope your voice hasn't changed yet. *(to the whole company)*—All of you are most welcome here. We'll get right to business. First, a speech. Come on, give us a little speech to whet our appetites. A passionate speech, please.

FIRST PLAYER

Which speech, my lord?

HAMLET

I heard you recite a speech for me once that was never acted out, or if it was, it was performed only once, since the play was not popular—like caviar for a slob who couldn't appreciate it. But the critics and I found it to be an excellent play, with well-ordered scenes that

Hamlet means that if Polonius has a daughter, it isn't because Hamlet called him Jephthah.

Boys played female dramatic roles in Shakespeare's day.

digested in the scenes, set down with as much modesty as
cunning. I remember, one said there were no sallets in the
lines to make the matter savory, nor no matter in the phrase
425   that might indict the author of affectation, but called it an
honest method, as wholesome as sweet, and by very much
more handsome than fine. One speech in it I chiefly loved.
'Twas Aeneas' tale to Dido and thereabout of it, especially
where he speaks of Priam's slaughter. If it live in your
430   memory, begin at this line—Let me see, let me see—
The rugged Pyrrhus, like th' Hyrcanian beast—
It is not so. It begins with Pyrrhus—
The rugged Pyrrhus, he whose sable arms,
Black as his purpose, did the night resemble
435   *When he lay couchèd in the ominous horse,*
Hath now this dread and black complexion smeared
With heraldry more dismal. Head to foot
Now is he total gules, horridly tricked
With blood of fathers, mothers, daughters, sons,
440   *Baked and impasted with the parching streets,*
That lend a tyrannous and damnèd light
To their lord's murder. Roasted in wrath and fire,
And thus o'ersizèd with coagulate gore,
With eyes like carbuncles, the hellish Pyrrhus
445   *Old grandsire Priam seeks.*
So, proceed you.

POLONIUS
'Fore God, my lord, well spoken, with good accent and
good discretion.

FIRST PLAYER
                      Anon he finds him
Striking too short at Greeks. His antique sword,
450   *Rebellious to his arm, lies where it falls,*
Repugnant to command. Unequal matched,
Pyrrhus at Priam drives, in rage strikes wide,
But with the whiff and wind of his fell sword
The unnerved father falls. Then senseless Ilium,

Dido, Priam, and Aeneas are characters in the Roman poet's epic called The Aeneid, *which produced the dramatic spin-off* Hamlet *is referring to here.*

were clever but not fancy. I remember one critic said there was no vulgar language to spice up the dialogue, and showing off on playwright's part. That critic called it an excellent play, containing things to reflect upon as well as sweet music to enjoy. I loved one speech in particular. It was when Aeneas told Dido about Priam's murder. If you happen to remember this scene, begin at line—let me see, how does it go?

Pyrrhus, the son of the Greek hero Achilles, came to Troy at the end of the Trojan War to avenge his father's death by killing Priam, king of Troy. Pyrrhus hid inside the Trojan Horse with the other Greek heroes.

> *The rugged Pyrrhus, strong as a tiger—*

No, that's wrong; it begins like this:

> *Savage Pyrrhus, whose black armor was*
> *As dark plans, and was like the night*
> *When he crouched inside the Trojan Horse,*
> *Has now smeared his dark armor*
> *With something worse. From head to foot*
> *He's now covered in red, decorated horribly*
> *With the blood of fathers, mothers, daughters, sons.*
> *The blood is baked to a paste by fires he set in the streets,*
> *Fires that lend a terrible light to his horrible murders.*
> *Boiling with anger and fire,*
> *And coated thick with hard-baked blood,*
> *His eyes glowing like rubies, the hellish Pyrrhus*
> *Goes looking for grandfather Priam.*

Sir, take it from there.

POLONIUS

My God, that was well done, my lord, with the right accent and a good ear.

FIRST PLAYER

>   *Soon he finds Priam*
> *Failing in his battle against the Greeks. His old sword,*
> *Which Priam cannot wield anymore, lies where it fell.*
> *An unfair opponent,*
> *Pyrrhus rushes at Priam, and in his rage he misses;*
> *But the wind created by his sword is enough to make*
> *The weakened old man fall. Just then the city of Ilium,*

455 *Seeming to feel this blow, with flaming top*
Stoops to his base, and with a hideous crash
Takes prisoner Pyrrhus' ear. For, lo, his sword,
Which was declining on the milky head
Of reverend Priam, seemed i' th' air to stick.
460 *So as a painted tyrant Pyrrhus stood,*
And, like a neutral to his will and matter,
Did nothing.
But as we often see against some storm
A silence in the heavens, the rack stand still,
465 *The bold winds speechless, and the orb below*
As hush as death, anon the dreadful thunder
Doth rend the region. So, after Pyrrhus' pause,
Aroused vengeance sets him new a-work.
And never did the Cyclops' hammers fall
470 *On Mars's armor forged for proof eterne*
With less remorse than Pyrrhus' bleeding sword
Now falls on Priam.
Out, out, thou strumpet Fortune! All you gods
In general synod take away her power,
475 *Break all the spokes and fellies from her wheel,*
And bowl the round nave down the hill of heaven,
As low as to the fiends!

POLONIUS
This is too long.

HAMLET
It shall to the barber's, with your beard.—Prithee, say on.
480 He's for a jig or a tale of bawdry, or he sleeps. Say on. Come
to Hecuba.

FIRST PLAYER
But who, ah woe, who had seen the mobled queen—

HAMLET
"The mobled queen"?

As if feeling this fatal blow to its ruler,
Collapses in flames, and the crash
Captures Pyrrhus's attention. His sword,
Which was falling onto Priam's white-haired head
Seemed to hang in the air.
Pyrrhus stood there like a man in a painting,
Doing nothing.
But just as a raging thunderstorm
Is often interrupted by a moment's silence,
And then soon after the region is split apart by dreadful
thunderclaps,
In the same way, after Pyrrhus paused,
His newly awakened fury set him to work again.
When the Cyclopses were making unbreakable armor
For the god of war, their hammers never fell
So mercilessly as Pyrrhus's bloody sword
Now falls on Priam.
Get out of here, Lady Luck, you whore! All you gods
Should come together to rob her of her powers,
Break all the spokes on her wheel of fortune,
And send it rolling down the hills of heaven
Into the depths of hell.

POLONIUS

This speech is going on too long.

HAMLET

We'll have the barber trim it later, along with your beard. Please, continue, players. This old man only likes the dancing or the sex scenes; he sleeps through all the rest. Go on, come to the part about Hecuba.

FIRST PLAYER

But who—ah, the sadness—had seen the muffled queen—

HAMLET

"The muffled queen"?

POLONIUS
That's good. "Moblèd queen" is good.

FIRST PLAYER
485 *Run barefoot up and down, threatening the flames*
With bisson rheum, a clout upon that head
Where late the diadem stood, and for a robe,
About her lank and all o'erteemèd loins,
A blanket, in the alarm of fear caught up—
490 *Who this had seen, with tongue in venom steeped,*
'Gainst fortune's state would treason have pronounced.
But if the gods themselves did see her then
When she saw Pyrrhus make malicious sport
In mincing with his sword her husband's limbs,
495 *The instant burst of clamor that she made,*
(Unless things mortal move them not at all)
Would have made milch the burning eyes of heaven,
And passion in the gods.

POLONIUS
Look whe'e he has not turned his color and has
500 tears in 's eyes.—Prithee, no more.

HAMLET
(*to* **FIRST PLAYER**) 'Tis well. I'll have thee speak out the rest
soon. (*to* **POLONIUS**) Good my lord, will you see the players
well bestowed? Do you hear, let them be well used, for they
are the abstract and brief chronicles of the time. After your
505 death you were better have a bad epitaph than their ill
report while you live.

POLONIUS
My lord, I will use them according to their desert.

HAMLET
God's bodykins, man, much better. Use every man after his
desert, and who should 'scape whipping? Use them after
510 your own honor and dignity. The less they deserve, the
more merit is in your bounty. Take them in.

POLONIUS

That's good. "The muffled queen" is good.

FIRST PLAYER

Running back and forth, spraying the flames with her tears, a cloth on that head where a crown had recently sat and a blanket instead of a robe wrapped around her body, which has withered from childbearing: anyone seeing her in such a state, no matter how spiteful he was, would have cursed Lady Luck for bringing her down like that. If the gods had seen her while she watched Pyrrhus chopping her husband into bits, the terrible cry she uttered would have made all the eyes in heaven burn with hot tears—unless the gods don't care at all about human affairs.

POLONIUS

Look how flushed the actor is, with tears in his eyes. All right, that's enough, please.

HAMLET

(to FIRST PLAYER) Very fine. I'll have you perform the rest of it soon. *(to POLONIUS)*—My lord, will you make sure the actors are made comfortable? Make sure you're good to them, since what they say about us later will go down in history. It'd be better to have a bad epitaph on our graves than to have their ill will while we're alive.

POLONIUS

My lord, I will give them all they deserve.

HAMLET

Good heavens, man, give them more than that! If you pay everyone what they deserve, would anyone ever escape a whipping? Treat them with honor and dignity. The less they deserve, the more your generosity is worth. Lead them inside.

POLONIUS
Come, sirs.

HAMLET
Follow him, friends. We'll hear a play tomorrow. *(to* FIRST
PLAYER*)*— Dost thou hear me, old friend? Can you play *The*
515   *Murder of Gonzago*?

FIRST PLAYER
Ay, my lord.

HAMLET
We'll ha 't tomorrow night. You could, for a need, study a
speech of some dozen or sixteen lines which I would set
down and insert in 't, could you not?

FIRST PLAYER
520   Ay, my lord.

HAMLET
Very well. Follow that lord, and look you mock him not.
                                    Exeunt POLONIUS *and the* PLAYERS
My good friends, I'll leave you till night. You are welcome
to Elsinore.

ROSENCRANTZ
Good my lord.

HAMLET
525   Ay, so. Good-bye to you.
                                    Exeunt ROSENCRANTZ *and* GUILDENSTERN
                                    Now I am alone.
Oh, what a rogue and peasant slave am I!
Is it not monstrous that this player here,
But in a fiction, in a dream of passion,
Could force his soul so to his own conceit
530   That from her working all his visage wanned,
Tears in his eyes, distraction in his aspect,
A broken voice, and his whole function suiting
With forms to his conceit? And all for nothing—
For Hecuba!

POLONIUS

Come, everyone.

HAMLET

Follow him, friends. We'll watch a whole play tomorrow. *(to* FIRST PLAYER*)* My friend, can you perform *The Murder of Gonzago?*

FIRST PLAYER

Yes, my lord.

HAMLET

Then we'll see that tomorrow night. By the way, if I were to compose an extra speech of twelve to sixteen lines and stick it into the play, you could learn it by heart for tomorrow, right?

FIRST PLAYER

Yes, my lord.

HAMLET

Very well. Follow that gentleman now, and be careful not to make fun of him.

> POLONIUS *and the* PLAYERS *exit.*

My good friends, I'll see you tomorrow. Welcome to Elsinore.

ROSENCRANTZ

Yes, my lord.

HAMLET

Ah yes, good-bye to you both.

> ROSENCRANTZ *and* GUILDENSTERN *exit.*

Now I'm alone. Oh, what a mean low-life I am! It's awful that this actor could force his soul to feel made-up feelings in a work of make-believe. He grew pale, shed real tears, became overwhelmed, his voice breaking with feeling and his whole being, even, meeting the needs of his act—and all for nothing. For Hecuba!

535   What's Hecuba to him or he to Hecuba
     That he should weep for her? What would he do
     Had he the motive and the cue for passion
     That I have? He would drown the stage with tears
     And cleave the general ear with horrid speech,
540   Make mad the guilty and appall the free,
     Confound the ignorant, and amaze indeed
     The very faculties of eyes and ears. Yet I,
     A dull and muddy-mettled rascal, peak
     Like John-a-dreams, unpregnant of my cause,
545   And can say nothing—no, not for a king,
     Upon whose property and most dear life
     A damned defeat was made. Am I a coward?
     Who calls me "villain"? Breaks my pate across?
     Plucks off my beard and blows it in my face?
550   Tweaks me by the nose? Gives me the lie i' th' throat
     As deep as to the lungs? Who does me this?
     Ha!
     'Swounds, I should take it, for it cannot be
     But I am pigeon-livered and lack gall
555   To make oppression bitter, or ere this
     I should have fatted all the region kites
     With this slave's offal. Bloody, bawdy villain!
     Remorseless, treacherous, lecherous, kindless villain!
     O vengeance!
560   Why, what an ass am I! This is most brave,
     That I, the son of a dear father murdered,
     Prompted to my revenge by heaven and hell,
     Must, like a whore, unpack my heart with words
     And fall a-cursing like a very drab,
565   A scullion! Fie upon 't, foh!
     About, my brain.—Hum, I have heard
     That guilty creatures sitting at a play
     Have, by the very cunning of the scene,
     Been struck so to the soul that presently
570   They have proclaimed their malefactions.

What is Hecuba to him, or he to Hecuba, that he would weep for her? Just imagine what he would do if he had the cause for feeling that I do. He would drown the stage with his tears and burst the audience's ears with his terrible words, drive the guilty spectators crazy, terrify the innocent ones, confuse the ignorant ones, and astound absolutely everyone's eyes and ears. But what do I, a grim and uncourageous rascal, do? Mope around like a dreamer, not even bothering with plans for revenge, and I can say nothing—nothing at all—on behalf of a king whose dear life was stolen. Am I a coward? Is there anyone out there who'll call me "villain" and slap me hard? Pull off my beard? Pinch my nose? Call me the worst liar? By God, if someone would do that to me, I'd take it, because I'm a lily-livered man—otherwise, I would've fattened up the local vultures with the intestines of that low-life king a long time ago. Bloody, inhuman villain! Remorseless, treacherous, sex-obsessed, unnatural villain! Ah, revenge! What an ass I am. I'm so damn brave. My dear father's been murdered, and I've been urged to seek revenge by heaven and hell, and yet all I can do is stand around cursing like a whore in the streets. Damn it! I need to get myself together here! Hmm. . . . I've heard that guilty people watching a play have been so affected by the artistry of the scene that they are driven to confess their crimes out loud.

For murder, though it have no tongue, will speak
With most miraculous organ. I'll have these players
Play something like the murder of my father
575 Before mine uncle. I'll observe his looks.
I'll tent him to the quick. If he do blench,
I know my course. The spirit that I have seen
May be the devil, and the devil hath power
T' assume a pleasing shape. Yea, and perhaps
580 Out of my weakness and my melancholy,
As he is very potent with such spirits,
Abuses me to damn me. I'll have grounds
More relative than this. The play's the thing
Wherein I'll catch the conscience of the king.

Exit

Murder has no tongue, but miraculously it still finds a way to speak. I'll have these actors perform something like my father's murder in front of my uncle. I'll watch my uncle. I'll probe his conscience and see if he flinches. If he becomes pale, I know what to do. The ghost I saw may be the devil, and the devil has the power to assume a pleasing disguise, and so he may be taking advantage of my weakness and sadness to bring about my damnation. I need better evidence than the ghost to work with. The play's the thing to uncover the conscience of the king.

HAMLET *exits.*

ACT THREE

SCENE 1

Enter CLAUDIUS, GERTRUDE, POLONIUS, OPHELIA, ROSENCRANTZ, *and* GUILDENSTERN

CLAUDIUS
And can you by no drift of conference
Get from him why he puts on this confusion,
Grating so harshly all his days of quiet
With turbulent and dangerous lunacy?

ROSENCRANTZ
5   He does confess he feels himself distracted.
But from what cause he will by no means speak.

GUILDENSTERN
Nor do we find him forward to be sounded.
But with a crafty madness keeps aloof
When we would bring him on to some confession
10   Of his true state.

GERTRUDE
               Did he receive you well?

ROSENCRANTZ
Most like a gentleman.

GUILDENSTERN
But with much forcing of his disposition.

ROSENCRANTZ
Niggard of question, but of our demands
Most free in his reply.

GERTRUDE
               Did you assay him?
15   To any pastime?

ROSENCRANTZ
Madam, it so fell out, that certain players
We o'erraught on the way. Of these we told him,
And there did seem in him a kind of joy

ACT THREE
SCENE 1

CLAUDIUS, GERTRUDE, POLONIUS, OPHELIA, ROSENCRANTZ, *and* GUILDENSTERN *enter*.

CLAUDIUS

And you can't put your heads together and figure out why he's acting so dazed and confused, ruining his peace and quiet with such dangerous displays of lunacy?

ROSENCRANTZ

He admits he feels confused, but refuses to say why.

GUILDENSTERN

And he's not exactly eager to be interrogated. He's very sly and dances around our questions when we try to get him to talk about how he feels.

GERTRUDE

Did he treat you well when you saw him?

ROSENCRANTZ

Yes, in a very gentlemanly way.

GUILDENSTERN

But it seemed like he had to force himself to be nice to us.

ROSENCRANTZ

He didn't ask questions, but answered ours at length.

GERTRUDE

Did you try tempting him with some entertainment?

ROSENCRANTZ

Madam, some actors happened to cross our paths on the way here. We told Hamlet about them, and that seemed to do him good.

To hear of it. They are about the court,
20 And, as I think, they have already order
This night to play before him.

POLONIUS
                              'Tis most true,
And he beseeched me to entreat your Majesties
To hear and see the matter.

CLAUDIUS
With all my heart, and it doth much content me
25 To hear him so inclined.
Good gentlemen, give him a further edge,
And drive his purpose on to these delights.

ROSENCRANTZ
We shall, my lord.

Exeunt ROSENCRANTZ *and* GUILDENSTERN

CLAUDIUS
Sweet Gertrude, leave us too,
30 For we have closely sent for Hamlet hither,
That he, as 'twere by accident, may here
Affront Ophelia.
Her father and myself (lawful espials)
Will so bestow ourselves that, seeing unseen,
35 We may of their encounter frankly judge,
And gather by him, as he is behaved,
If 't be the affliction of his love or no
That thus he suffers for.

GERTRUDE
                              I shall obey you.
And for your part, Ophelia, I do wish
40 That your good beauties be the happy cause
Of Hamlet's wildness. So shall I hope your virtues
Will bring him to his wonted way again,
To both your honors.

OPHELIA
                    Madam, I wish it may.

Exit GERTRUDE

They are here at court now, and I believe they've been told to give a performance for him tonight.

POLONIUS

It's true, and he asked me to beg you both to attend.

CLAUDIUS

It makes me very happy to hear he's so interested. Gentlemen, please try to sharpen his interest even more, and let this play do him some good.

ROSENCRANTZ

We will, my lord.

ROSENCRANTZ *and* GUILDENSTERN *exit.*

CLAUDIUS

Dear Gertrude, please give us a moment alone. We've secretly arranged for Hamlet to come here so that he can run into Ophelia. Her father and I, justifiably acting as spies, will hide in the room and observe Hamlet's behavior, to determine whether it's love that's making him suffer.

GERTRUDE

Yes, I'll go. As for you, Ophelia, I hope that your beauty is the reason for Hamlet's insane behavior, just as I hope your virtues will return him to normal some day, for the good of both of you.

OPHELIA

I hope so too, Madam.

GERTRUDE *exits.*

POLONIUS

Ophelia, walk you here. *(to* CLAUDIUS*)* Gracious, so please
you,

45   We will bestow ourselves. *(to* OPHELIA*)*Read on this book
That show of such an exercise may color
Your loneliness.—We are oft to blame in this,
'Tis too much proved, that with devotion's visage
And pious action we do sugar o'er

50   The devil himself.

CLAUDIUS

(aside)   Oh, 'tis too true!
How smart a lash that speech doth give my conscience!
The harlot's cheek, beautied with plastering art,
Is not more ugly to the thing that helps it
Than is my deed to my most painted word.

55   O heavy burden!

POLONIUS

I hear him coming. Let's withdraw, my lord.

                     CLAUDIUS *and* POLONIUS *withdraw*
                     Enter HAMLET

HAMLET

To be, or not to be? That is the question—
Whether 'tis nobler in the mind to suffer
The slings and arrows of outrageous fortune,

60   Or to take arms against a sea of troubles,
And, by opposing, end them? To die, to sleep—
No more—and by a sleep to say we end
The heartache and the thousand natural shocks
That flesh is heir to—'tis a consummation

65   Devoutly to be wished! To die, to sleep.
To sleep, perchance to dream—ay, there's the rub,
For in that sleep of death what dreams may come
When we have shuffled off this mortal coil,
Must give us pause. There's the respect

70   That makes calamity of so long life.

POLONIUS

Ophelia, come here.—*(to* CLAUDIUS*)* Your Majesty, we will hide. *(to* OPHELIA*)*—Read from this prayer book, so it looks natural that you're all alone. Come to think of it, this happens all the time—people act devoted to God to mask their bad deeds.

CLAUDIUS

(to himself) How right he is! His words whip up my guilty feelings. The whore's pockmarked cheek made pretty with make-up is just like the ugly actions I'm disguising with fine words. What a terrible guilt I feel!

POLONIUS

I hear him coming. Quick, let's hide, my lord.

CLAUDIUS *and* POLONIUS *hide.*
HAMLET *enters.*

HAMLET

The question is: is it better to be alive or dead? Is it nobler to put up with all the nasty things that luck throws your way, or to fight against all those troubles by simply putting an end to them once and for all? Dying, sleeping—that's all dying is—a sleep that ends all the heartache and shocks that life on earth gives us—that's an achievement to wish for. To die, to sleep—to sleep, maybe to dream. Ah, but there's the catch: in death's sleep who knows what kind of dreams might come, after we've put the noise and commotion of life behind us. That's certainly something to worry about. That's the consideration that makes us stretch out our sufferings so long.

For who would bear the whips and scorns of time,
Th' oppressor's wrong, the proud man's contumely,
The pangs of despised love, the law's delay,
The insolence of office, and the spurns
75 That patient merit of th' unworthy takes,
When he himself might his quietus make
With a bare bodkin? Who would fardels bear,
To grunt and sweat under a weary life,
But that the dread of something after death,
80 The undiscovered country from whose bourn
No traveler returns, puzzles the will
And makes us rather bear those ills we have
Than fly to others that we know not of?
Thus conscience does make cowards of us all,
85 And thus the native hue of resolution
Is sicklied o'er with the pale cast of thought,
And enterprises of great pith and moment
With this regard their currents turn awry,
And lose the name of action.—Soft you now,
90 The fair Ophelia!—Nymph, in thy orisons
Be all my sins remembered.

OPHELIA
Good my lord,
How does your honor for this many a day?

HAMLET
I humbly thank you. Well, well, well.

OPHELIA
95 My lord, I have remembrances of yours
That I have longèd long to redeliver.
I pray you now receive them.

HAMLET
No, not I. I never gave you aught.

OPHELIA
My honored lord, you know right well you did,
100 And with them, words of so sweet breath composed
As made the things more rich. Their perfume lost,

After all, who would put up with all life's humiliations—the abuse from superiors, the insults of arrogant men, the pangs of unrequited love, the inefficiency of the legal system, the rudeness of people in office, and the mistreatment good people have to take from bad—when you could simply take out your knife and call it quits? Who would choose to grunt and sweat through an exhausting life, unless they were afraid of something dreadful after death, the undiscovered country from which no visitor returns, which we wonder about without getting any answers from and which makes us stick to the evils we know rather than rush off to seek the ones we don't? Fear of death makes us all cowards, and our natural boldness becomes weak with too much thinking. Actions that should be carried out at once get misdirected, and stop being actions at all. But *shh*, here comes the beautiful Ophelia. Pretty lady, please remember me when you pray.

OPHELIA

Hello, my lord, how have you been doing lately?

HAMLET

Very well, thank you. Well, well, well.

OPHELIA

My lord, I have some mementos of yours that I've been meaning to give back to you for a long time now. Please take them.

HAMLET

No, it wasn't me. I never gave you anything.

OPHELIA

My lord, you know very well that you did, and wrote letters to go along with them, letters so sweetly written that they made your gifts even more valuable. Their

Take these again, for to the noble mind
Rich gifts wax poor when givers prove unkind.
There, my lord.

HAMLET

105   Ha, ha, are you honest?

OPHELIA

My lord?

HAMLET

Are you fair?

OPHELIA

What means your lordship?

HAMLET

That if you be honest and fair, your honesty should admit
110   no discourse to your beauty.

OPHELIA

Could beauty, my lord, have better commerce than with
honesty?

HAMLET

Ay, truly, for the power of beauty will sooner transform
honesty from what it is to a bawd than the force of honesty
115   can translate beauty into his likeness. This was sometime a
paradox, but now the time gives it proof. I did love you
once.

OPHELIA

Indeed, my lord, you made me believe so.

HAMLET

You should not have believed me, for virtue cannot so
120   inoculate our old stock but we shall relish of it. I loved you
not.

OPHELIA

I was the more deceived.

HAMLET

Get thee to a nunnery. Why wouldst thou be a breeder of
sinners? I am myself indifferent honest, but yet I could
125   accuse me of such things that it were better my mother had
not borne me. I am very proud, revengeful, ambitious, with

perfume is gone now, so take them back. Nice gifts lose their value when the givers turn out not to be so nice. There, my lord.

HAMLET

Ha ha, are you good?

OPHELIA

Excuse me?

HAMLET

Are you beautiful?

OPHELIA

My lord, what are you talking about?

HAMLET

I'm just saying that if you're good and beautiful, your goodness should have nothing to do with your beauty.

OPHELIA

But could beauty be related to anything better than goodness?

HAMLET

Sure, since beauty's power can more easily change a good girl into a whore than the power of goodness can change a beautiful girl into a virgin. This used to be a great puzzle, but now I've solved it. I used to love you.

OPHELIA

You certainly made me believe you did, my lord.

HAMLET

You shouldn't have believed me, since we're all rotten at the core, no matter how hard we try to be virtuous. I didn't love you.

OPHELIA

Then I guess I was misled.

HAMLET

"Nunnery" could mean either convent or brothel.

Get yourself to a convent at once. Why would you want to give birth to more sinners? I'm fairly good myself, but even so I could accuse myself of such horrible crimes that it would've been better if my mother more offences at my beck than I have thoughts to put them in, imagination to give them shape, or time to act them in. What should such fellows as I do crawling between earth and heaven? We are arrant knaves, all. Believe none of us. Go thy ways to a nunnery. Where's your father?

OPHELIA
At home, my lord.

HAMLET
Let the doors be shut upon him, that he may play the fool no where but in 's own house. Farewell.

OPHELIA
O, help him, you sweet heavens!

HAMLET
If thou dost marry, I'll give thee this plague for thy dowry. Be thou as chaste as ice, as pure as snow, thou shalt not escape calumny. Get thee to a nunnery, go. Farewell. Or, if thou wilt needs marry, marry a fool, for wise men know well enough what monsters you make of them. To a nunnery, go, and quickly too. Farewell.

OPHELIA
Heavenly powers, restore him!

HAMLET
I have heard of your paintings too, well enough. God has given you one face and you make yourselves another. You jig and amble, and you lisp, you nickname God's creatures and make your wantonness your ignorance. Go to, I'll no more on 't. It hath made me mad. I say, we will have no more marriages. Those that are married already, all but one, shall live. The rest shall keep as they are. To a nunnery, go.

Exit **HAMLET**

had never given birth to me. I am arrogant, vengeful, and ambitious, with more ill will in me than I can fit into my thoughts, and more than I have time to carry it out in. Why should people like me be crawling around between earth and heaven? Every one of us is a criminal. Don't believe any of us. Hurry to a convent. Where's your father?

OPHELIA

He's at home, my lord.

HAMLET

Lock him in, so he can play the fool in his own home only. Good-bye.

OPHELIA

Oh, dear God, please help him!

HAMLET

If you marry, I'll give you this curse as your wedding present—be as clean as ice, as pure as the driven snow, and you'll still get a bad reputation. Get yourself to a convent, at once. Good-bye. Or if you have to get married, marry a fool, since wise men know far too well that you'll cheat on them. Good-bye.

OPHELIA

Dear God, please make him normal again!

HAMLET

I've heard all about you women and your cosmetics too. God gives you one face, but you paint another on top of it. You dance and prance and lisp; you call God's creations by pet names, and you excuse your sexpot ploys by pleading ignorance. Come on, I won't stand for it anymore. It's driven me crazy. I hereby declare we will have no more marriage. Whoever is already married (except one person I know) will stay married—all but one person. Everyone else will have to stay single. Get yourself to a convent, fast.

HAMLET *exits.*

OPHELIA
150   Oh, what a noble mind is here o'erthrown!—
The courtier's, soldier's, scholar's, eye, tongue, sword,
Th' expectancy and rose of the fair state,
The glass of fashion and the mould of form,
Th' observed of all observers, quite, quite down!
155   And I, of ladies most deject and wretched,
That sucked the honey of his music vows,
Now see that noble and most sovereign reason
Like sweet bells jangled, out of tune and harsh;
That unmatched form and feature of blown youth
160   Blasted with ecstasy. Oh, woe is me,
T' have seen what I have seen, see what I see!

CLAUDIUS *and* POLONIUS *come forward*

CLAUDIUS
Love? His affections do not that way tend.
Nor what he spake, though it lacked form a little,
Was not like madness. There's something in his soul
165   O'er which his melancholy sits on brood,
And I do doubt the hatch and the disclose
Will be some danger—which for to prevent,
I have in quick determination
Thus set it down: he shall with speed to England
170   For the demand of our neglected tribute.
Haply the seas and countries different
With variable objects shall expel
This something-settled matter in his heart,
Whereon his brains still beating puts him thus
175   From fashion of himself. What think you on 't?

POLONIUS
It shall do well. But yet do I believe
The origin and commencement of his grief
Sprung from neglected love.—How now, Ophelia?
You need not tell us what Lord Hamlet said.

OPHELIA

Oh, how noble his mind used to be, and how lost he is now! He used to have a gentleman's grace, a scholar's wit, and a soldier's strength. He used to be the jewel of our country, the obvious heir to the throne, the one everyone admired and imitated. And now he has fallen so low! And of all the miserable women who once enjoyed hearing his sweet, seductive words, I am the most miserable. A mind that used to sing so sweetly is now completely out of tune, making harsh sounds instead of fine notes. The unparalleled appearance and nobility he had in the full bloom of his youth has been ruined by madness. O, how miserable I am to see Hamlet now and know what he was before!

CLAUDIUS *and* POLONIUS *come forward.*

CLAUDIUS

Love? His feelings don't move in that direction. And his words, although they were a little disorganized, weren't crazy. No, his sadness is hatching something, like a hen does sitting on an egg. What hatches very well may be dangerous. So to prevent any harm being done, I've made a quick executive decision: he'll be sent to England to try to get back the money they owe us. With any luck, the sea and new countries will push out these thoughts that have somehow taken root in his mind. What do you think of this plan?

POLONIUS

It should work. But I still believe that his madness was caused by unrequited love.—Hello, Ophelia. You don't have to tell us what Lord Hamlet said.

180   We heard it all.—My lord, do as you please.
But, if you hold it fit, after the play
Let his queen mother all alone entreat him
To show his grief. Let her be round with him,
And I'll be placed, so please you, in the ear
185   Of all their conference. If she find him not,
To England send him or confine him where
Your wisdom best shall think.

CLAUDIUS
It shall be so.
Madness in great ones must not unwatched go.

Exeunt

    ORIGINAL TEXT

We heard everything.—My lord, do whatever you like, but if you like this idea, let his mother the queen get him alone and beg him to share his feelings with her. I'll hide and listen in. If she can't find out what his secret is, then send him off to England or wherever you think best.

CLAUDIUS

That's how we'll do it, then. When important people start to show signs of insanity, you have to watch them closely.

They all exit.

ACT 3, SCENE 2

Enter HAMLET *and* PLAYERS

HAMLET

Speak the speech, I pray you, as I pronounced it to you,
trippingly on the tongue. But if you mouth it, as many of
your players do, I had as lief the town crier spoke my lines.
Nor do not saw the air too much with your hand thus, but

5   use all gently, for in the very torrent, tempest, and (as I may
say) whirlwind of passion, you must acquire and beget a
temperance that may give it smoothness. Oh, it offends me
to the soul to hear a robustious periwig-pated fellow tear a
passion to tatters, to very rags, to split the ears of the

10 groundlings, who for the most part are capable of nothing
but inexplicable dumb-shows and noise. I would have such
a fellow whipped for o'erdoing Termagant. It out-Herods
Herod. Pray you, avoid it.

FIRST PLAYER

I warrant your honor.

HAMLET

15 Be not too tame neither, but let your own discretion be your
tutor. Suit the action to the word, the word to the action,
with this special observance that you o'erstep not the
modesty of nature. For anything so overdone is from the
purpose of playing, whose end, both at the first and now,

20 was and is to hold, as 'twere, the mirror up to nature, to
show virtue her own feature, scorn her own image, and the
very age and body of the time his form and pressure. Now
this overdone or come tardy off, though it make the
unskillful laugh, cannot but make the judicious grieve, the

25 censure of the which one must in your allowance o'erweigh
a whole theatre of others.

ACT 3, SCENE 2

HAMLET *and the* PLAYERS *enter.*

HAMLET

Perform the speech just as I taught you, musically and smoothly. If you exaggerate the words the way some actors do, I might as well have some newscaster read the lines. Don't use too many hand gestures; just do a few, gently, like this. When you get into a whirlwind of passion on stage, remember to keep the emotion moderate and smooth. I hate it when I hear a blustery actor in a wig tear a passion to shreds, bursting everyone's eardrums so as to impress the audience on the lower levels of the playhouse, who for the most part can only appreciate loud noises and pantomime shows. I would whip a guy for making a tyrant sound too tyrannical. That's as bad as those old plays in which King Herod ranted. Please avoid doing that.

FIRST PLAYER

I will, sir.

HAMLET

But don't be too tame, either—let your good sense guide you. Fit the action to the word and the word to the action. Act natural at all costs. Exaggeration has no place in the theater, where the purpose is to represent reality, holding a mirror up to virtue, to vice, and to the spirit of the times. If you handle this badly, it just makes ignorant people laugh while regular theater-goers are miserable—and they're the ones you should be keeping happy.

Oh, there be players that I have seen play and heard others praise (and that highly), not to speak it profanely, that, neither having th' accent of Christians nor the gait of

30   Christian, pagan, nor man, have so strutted and bellowed that I have thought some of nature's journeymen had made men and not made them well, they imitated humanity so abominably.

FIRST PLAYER

I hope we have reformed that indifferently with us, sir.

HAMLET

35   O, reform it altogether! And let those that play your clowns speak no more than is set down for them, for there be of them that will themselves laugh to set on some quantity of barren spectators to laugh too, though in the meantime some necessary question of the play be then to be

40   considered. That's villainous, and shows a most pitiful ambition in the fool that uses it. Go, make you ready.

Exeunt PLAYERS

Enter POLONIUS, ROSENCRANTZ, *and* GUILDENSTERN

How now, my lord! Will the king hear this piece of work?

POLONIUS

And the queen too, and that presently.

HAMLET

Bid the players make haste.

Exit POLONIUS

45   Will you two help to hasten them?

ROSENCRANTZ

Ay, my lord.

Exeunt ROSENCRANTZ *and* GUILDENSTERN

HAMLET

What ho, Horatio!

Enter HORATIO

I've seen actors who are highly praised, but who—not to be too rude here—can't even talk or walk like human beings. They bellow and strut about like weird animals that were made to look like men, but very badly.

FIRST PLAYER

I hope we've corrected that fault pretty well in our company, sir.

HAMLET

Oh, correct it completely. Make sure that the clowns do not ad-lib, since some of them will make certain dumb audience members laugh mindlessly at them, while an important issue in the play needs to be addressed. It's bad behavior for an actor, anyway, and displays a pitiful ambition to hog the limelight on stage.

The PLAYERS *exit.*
POLONIUS, GUILDENSTERN, *and* ROSENCRANTZ *enter.*

So, my lord, will the king be attending the performance?

POLONIUS

Yes, he will, and the queen as well.

HAMLET

Tell the actors to hurry.

POLONIUS *exits.*

Will you two help them get ready?

ROSENCRANTZ

Yes, my lord.

ROSENCRANTZ *and* GUILDENSTERN *exit.*

HAMLET

Well, hello there, Horatio!

HORATIO *enters.*

HORATIO
                  Here, sweet lord, at your service.

HAMLET
Horatio, thou art e'en as just a man
As e'er my conversation coped withal.

HORATIO
O my dear lord—

HAMLET
               Nay, do not think I flatter.
50   For what advancement may I hope from thee
That no revenue hast but thy good spirits,
To feed and clothe thee? Why should the poor be flattered?
No, let the candied tongue lick absurd pomp,
And crook the pregnant hinges of the knee
55   Where thrift may follow fawning. Dost thou hear?
Since my dear soul was mistress of her choice
And could of men distinguish, her election
Hath sealed thee for herself, for thou hast been—
As one in suffering all that suffers nothing—
60   A man that Fortune's buffets and rewards
Hast ta'en with equal thanks. And blessed are those
Whose blood and judgment are so well commingled,
That they are not a pipe for Fortune's finger
To sound what stop she please. Give me that man
65   That is not passion's slave, and I will wear him
In my heart's core, ay, in my heart of heart,
As I do thee.—Something too much of this.—
There is a play tonight before the king.
One scene of it comes near the circumstance
70   Which I have told thee of my father's death.
I prithee, when thou seest that act afoot,
Even with the very comment of thy soul
Observe mine uncle. If his occulted guilt
Do not itself unkennel in one speech,
75   It is a damnèd ghost that we have seen,
And my imaginations are as foul

HORATIO

Here I am at your service, my dear lord.

HAMLET

Horatio, you're the best man I've ever known.

HORATIO

Oh, sir—

HAMLET

Don't think I'm flattering you. What could I hope to get from you, who've got nothing but your charm to support you in life? Why would anyone flatter a poor person? No, keep flattery for kissing the hands of those who can pay well. You understand? Ever since I've been a free agent in my choice of friends, I've chosen you because you take everything life hands you with calm acceptance, grateful for both good and bad. Blessed are those who mix emotion with reason in just the right proportion, making them strong enough to resist the whims of Lady Luck. Show me the person who's master of his emotions, and I'll put him close to my heart—in my heart of hearts—as I do you. But I'm talking too much. The point is, there's a play being performed for the king tonight. One of the scenes comes very close to depicting the circumstances of my father's death, as I described them to you. Watch my uncle carefully when that scene begins. If his guilty secret does not reveal itself, then that ghost was just a devil, and my hunch wasn't, in fact, worth anything.

As Vulcan's stithy. Give him heedful note.
For I mine eyes will rivet to his face,
And after we will both our judgments join
80 In censure of his seeming.

HORATIO

Well, my lord.
If he steal aught the whilst this play is playing,
And 'scape detecting, I will pay the theft.

Danish march. Sound a flourish. Enter King CLAUDIUS,
Queen GERTRUDE, POLONIUS, OPHELIA, ROSENCRANTZ,
GUILDENSTERN, *and other lords attendant with* CLAUDIUS'S
guard carrying torches

HAMLET

They are coming to the play. I must be idle.
Get you a place.

CLAUDIUS

85 How fares our cousin Hamlet?

HAMLET

Excellent, i' faith, of the chameleon's dish. I eat
the air, promise-crammed. You cannot feed capons so.

CLAUDIUS

I have nothing with this answer, Hamlet. These words
are not mine.

HAMLET

90 No, nor mine now. *(To* POLONIUS*)* My lord, you played once
i' th' university, you say?

POLONIUS

That did I, my lord, and was accounted a good actor.

HAMLET

What did you enact?

POLONIUS

I did enact Julius Caesar. I was killed i' th' Capitol. Brutus
95 killed me.

Watch him closely. I'll stare at him too, and afterward we'll compare notes on him.

HORATIO

My lord, I'll watch him as closely as I would a thief. I won't miss a trick.

Trumpets play. CLAUDIUS *enters with* GERTRUDE, POLONIUS, OPHELIA, ROSENCRANTZ, GUILDENSTERN, *and other lords attendant with* CLAUDIUS'S *guard carrying torches.*

HAMLET

They're coming. I can't talk now. Take your seat.

CLAUDIUS

So how's my nephew Hamlet doing?

HAMLET

Wonderful! I eat the air, like chameleons do. I'm positively stuffed with air, I eat so much of it.

CLAUDIUS

I have no idea what you're talking about, Hamlet. You're not answering my question.

HAMLET

Mine, neither. *(to* POLONIUS*)* My lord, you performed in amateur dramatic productions in college, right?

POLONIUS

Indeed I did, my lord. I was considered to be quite a good actor.

HAMLET

What role did you play?

POLONIUS

I played Julius Caesar. I was killed in the Capitol. Brutus killed me.

HAMLET

It was a brute part of him to kill so capital a calf there.—Be the players ready?

ROSENCRANTZ

Ay, my lord. They stay upon your patience.

GERTRUDE

Come hither, my dear Hamlet, sit by me.

HAMLET

100 No, good mother. Here's metal more attractive. *(sits next to* OPHELIA*)*

POLONIUS

(to CLAUDIUS*)* Oh, ho, do you mark that?

HAMLET

Lady, shall I lie in your lap?

OPHELIA

No, my lord.

HAMLET

I mean, my head upon your lap?

OPHELIA

105 Ay, my lord.

HAMLET

Do you think I meant country matters?

OPHELIA

I think nothing, my lord.

HAMLET

That's a fair thought to lie between maids' legs.

OPHELIA

What is, my lord?

HAMLET

110 Nothing.

OPHELIA

You are merry, my lord.

HAMLET

Who, I?

OPHELIA

Ay, my lord.

HAMLET

That was brutish of them, to kill so capital a guy. —
Are the actors ready?

ROSENCRANTZ

Yes, my lord. They're ready whenever you are.

GERTRUDE

Come here, my dear Hamlet. Sit by me.

HAMLET

No thanks, my good mother. There's a nicer piece of
work right here. *(he sits down near* OPHELIA*)*

POLONIUS

(to CLAUDIUS*)* Hey, did you notice that?

HAMLET

My lady, should I lie in your lap?

OPHELIA

No, my lord.

HAMLET

I mean, with my head in your lap?

OPHELIA

Yes, my lord.

HAMLET

Did you think I was talking about sex?

OPHELIA

I think nothing, my lord.

HAMLET

That's a nice thought to lie between a girl's legs.

In Shakespeare's time, "nothing" (or "0") was slang for the vagina.

OPHELIA

What is, my lord?

HAMLET

Nothing.

OPHELIA

You're in a good mood tonight, my lord.

HAMLET

Who, me?

OPHELIA

Yes, my lord.

HAMLET

115   O God, your only jig-maker. What should a man do
but be merry? For, look you, how cheerfully my
mother looks, and my father died within these two hours.

OPHELIA

Nay, 'tis twice two months, my lord.

HAMLET

So long? Nay then, let the devil wear black, for I'll have a
suit of sables. O heavens! Die two months ago and not
120   forgotten yet? Then there's hope a great man's memory may
outlive his life half a year. But, by 'r Lady, he must build
churches then, or else shall he suffer not thinking on, with
the hobby-horse, whose epitaph is "For, oh, for, oh, the
hobby-horse is forgot."

Trumpets sound. The dumb show begins

*Enter a King and a Queen very lovingly, the Queen embracing
him and he her. She kneels and makes show of protestation
unto him. He takes her up and declines his head upon her neck,
lays him down upon a bank of flowers. She, seeing him asleep,
leaves him. Anon comes in a fellow, takes off his crown, kisses
it, pours poison in the King's ears, and exits. The Queen
returns, finds the King dead, and makes passionate action.
The Poisoner, with some two or three Mutes, comes in again,
seeming to lament with her. The dead body is carried away. The
Poisoner woos the Queen with gifts. She seems loath and
unwilling awhile, but in the end accepts his love*

Exeunt PLAYERS

OPHELIA

125   What means this, my lord?

HAMLET

Marry, this is miching *malhecho*. It means mischief.

HAMLET

Oh God—who is, by the way, the best comic of them all. What can you do but be happy? Look how cheerful my mother is, only two hours after my father died.

OPHELIA

No, my lord, it's been four months.

HAMLET

As long as that? Well, in that case these mourning clothes can go to hell. I'll get myself a fur-trimmed suit. Good heavens, he died two months ago and hasn't been forgotten yet? In that case, there's reason to hope a man's memory may outlive him by six months. But he's got to build churches for that to happen, my lady, or else he'll have to put up with being forgotten, like the hobby-horse in the popular song that goes, "Heigh-ho, heigh-ho, the hobby-horse is forgotten."

Trumpets play. The pantomime show begins. A king and queen enter and embrace lovingly. She kneels before him and resists his passion. He lifts her up and lays his head on her neck. He lies down on a bank of flowers. When she sees him sleeping, she leaves. Another man comes in, takes the crown from the king, pours poison in the sleeping man's ear, and leaves. The queen returns and finds the king dead. She becomes hysterical. The killer comes back with three others and calms the queen. The body is carried away. The killer woos the queen with gifts. She is cold toward him for a while but then relents and accepts his advances.

The PLAYERS *exit.*

OPHELIA

What does this mean, my lord?

HAMLET

This means we're having some mischievous fun.

OPHELIA
> Belike this show imports the argument of the play.

Enter PROLOGUE

HAMLET
> We shall know by this fellow. The players cannot keep
> counsel. They'll tell all.

OPHELIA
130 > Will he tell us what this show meant?

HAMLET
> Ay, or any show that you will show him. Be not you
> ashamed to show, he'll not shame to tell you what it means.

OPHELIA
> You are naught, you are naught. I'll mark the play.

PROLOGUE
> *For us and for our tragedy,*
135 > *Here stooping to your clemency,*
> *We beg your hearing patiently.*

Exit PROLOGUE

HAMLET
> Is this a prologue or the posy of a ring?

OPHELIA
> 'Tis brief, my lord.

HAMLET
> As woman's love.

Enter PLAYER KING *and* PLAYER QUEEN

OPHELIA

This pantomime was probably a summary of the play.

The PROLOGUE—*the actor who will introduce the play—enters.*

HAMLET

This guy will tell us everything. Actors can't keep a secret. They'll tell all.

OPHELIA

Will he tell us what that pantomime meant?

HAMLET

Sure, or anything else you show him. As long as you aren't ashamed to show it, he won't be ashamed to tell you what it means.

OPHELIA

You're naughty. I'm watching the play.

PROLOGUE

We beg you most courteously
To be patient with us
And watch our humble tragedy.

The PROLOGUE *exits.*

HAMLET

Was that the prologue or the inscription on some wedding ring?

OPHELIA

It was a bit short, my lord.

HAMLET

Yes, as short as a woman's love.

Actors playing the roles of KING *and* QUEEN *enter.*

PLAYER KING

140   *Full thirty times hath Phoebus' cart gone round*
     Neptune's salt wash and Tellus' orbèd ground,
     And thirty dozen moons with borrowed sheen
     About the world have times twelve thirties been,
     Since love our hearts and Hymen did our hands
145   *Unite commutual in most sacred bands.*

PLAYER QUEEN

     So many journeys may the sun and moon
     Make us again count o'er ere love be done.
     But woe is me! You are so sick of late,
     So far from cheer and from your former state,
150   *That I distrust you. Yet though I distrust,*
     Discomfort you, my lord, it nothing must.
     For women fear too much, even as they love,
     And women's fear and love hold quantity,
     In neither aught, or in extremity.
155   *Now what my love is, proof hath made you know,*
     And as my love is sized, my fear is so:
     Where love is great, the littlest doubts are fear.
     Where little fears grow great, great love grows there.

PLAYER KING

     Faith, I must leave thee, love, and shortly too.
160   *My operant powers their functions leave to do.*
     And thou shalt live in this fair world behind,
     Honored, beloved, and haply one as kind
     For husband shalt thou—

PLAYER QUEEN

                 Oh, confound the rest!
     Such love must needs be treason in my breast.
165   *In second husband let me be accursed!*
     None wed the second but who killed the first.

HAMLET

     (aside) Wormwood, wormwood.

PLAYER KING

It's been a full thirty years since we were married.

PLAYER QUEEN

I hope we stay in love for thirty more years! But I'm sad. You've been so gloomy lately, so unlike your usual cheerful self, that I worry something is wrong. But don't let this upset you, since women are too afraid in love—for them, love and fear go hand in hand. You know very well how much I love you, and my fear is just as deep. When someone's love is great, the little worries become very big. So when you see someone who worries a lot about little things, you know they're really in love.

PLAYER KING

My love, I will have to leave you soon. My body is growing weak, and I will leave you behind in this beautiful world, honored and much loved. Perhaps you'll find another husband—

PLAYER QUEEN

Oh, damn everyone else! Remarrying would be treason to my heart. Curse me if I take a second husband. When a woman takes a second husband, it's because she's killed off the first.

HAMLET

(to himself) Harsh!

PLAYER QUEEN
> The instances that second marriage move
> Are base respects of thrift, but none of love.
> ₁₇₀ A second time I kill my husband dead
> When second husband kisses me in bed.

PLAYER KING
> I do believe you think what now you speak,
> But what we do determine oft we break.
> Purpose is but the slave to memory,
> Of violent birth, but poor validity,
> Which now, like fruit unripe, sticks on the tree,
> But fall, unshaken, when they mellow be.
> Most necessary 'tis that we forget
> To pay ourselves what to ourselves is debt.
> What to ourselves in passion we propose,
> The passion ending, doth the purpose lose.
> The violence of either grief or joy
> Their own enactures with themselves destroy.
> Where joy most revels, grief doth most lament.
> Grief joys, joy grieves on slender accident.
> This world is not for aye, nor 'tis not strange
> That even our loves should with our fortunes change.
> For 'tis a question left us yet to prove,
> Whether love lead fortune, or else fortune love.
> The great man down, you mark his favorite flies.
> The poor advanced makes friends of enemies.
> And hitherto doth love on fortune tend,
> For who not needs shall never lack a friend,
> And who in want a hollow friend doth try,
> Directly seasons him his enemy.
> But, orderly to end where I begun,
> Our wills and fates do so contrary run
> That our devices still are overthrown.
> Our thoughts are ours, their ends none of our own.
> So think thou wilt no second husband wed,
> But die thy thoughts when thy first lord is dead.

PLAYER QUEEN

> *Someone might marry a second time for money, but never for love. Any time I kissed my second husband in bed, I'd kill the first one all over again.*

PLAYER KING

> *I know that's what you think now, but people change their minds. Often our intentions are strong at first, but as time goes on they weaken, just like an apple sticks to the tree when it is unripe but falls to the ground once it ripens. The promises we make to ourselves in emotional moments lose their power once the emotion passes. Great grief and joy may rouse us to action, but when the grief or joy have passed, we're no longer motivated to act. Joy turns to grief in the blink of an eye, and grief becomes joy just as quickly. This world is not made for either one to last long in, and it's no surprise that even our loves change along with our luck. It's still a mystery to be solved whether luck controls love, or love controls luck. When a great man has a run of bad luck, watch how followers desert him, and when a poor man advances to an important position, he makes friends with the people he used to hate. Love is unreliable. A person with lots of money will always have friends, while one fallen on hard times makes an enemy of any friend he turns to for money. But back to my original point—what we want and what we get are always at odds. We can have our little dreams, but the fates decide our futures. You think now you'll never remarry, but that thought will die with me, your first husband.*

PLAYER QUEEN
> *Nor earth to me give food, nor heaven light.*
> *Sport and repose lock from me day and night.*
> *To desperation turn my trust and hope.*
205 *An anchor's cheer in prison be my scope.*
> *Each opposite that blanks the face of joy*
> *Meet what I would have well and it destroy.*
> *Both here and hence pursue me lasting strife*
> *If, once a widow, ever I be wife!*

HAMLET
210 If she should break it now!

PLAYER KING
> *'Tis deeply sworn. Sweet, leave me here awhile.*
> *My spirits grow dull, and fain I would beguile*
> *The tedious day with sleep.*

The PLAYER KING *sleeps*

PLAYER QUEEN
> *Sleep rock thy brain,*
> *And never come mischance between us twain.*

Exit PLAYER QUEEN

HAMLET
215 Madam, how like you this play?

GERTRUDE
The lady protests too much, methinks.

HAMLET
Oh, but she'll keep her word.

CLAUDIUS
Have you heard the argument? Is there no offense in 't?

HAMLET
No, no, they do but jest. Poison in jest. No offense i' th'
220 world.

CLAUDIUS
What do you call the play?

PLAYER QUEEN

> *May the earth refuse me food and the heavens go dark,*
> *may I have no rest day and night, may my trust and hope*
> *turn to despair—may the gloom of a prison overtake me,*
> *and may my every joy be turned to sorrow. May I know*
> *no peace either in this life or the next one, if I become a*
> *wife again after I am a widow.*

HAMLET

> Nice vow, but what if she breaks it?

PLAYER KING

> *You have made this vow with deep sincerity. My dear,*
> *leave me alone now awhile. My mind is getting foggy,*
> *and I would like to sleep and escape this endless day.*

> *The PLAYER KING sleeps.*

PLAYER QUEEN

> *Sleep tight, and may nothing come between us.*
> *The PLAYER QUEEN exits.*

HAMLET

> Madam, how are you liking this play?

GERTRUDE

> The lady's overdoing it, I think.

HAMLET

> Oh, but she'll keep her word.

CLAUDIUS

> Do you know the plot? Is there anything offensive in it?

HAMLET

> No, no, it's just a joke, a little jibe but all in good fun.
> Not offensive at all.

CLAUDIUS

> What's the play called?

HAMLET

> *The Mousetrap.* Marry, how? Tropically. This play is the image of a murder done in Vienna. Gonzago is the duke's name, his wife Baptista. You shall see anon. 'Tis a knavish
>
225 > piece of work, but what o' that? Your majesty and we that have free souls, it touches us not. Let the galled jade wince, our withers are unwrung.

> *Enter* LUCIANUS

> This is one Lucianus, nephew to the king.

OPHELIA

> You are as good as a chorus, my lord.

HAMLET

230 > I could interpret between you and your love, if I could see the puppets dallying.

OPHELIA

> You are keen, my lord, you are keen.

HAMLET

> It would cost you a groaning to take off mine edge.

OPHELIA

> Still better and worse.

HAMLET

235 > So you must take your husbands.—Begin, murderer. Pox, leave thy damnable faces, and begin. Come, "The croaking raven doth bellow for revenge—"

LUCIANUS

> *Thoughts black, hands apt, drugs fit, and time agreeing,*
> *Confederate season, else no creature seeing,*
240 > *Thou mixture rank, of midnight weeds collected,*
> *With Hecate's ban thrice blasted, thrice infected,*

HAMLET

The Mousetrap. Why on earth is it called that, you ask?
It's a metaphor. This play is about a murder committed in Vienna. Gonzago is the duke's name, and his
wife is Baptista. You'll see soon enough. It's a piece of
garbage, but who cares? You and I have free souls, so
it doesn't concern us. Let the guilty wince. We can
watch without being bothered.

LUCIANUS *enters.*

This is Lucianus, the king's nephew in the play.

OPHELIA

You're an expert commentator, aren't you?

HAMLET

Yes. I could even supply the dialogue between you and
your lover if you did your little puppet show of love for
me.

OPHELIA

Ooh, you're sharp.

HAMLET

Yes, pointy, but you could take the edge off me—
though it might make you moan a little.

OPHELIA

You get better in your jokes and worse in your
manners.

HAMLET

That's what you women get when you trick us into
marriage.—Let's get started, murderer on stage,
please! Damn it, stop fussing with the makeup, and
get going. We're all waiting for the revenge!

LUCIANUS

*Evil thoughts, ready hands, the right poison, and the
time is right too. The dark night is on my side, for no one
can see me. You deadly mixture of weeds and plants,
which Hecate, goddess of witchcraft, has put a spell on,*

> *Thy natural magic and dire property*
> *On wholesome life usurp immediately.*
> *(pours poison into* PLAYER KING'S *ears)*

HAMLET

245 He poisons him i' th' garden for 's estate. His name's Gonzago. The story is extant, and writ in choice Italian. You shall see anon how the murderer gets the love of Gonzago's wife.

CLAUDIUS *stands up*

OPHELIA

The king rises.

HAMLET

What, frighted with false fire?

GERTRUDE

250 How fares my lord?

POLONIUS

Give o'er the play.

CLAUDIUS

Give me some light, away!

POLONIUS

Lights, lights, lights!

> *Commotion. Exeunt all but* HAMLET *and* HORATIO

HAMLET

> *Why, let the stricken deer go weep,*
> 255 *The hart ungallèd play.*
> *For some must watch while some must sleep.*
> *So runs the world away.*

Would not this, sir, and a forest of feathers—if the rest of my fortunes turn Turk with me—with two Provincial roses
260 on my razed shoes, get me a fellowship in a cry of players?

HORATIO

Half a share.

HAMLET

A whole one, I.

use your magic to steal this healthy person's life away.
(pours the poison into the PLAYER KING's *ears)*

HAMLET

You see, he poisons the king in his own garden to get
the kingdom for himself. The king's name is Gonzago.
The original story was written in the finest Italian.
You'll see shortly how the murderer wins the love of
Gonzago's wife.

CLAUDIUS *stands up.*

OPHELIA

The king is getting up.

HAMLET

What—is he scared of a gun that only fired a blank?

GERTRUDE

My lord, how are you feeling?

POLONIUS

Stop the play.

CLAUDIUS

Turn on the lights. Get me out of here!

POLONIUS

Lights, lights, get us some lights!
Everyone except HAMLET *and* HORATIO *exits.*

HAMLET

Let the deer that's been shot go off and weep,
While the unharmed deer happily plays.
For some must watch while other must sleep,
That's how the world goes.
Couldn't I get work as an actor (if I hit a run of bad
luck) in some acting company, and wear flowers on my
shoes?

HORATIO

They might even give you half a share of the company.

HAMLET

No, a whole share for me.

> For thou dost know, O Damon dear,
> This realm dismantled was
265 Of Jove himself. And now reigns here
> A very, very—pajock.

HORATIO
You might have rhymed.

HAMLET
O good Horatio, I'll take the ghost's word for a thousand
pound. Didst perceive?

HORATIO
270 Very well, my lord.

HAMLET
Upon the talk of the poisoning?

HORATIO
I did very well note him.

HAMLET
Ah ha! Come, some music! Come, the recorders!
> For if the king like not the comedy,
275 Why then, belike, he likes it not, perdy.
Come, some music!

Enter ROSENCRANTZ *and* GUILDENSTERN

GUILDENSTERN
Good my lord, vouchsafe me a word with you.

HAMLET
Sir, a whole history.

GUILDENSTERN
The king, sir—

HAMLET
280 Ay, sir, what of him?

GUILDENSTERN
Is in his retirement marvelous distempered.

For you know, my dearest Damon,
That Jove, king of the gods, was
Thrown out of power here, and
Who's in charge? A big—peacock.

HORATIO

The obvious rhyme is "ass."

You could have at least rhymed.

HAMLET

Oh, Horatio, I'll bet you a thousand bucks the ghost was right. Did you notice?

HORATIO

Yes, I did, my lord.

HAMLET

When the actors were talking about poison?

HORATIO

I watched him very closely.

HAMLET

Ah ha! Hey, let's have some music here! Play your flutes!

For if the king doesn't like the play,
Then he doesn't like it, we may say.

Come on, music!

ROSENCRANTZ *and* GUILDENSTERN *enter.*

GUILDENSTERN

My lord, could I have a word with you?

HAMLET

You can have a whole story, not just a word.

GUILDENSTERN

Sir, the king—

HAMLET

Yes, what about him?

GUILDENSTERN

He's in his chambers now, and he's extremely upset.

HAMLET
With drink, sir?

GUILDENSTERN
No, my lord, with choler.

HAMLET
Your wisdom should show itself more richer to signify this
285   to the doctor. For, for me to put him to his purgation would
perhaps plunge him into far more choler.

GUILDENSTERN
Good my lord, put your discourse into some frame and start
not so wildly from my affair.

HAMLET
I am tame, sir. Pronounce.

GUILDENSTERN
290   The queen your mother, in most great affliction of spirit,
hath sent me to you.

HAMLET
You are welcome.

GUILDENSTERN
Nay, good my lord, this courtesy is not of the right breed. If
it shall please you to make me a wholesome answer, I will do
295   your mother's commandment. If not, your pardon and my
return shall be the end of my business.

HAMLET
Sir, I cannot.

GUILDENSTERN
What, my lord?

HAMLET
Make you a wholesome answer. My wit's diseased. But, sir,
300   such answer as I can make, you shall command. Or, rather,
as you say, my mother. Therefore no more but to the matter.
My mother, you say—

ROSENCRANTZ
Then thus she says: your behavior hath struck her into
amazement and admiration.

HAMLET

What, an upset stomach from too much booze?

GUILDENSTERN

No, sir, he's angry.

HAMLET

You should be smart enough to tell this to a doctor, not me, since if I treated him, he'd just get angrier.

GUILDENSTERN

My lord, please try to stick to the subject at hand.

HAMLET

I'll be good, sir. Go ahead.

GUILDENSTERN

The queen your mother is upset, and sent me to see you.

HAMLET

It's lovely to see you.

GUILDENSTERN

No, my lord, your polite words are not to the point. If you could please stop fooling around, I'll tell you what your mother wants. If not, I'll leave you alone and that'll be the end of my business.

HAMLET

Sir, I can't.

GUILDENSTERN

Can't what, my lord?

HAMLET

Stop fooling around. My mind is confused. But I'll do my best to give you a straight answer, as you wish—or rather, as my mother wishes. Okay, to the point. My mother, you say . . . ?

ROSENCRANTZ

She says that your behavior has astonished her.

HAMLET

305   O wonderful son that can so 'stonish a mother! But is there
          no sequel at the heels of this mother's admiration? Impart.

ROSENCRANTZ

          She desires to speak with you in her closet ere you go to bed.

HAMLET

          We shall obey, were she ten times our mother. Have you any
          further trade with us?

ROSENCRANTZ

310   My lord, you once did love me.

HAMLET

          And do still, by these pickers and stealers.

ROSENCRANTZ

          Good my lord, what is your cause of distemper? You do
          surely bar the door upon your own liberty if you deny your
          griefs to your friend.

HAMLET

315   Sir, I lack advancement.

ROSENCRANTZ

          How can that be, when you have the voice of the king
          himself for your succession in Denmark?

Reenter the PLAYERS *with recorders*

HAMLET

          Ay, sir, but "While the grass grows—" The proverb
          is something musty.—Oh, the recorders! Let me see one.
          (takes a recorder)
          (aside to ROSENCRANTZ *and* GUILDENSTERN*)*
320   To withdraw with you, why do you go about to recover the
          wind of me as if you would drive me into a toil?

GUILDENSTERN

          O my lord, if my duty be too bold, my love is too
          unmannerly.

HAMLET

Oh, what a wonderful son, I can impress my mother! But what's the upshot of her admiration? Do tell.

ROSENCRANTZ

She wants to have a word with you in her bedroom before you go to bed.

HAMLET

I'd obey even if she were my mother ten times over. Is there anything else I can do for you?

ROSENCRANTZ

My lord, you used to like me.

HAMLET

And still do, I swear by my hands.

ROSENCRANTZ

My lord, what's wrong with you? You're not doing yourself any good by refusing to tell your friends what's bothering you.

HAMLET

Sir, I have no future ahead of me.

ROSENCRANTZ

A recorder is a wind instrument that sounds like a flute

But how can you say that, when the king himself says you're the heir to the Danish throne?

The PLAYERS *enter with recorders.*

HAMLET

The rest of the proverb goes, ". . . the horse starves."

Yes, eventually, but as the proverb goes, "While the grass grows . . ." But that's a tired old proverb. Oh, the recorders! Let me see one. *(he takes a recorder and turns to* GUILDENSTERN*)* Why are you hovering so close, as if you want to ambush me?

GUILDENSTERN

Oh, my lord, I'm sorry if I'm forgetting my manners. It's just that I'm worried about you.

HAMLET
I do not well understand that. Will you play upon this pipe?

GUILDENSTERN
325   My lord, I cannot.

HAMLET
I pray you.

GUILDENSTERN
Believe me, I cannot.

HAMLET
I do beseech you.

GUILDENSTERN
I know no touch of it, my lord.

HAMLET
330   It is as easy as lying. Govern these ventages with your fingers and thumb, give it breath with your mouth, and it will discourse most eloquent music. Look you, these are the stops.

GUILDENSTERN
But these cannot I command to any utterance of harmony.
335   I have not the skill.

HAMLET
Why, look you now, how unworthy a thing you make of me! You would play upon me. You would seem to know my stops. You would pluck out the heart of my mystery. You would sound me from my lowest note to the top of my
340   compass. And there is much music, excellent voice, in this little organ, yet cannot you make it speak? 'Sblood, do you think I am easier to be played on than a pipe? Call me what instrument you will, though you can fret me, yet you cannot play upon me.

HAMLET

I don't really understand what you mean. Will you play this recorder?

GUILDENSTERN

I can't, my lord.

HAMLET

Please.

GUILDENSTERN

I'm serious, I can't.

HAMLET

I'm begging you.

GUILDENSTERN

I have no idea how.

HAMLET

Oh, it's as easy as lying. Just put your fingers and thumb over the holes and blow into it, and it'll produce the most moving music. Here, the holes are here.

GUILDENSTERN

But I can't play a melody. I don't know how.

HAMLET

Well, look how you play me—as if you knew exactly where to put your fingers, to blow the mystery out of me, playing all the octaves of my range—and yet you can't even produce music from this little instrument? My God, do you think I'm easier to manipulate than a pipe? You can push my buttons, but you can't play me for a fool.

Enter POLONIUS

345   God bless you, sir.

POLONIUS
     My lord, the queen would speak with you, and presently.

HAMLET
     Do you see yonder cloud that's almost in shape of a camel?

POLONIUS
     By th' mass, and 'tis like a camel indeed.

HAMLET
     Methinks it is like a weasel.

POLONIUS
350   It is backed like a weasel.

HAMLET
     Or like a whale.

POLONIUS
     Very like a whale.

HAMLET
     Then I will come to my mother by and by. *(aside)* They fool
     me to the top of my bent.—I will come by and by.

POLONIUS
360   I will say so.

HAMLET
     "By and by" is easily said.

Exit POLONIUS

     Leave me, friends.

Exeunt all but HAMLET

     'Tis now the very witching time of night,
     When churchyards yawn and hell itself breathes out
365   Contagion to this world. Now could I drink hot blood
     And do such bitter business as the bitter day
     Would quake to look on. Soft, now to my mother.—
     O heart, lose not thy nature, let not ever
     The soul of Nero enter this firm bosom.
370   Let me be cruel, not unnatural.

POLONIUS *enters.*

Hello and God bless you, sir.

POLONIUS

My lord, the queen wants to speak with you right away.

HAMLET

Do you see that cloud up there that looks like a camel?

POLONIUS

By God, it does look like a camel.

HAMLET

To me it looks like a weasel.

POLONIUS

It does have a back like a weasel's.

HAMLET

Or like a whale.

POLONIUS

Yes, very much like a whale.

HAMLET

I'll go see my mother soon. (*to himself*) They're trying as hard as they can to mess with me.—I will go soon.

POLONIUS

I'll tell her.

HAMLET

It's easy enough to say "soon."

POLONIUS *exits.*

Now please leave me alone, my friends.

Everyone except HAMLET *exits.*

This is the time of night when witches come out, when graveyards yawn open and the stench of hell seeps out. I could drink hot blood and do such terrible deeds that people would tremble even in the daylight. But I've got to go see my mother.—Oh, heart, don't grow weak, like Nero. Let me be cruel, but not inhuman.

Nero was a Roman emperor known for his extreme cruelty.

I will speak daggers to her but use none.
My tongue and soul in this be hypocrites.
How in my words somever she be shent,
To give them seals never, my soul, consent!

Exit

I'll speak as sharp as a dagger to her, but I won't use one on her. And so, my words and thoughts will be at odds.

HAMLET *exits.*

ACT 3, SCENE 3

Enter CLAUDIUS, ROSENCRANTZ, *and* GUILDENSTERN

CLAUDIUS
     I like him not, nor stands it safe with us
     To let his madness range. Therefore prepare you.
     I your commission will forthwith dispatch,
     And he to England shall along with you.
5   The terms of our estate may not endure
     Hazard so dangerous as doth hourly grow
     Out of his lunacies.

GUILDENSTERN
                      We will ourselves provide.
     Most holy and religious fear it is
     To keep those many, many bodies safe
10   That live and feed upon your majesty.

ROSENCRANTZ
     The single and peculiar life is bound
     With all the strength and armor of the mind
     To keep itself from noyance, but much more
     That spirit upon whose weal depend and rest
15   The lives of many. The cease of majesty
     Dies not alone, but, like a gulf, doth draw
     What's near it with it. It is a massy wheel
     Fixed on the summit of the highest mount,
     To whose huge spokes ten thousand lesser things
20   Are mortised and adjoined, which, when it falls,
     Each small annexment, petty consequence,
     Attends the boisterous ruin. Never alone
     Did the king sigh, but with a general groan.

CLAUDIUS
     Arm you, I pray you, to this speedy voyage.
25   For we will fetters put upon this fear,
     Which now goes too free-footed.

ACT 3, SCENE 3

CLAUDIUS, ROSENCRANTZ, *and* GUILDENSTERN *enter.*

CLAUDIUS

> I don't like the way he's acting, and it's not safe for me to let his insanity get out of control. So get prepared. I'm sending you to England on diplomatic business, and Hamlet will go with you. As king, I cannot risk the danger he represents as he grows crazier by the hour.

GUILDENSTERN

> We'll take care of it. It's a sacred duty to protect the lives of all those who depend on Your Highness.

ROSENCRANTZ

> Everyone tries to avoid harm, but the public figure demands even more protection. When a great leader dies he doesn't die alone but, like a whirlpool, draws others with him. He's like a huge wheel on the top of the highest mountain whose spokes touch the rim of ten thousand smaller things—when it falls down the mountain, every little object goes down with it. Whenever a king sighs, everyone groans.

CLAUDIUS

> Prepare yourself, please, for this trip. We'll put a leash on this danger that's now running wild.

ROSENCRANTZ, GUILDENSTERN
We will haste us.

Exeunt ROSENCRANTZ *and* GUILDENSTERN

Enter POLONIUS

POLONIUS
My lord, he's going to his mother's closet.
Behind the arras I'll convey myself

30 To hear the process. I'll warrant she'll tax him home.
And, as you said (and wisely was it said)
'Tis meet that some more audience than a mother—
Since nature makes them partial—should o'erhear
The speech, of vantage. Fare you well, my liege.

35 I'll call upon you ere you go to bed
And tell you what I know.

CLAUDIUS
                              Thanks, dear my lord.

Exit POLONIUS

Oh, my offence is rank. It smells to heaven.
It hath the primal eldest curse upon 't,
A brother's murder. Pray can I not.

40 Though inclination be as sharp as will,
My stronger guilt defeats my strong intent,
And, like a man to double business bound,
I stand in pause where I shall first begin,
And both neglect. What if this cursèd hand

45 Were thicker than itself with brother's blood?
Is there not rain enough in the sweet heavens
To wash it white as snow? Whereto serves mercy
But to confront the visage of offence?
And what's in prayer but this twofold force,

50 To be forestallèd ere we come to fall
Or pardoned being down? Then I'll look up.
My fault is past. But oh, what form of prayer
Can serve my turn, "Forgive me my foul murder"?

ROSENCRANTZ, GUILDENSTERN

We'll hurry.

ROSENCRANTZ and GUILDENSTERN exit.
POLONIUS *enters.*

POLONIUS

My lord, Hamlet's going to his mother's room. I'll hide behind the tapestry to hear what they say. I bet she'll chew him out. And as you said (and you said it wisely), it's good to have someone other than a mother listening in on them, since she can be too partial to him. Goodbye, my lord. I'll stop by before you go to bed, and tell you what I've heard.

CLAUDIUS

Thanks, my dear lord.

POLONIUS exits.

Oh, my crime is so rotten it stinks all the way to heaven. It has the mark of Cain on it, a brother's murder. I can't pray, though I want to desperately. My guilt is stronger even than my intentions. And like a person with two opposite things to do at once, I stand paralyzed and neglect them both. So what if this cursed hand of mine is coated with my brother's blood? Isn't there enough rain in heaven to wash it clean as snow? Isn't that what God's mercy is for? And doesn't prayer serve these two purposes—to keep us from sinning and to bring us forgiveness when we have sinned? So I'll pray. I've already committed my sin. But, oh, what kind of prayer is there for me? "Dear Lord, forgive me for my horrible murder"?

In the Bible, Cain was the first murderer, killing his brother in Genesis 4:10-12.

That cannot be, since I am still possessed
55 Of those effects for which I did the murder:
My crown, mine own ambition, and my queen.
May one be pardoned and retain th' offense?
In the corrupted currents of this world
Offense's gilded hand may shove by justice,
60 And oft 'tis seen the wicked prize itself
Buys out the law. But 'tis not so above.
There is no shuffling. There the action lies
In his true nature, and we ourselves compelled,
Even to the teeth and forehead of our faults,
65 To give in evidence. What then? What rests?
Try what repentance can. What can it not?
Yet what can it when one can not repent?
O wretched state! O bosom black as death!
O limèd soul that, struggling to be free,
70 Art more engaged! Help, angels. Make assay.
Bow, stubborn knees, and, heart with strings of steel,
Be soft as sinews of the newborn babe.
All may be well. *(kneels)*

Enter HAMLET

HAMLET
Now might I do it pat. Now he is a-praying.
75 And now I'll do 't. And so he goes to heaven.
And so am I revenged.—That would be scanned.
A villain kills my father, and, for that,
I, his sole son, do this same villain send
To heaven.
80 Oh, this is hire and salary, not revenge.
He took my father grossly, full of bread,
With all his crimes broad blown, as flush as May.
And how his audit stands who knows save heaven?
But in our circumstance and course of thought
85 'Tis heavy with him. And am I then revenged

That won't work, since I'm still reaping the rewards of that murder: my crown and my queen. Can a person be forgiven and still keep the fruits of his crime? In this wicked world, criminals often take the money they stole and use it to buy off the law, shoving justice aside. But not in heaven. Up there, every action is judged for exactly what it's worth, and we're forced to confront our crimes. So what can I do? What is there left to do? Offer whatever repentance I can—that couldn't hurt. But it can't help either! Oh, what a lousy situation I'm in. My heart's as black as death. My soul is stuck to sin, and the more it struggles to break free, the more it sticks. Help me, angels! C'mon, make an effort. Bend, stubborn knees. Steely heart, be soft as a newborn babe, so I can pray. Perhaps everything will turn out okay after all. (*he kneels*)

HAMLET *enters.*

HAMLET

I could do it easily now. He's praying now. And now I'll do it. (*he draws out his sword*) And there he goes, off to heaven. And that's my revenge. I'd better think about this more carefully. A villain kills my father, and I, my father's only son, send this same villain to heaven. Seems like I just did him a favor. He killed my father when my father was enjoying life, with all his sins in full bloom, before my father could repent for any of them. Only God knows how many sins my father has to pay for. As for me, I don't think his prospects look so good.

To take him in the purging of his soul
When he is fit and seasoned for his passage?
No.
Up, sword, and know thou a more horrid hent.
90 When he is drunk asleep, or in his rage,
Or in th' incestuous pleasure of his bed,
At game a-swearing, or about some act
That has no relish of salvation in 't—
Then trip him, that his heels may kick at heaven,
95 And that his soul may be as damned and black
As hell, whereto it goes. My mother stays
This physic but prolongs thy sickly days.

Exit HAMLET

CLAUDIUS
(rises) My words fly up, my thoughts remain below.
Words without thoughts never to heaven go.

Exit

So is it really revenge for me if I kill Claudius right when he is confessing his sins, in perfect condition for a trip to heaven? No. Away, sword, and wait for a better moment to kill him. *(he puts his sword away)* When he's sleeping off some drunken orgy, or having incestuous sex, or swearing while he gambles, or committing some other act that has no goodness about it—that's when I'll trip him up and send him to hell with his heels kicking up at heaven. My mother's waiting. The king's trying to cure himself with prayer, but all he's doing is keeping himself alive a little longer.

HAMLET exits.

CLAUDIUS

(rising) My words fly up toward heaven, but my thoughts stay down here on earth. Words without thoughts behind them will never make it to heaven.

CLAUDIUS exits.

ACT 3, SCENE 4

Enter GERTRUDE *and* POLONIUS

POLONIUS
He will come straight. Look you lay home to him.
Tell him his pranks have been too broad to bear with,
And that your grace hath screened and stood between
Much heat and him. I'll silence me even here.
5   Pray you, be round with him.

HAMLET
(within) Mother, mother, mother!

GERTRUDE
I'll warrant you. Fear me not. Withdraw, I hear him
coming.

POLONIUS *hides behind the arras*
Enter HAMLET

HAMLET
Now mother, what's the matter?

GERTRUDE
10   Hamlet, thou hast thy father much offended.

HAMLET
Mother, you have my father much offended.

GERTRUDE
Come, come, you answer with an idle tongue.

HAMLET
Go, go, you question with a wicked tongue.

GERTRUDE
Why, how now, Hamlet?

HAMLET
                                    What's the matter now?

GERTRUDE
15   Have you forgot me?

ACT 3, SCENE 4

GERTRUDE *and* POLONIUS *enter.*

POLONIUS

He'll come right away. Make sure you lay into him. Tell him his pranks have caused too much trouble, and that Your Highness has taken a lot of heat for them. I'll be right here, silent. Please be blunt with him.

HAMLET

(offstage) Mother, mother, mother!

GERTRUDE

Don't worry, I'll do what you say. Now hide, I hear him coming.

POLONIUS *hides behind the tapestry.*
HAMLET *enters.*

HAMLET

Now mother, what's this all about?

GERTRUDE

Hamlet, you've insulted your father.

HAMLET

Mother, you've insulted my father.

GERTRUDE

Come on, you're answering me foolishly.

HAMLET

Go on, you're questioning me evilly.

GERTRUDE

Hamlet, what, why?

HAMLET

What's the problem now?

GERTRUDE

Have you forgotten who I am?

HAMLET

     No, by the rood, not so.
You are the queen, your husband's brother's wife,
And—would it were not so!—you are my mother.

GERTRUDE

Nay, then I'll set those to you that can speak.

HAMLET

Come, come, and sit you down. You shall not budge.
You go not till I set you up a glass
Where you may see the inmost part of you.

GERTRUDE

What wilt thou do? Thou wilt not murder me?
Help, help, ho!

POLONIUS

(from behind the arras) What, ho? Help, help, help!

HAMLET

How now, a rat? Dead for a ducat, dead!
(stabs his sword through the arras and kills POLONIUS*)*

POLONIUS

(from behind the arras) Oh, I am slain.

GERTRUDE

O me, what hast thou done?

HAMLET

Nay, I know not. Is it the king?

GERTRUDE

Oh, what a rash and bloody deed is this!

HAMLET

A bloody deed? Almost as bad, good mother,
As kill a king and marry with his brother.

GERTRUDE

As kill a king?

HAMLET

     Ay, lady, 'twas my word.
(draws back the arras and discovers POLONIUS*)*

HAMLET

For God's sake no, I haven't. You are the queen, your husband's brother's wife, and you are my mother, though I wish you weren't.

GERTRUDE

In that case I'll call in others who can still speak.

HAMLET

No, sit down. You won't budge until I hold a mirror up to you, where you will see what's deep inside you.

GERTRUDE

What are you going to do? You won't kill me, will you? Help!

POLONIUS

(from behind the tapestry) Hey! Help, help, help!

HAMLET

What's this, a rat? I'll bet a buck he's a dead rat now. *(he stabs his sword through the tapestry and kills* POLO-NIUS*)*

POLONIUS

(from behind the tapestry) Oh, I've been killed!

GERTRUDE

Oh my God, what have you done?

HAMLET

I don't know. Is it the king?

GERTRUDE

Oh, what a senseless, horrible act!

HAMLET

A horrible act—almost as bad, my good mother, as killing a king and marrying his brother.

GERTRUDE

Killing a king?

HAMLET

That's what I said, my good woman. *(he pulls back the tapestry and discovers* POLONIUS*)*

Thou wretched, rash, intruding fool, farewell.
I took thee for thy better. Take thy fortune.
Thou find'st to be too busy is some danger.
35 *(to* GERTRUDE*)* Leave wringing of your hands. Peace. Sit you
          down
And let me wring your heart. For so I shall
If it be made of penetrable stuff,
If damnèd custom have not brassed it so
That it is proof and bulwark against sense.

GERTRUDE
40 What have I done, that thou darest wag thy tongue
In noise so rude against me?

HAMLET
                              Such an act
That blurs the grace and blush of modesty,
Calls virtue hypocrite, takes off the rose
From the fair forehead of an innocent love
45 And sets a blister there, makes marriage vows
As false as dicers' oaths—oh, such a deed
As from the body of contraction plucks
The very soul, and sweet religion makes
A rhapsody of words. Heaven's face doth glow
50 O'er this solidity and compound mass
With tristful visage, as against the doom,
Is thought-sick at the act.

GERTRUDE
                              Ay me, what act
That roars so loud and thunders in the index?

HAMLET
Look here upon this picture and on this,
55 The counterfeit presentment of two brothers.
See, what a grace was seated on this brow?
Hyperion's curls, the front of Jove himself,
An eye like Mars to threaten and command,
A station like the herald Mercury
60 New-lighted on a heaven-kissing hill—

You low-life, nosy, busybody fool, goodbye. I thought you were somebody more important. You've gotten what you deserve. I guess you found out it's dangerous to be a busybody. *(to* GERTRUDE*)* Stop wringing your hands. Sit down and let me wring your heart instead, which I will do if it's still soft enough, if your evil lifestyle has not toughened it against feeling anything at all.

GERTRUDE

What have I done that you dare to talk to me so rudely?

HAMLET

A deed that destroys modesty, turns virtue into hypocrisy, replaces the blossom on the face of true love with a nasty blemish, makes marriage vows as false as a gambler's oath—oh, you've done a deed that plucks the soul out of marriage and turns religion into meaningless blather. Heaven looks down on this earth, as angry as if Judgment Day were here, and is sick at the thought of what you've done.

GERTRUDE

C'mon, what's this deed that sounds so awful even before I know what it is?

HAMLET

Look at this picture here, and that one there, the painted images of two brothers. Look how kind and gentlemanly this one is, with his curly hair and his forehead like a Greek god. His eye could command like the god of war. His body is as agile as Mercury just landing on a high hill.

Hamlet may be referring to miniatures they wear around their necks, or to pictures on the wall.

A combination and a form indeed
Where every god did seem to set his seal
To give the world assurance of a man.
This was your husband. Look you now, what follows.
65 Here is your husband, like a mildewed ear
Blasting his wholesome brother. Have you eyes?
Could you on this fair mountain leave to feed
And batten on this moor? Ha, have you eyes?
You cannot call it love, for at your age
70 The heyday in the blood is tame, it's humble,
And waits upon the judgment. And what judgment
Would step from this to this? Sense sure you have,
Else could you not have motion. But sure that sense
Is apoplexed, for madness would not err,
75 Nor sense to ecstasy was ne'er so thralled,
But it reserved some quantity of choice
To serve in such a difference. What devil was 't
That thus hath cozened you at hoodman-blind?
Eyes without feeling, feeling without sight,
80 Ears without hands or eyes, smelling sans all,
Or but a sickly part of one true sense
Could not so mope. O shame, where is thy blush?
Rebellious hell,
If thou canst mutine in a matron's bones,
85 To flaming youth let virtue be as wax
And melt in her own fire. Proclaim no shame
When the compulsive ardor gives the charge,
Since frost itself as actively doth burn,
And reason panders will.

GERTRUDE

O Hamlet, speak no more!
90 Thou turn'st mine eyes into my very soul,
And there I see such black and grainèd spots
As will not leave their tinct.

A figure and a combination of good qualities that seemed like every god had set his stamp on this man. That was your husband. Now look at this other one. Here is your present husband, like a mildewed ear of corn infecting the healthy one next to it. Do you have eyes? How could you leave the lofty heights of this man here and descend as low as this one? Ha! Do you have eyes? You cannot say you did it out of love, since at your age romantic passions have grown weak, and the heart obeys reason. But what reason could move you from this one to that one? You must have some sense in your head, since you're able to get around, but it seems to be paralyzed, since even if you were crazy you would know the difference between these two men. No one ever went so insane that they couldn't get an easy choice like this one right. What devil was it that blindfolded you? Eyes without feeling, feeling without sight, ears without hands or eyes, smell without anything else, the use of even one impaired sense would not permit such a mistake as yours. Oh, for shame, why aren't you blushing? If evil can overtake even an old mother's bones, then let it melt my own. It turns out it's no longer shameful to act on impulse— now that the old are doing so, and now that reason is a servant to desire.

GERTRUDE

Oh, Hamlet, stop! You're making me look into my very soul, where the marks of sin are so thick and black they will never be washed away.

HAMLET
                                   Nay, but to live
In the rank sweat of an enseamèd bed,
Stewed in corruption, honeying and making love
95   Over the nasty sty—

GERTRUDE
                              O, speak to me no more!
These words like daggers enter in my ears.
No more, sweet Hamlet.

HAMLET
                                   A murderer and a villain,
A slave that is not twentieth part the tithe
Of your precedent lord, a vice of kings,
100   A cutpurse of the empire and the rule,
That from a shelf the precious diadem stole,
And put it in his pocket—

GERTRUDE
No more!

HAMLET
A king of shreds and patches—

Enter GHOST

105   Save me and hover o'er me with your wings,
You heavenly guards!—What would your gracious figure?

GERTRUDE
Alas, he's mad!

HAMLET
Do you not come your tardy son to chide,
That, lapsed in time and passion, lets go by
110   The important acting of your dread command?
O, say!

GHOST
                         Do not forget. This visitation
Is but to whet thy almost blunted purpose.
But look, amazement on thy mother sits.

HAMLET

Yes, and you lie in the sweaty stench of your dirty sheets, wet with corruption, making love—

GERTRUDE

Oh, you must stop! Your words are like daggers. Please, no more, sweet Hamlet.

HAMLET

A murderer and a villain, a low-life who's not worth a twentieth of a tenth of your first husband—the worst of kings, a thief of the throne, who took the precious crown from a shelf and put it in his pocket—

GERTRUDE

Stop!

HAMLET

A ragtag king—

The GHOST *enters.*

Oh, angels in heaven, protect me with your wings!— What can I do for you, my gracious lord?

GERTRUDE

Oh no! Hamlet's gone completely crazy.

HAMLET

Have you come to scold your tardy son for straying from his mission, letting your important command slip by? Tell me!

GHOST

Don't forget. I've come to sharpen your somewhat dull appetite for revenge. But look, your mother is in shock.

O, step between her and her fighting soul.

115 Conceit in weakest bodies strongest works.

Speak to her, Hamlet.

HAMLET
How is it with you, lady?

GERTRUDE
                                    Alas, how is 't with you,
That you do bend your eye on vacancy
And with th' incorporal air do hold discourse?

120 Forth at your eyes your spirits wildly peep,
And, as the sleeping soldiers in th' alarm,
Your bedded hair, like life in excrements,
Starts up and stands on end. O gentle son,
Upon the heat and flame of thy distemper

125 Sprinkle cool patience. Whereon do you look?

HAMLET
On him, on him! Look you, how pale he glares!
His form and cause conjoined, preaching to stones,
Would make them capable.
(to GHOST*)* Do not look upon me,

130 Lest with this piteous action you convert
My stern effects. Then what I have to do
Will want true color—tears perchance for blood.

GERTRUDE
To whom do you speak this?

HAMLET
                                    Do you see nothing there?

GERTRUDE
Nothing at all, yet all that is I see.

HAMLET
135 Nor did you nothing hear?

GERTRUDE
                                    No, nothing but ourselves.

HAMLET
Why, look you there! Look how it steals away—
My father, in his habit as he lived—

Oh, keep her struggling soul from being over-whelmed by horrid visions. The imagination works strongest in those with the weakest bodies. Talk to her, Hamlet.

HAMLET

How are you doing, madam?

GERTRUDE

And how are *you* doing, staring into the empty air and talking to nobody? Your eyes give away your wild thoughts, and your hair is standing upright, like soldiers during a call to arms. Oh my dear son, calm yourself and cool off your overheated mind! What are you staring at?

HAMLET

At him, at him! Look how pale he is and how he glares at me. Preaching even at stones, he could get them to act. *(to the* GHOST*)* Don't look at me like that, unless you want me to cry instead of kill.

GERTRUDE

Who are you talking to?

HAMLET

You don't see anything?

GERTRUDE

Nothing at all, but I can see everything that's here.

HAMLET

And you don't hear anything?

GERTRUDE

No, nothing but us talking.

HAMLET

Look, look how it's sneaking away! My father, dressed just like he was when he was alive!

Look where he goes, even now, out at the portal!

Exit GHOST

GERTRUDE

This the very coinage of your brain.
140 This bodiless creation ecstasy
Is very cunning in.

HAMLET

Ecstasy?
My pulse as yours doth temperately keep time
And makes as healthful music. It is not madness
That I have uttered. Bring me to the test,
145 And I the matter will reword, which madness
Would gambol from. Mother, for love of grace,
Lay not that flattering unction to your soul
That not your trespass but my madness speaks.
It will but skin and film the ulcerous place
150 Whilst rank corruption, mining all within,
Infects unseen. Confess yourself to heaven.
Repent what's past. Avoid what is to come.
And do not spread the compost on the weeds
To make them ranker. Forgive me this my virtue,
155 For in the fatness of these pursy times
Virtue itself of vice must pardon beg,
Yea, curb and woo for leave to do him good.

GERTRUDE

O Hamlet, thou hast cleft my heart in twain.

HAMLET

Oh, throw away the worser part of it,
160 And live the purer with the other half.
Good night—but go not to mine uncle's bed.
Assume a virtue if you have it not.
That monster, custom, who all sense doth eat,
Of habits devil, is angel yet in this:
165 That to the use of actions fair and good
He likewise gives a frock or livery
That aptly is put on. Refrain tonight,

Look, he's going out the door right now!

The GHOST *exits.*

GERTRUDE

This is only a figment of your imagination. Madness is good at creating hallucinations.

HAMLET

Madness? My heart beats just as evenly as yours does. There's nothing crazy in what I've just uttered. Put me to the test. I'll rephrase everything I've just said, which a lunatic couldn't do. Mother, for the love of God, don't flatter yourself into believing that it's my madness, not your crime, that's the problem. You'd just be concealing the rot that's eating you from the inside. Confess your sins to heaven. Repent and avoid damnation. Don't spread manure over the weeds in your heart; it'll only make them more filthy. Forgive me my good intentions here since in these fat and spoiled times, virtuous people have to say, "Beg your pardon" to vile ones and beg for the chance to do any good.

GERTRUDE

Oh Hamlet, you've broken my heart in two!

HAMLET

Then throw away the worse half, and live a purer life with the other! Good night to you. But don't go to my uncle's bed tonight. At least pretend to be virtuous, even if you're not. Habit is a terrible thing, in that it's easy to get used to doing evil without feeling bad about it. But it's also a good thing, in that being good can also become a habit.

And that shall lend a kind of easiness
To the next abstinence, the next more easy.
170   For use almost can change the stamp of nature,
And either rein the devil or throw him out
With wondrous potency. Once more, good night,
And when you are desirous to be blessed,
I'll blessing beg of you. *(points to* POLONIUS*)*
175   For this same lord,
I do repent. But heaven hath pleased it so,
To punish me with this and this with me,
That I must be their scourge and minister.
I will bestow him and will answer well
180   The death I gave him. So, again, good night.
I must be cruel only to be kind.
Thus bad begins and worse remains behind.
One word more, good lady—

GERTRUDE
What shall I do?

HAMLET
185   Not this, by no means, that I bid you do—
Let the bloat king tempt you again to bed,
Pinch wanton on your cheek, call you his mouse,
And let him, for a pair of reechy kisses
Or paddling in your neck with his damned fingers,
190   Make you to ravel all this matter out:
That I essentially am not in madness
But mad in craft. 'Twere good you let him know,
For who that's but a queen, fair, sober, wise,
Would from a paddock, from a bat, a gib,
195   Such dear concernings hide? Who would do so?
No, in despite of sense and secrecy,
Unpeg the basket on the house's top.
Let the birds fly, and like the famous ape,
To try conclusions, in the basket creep
200   And break your own neck down.

Say no to sex tonight, and that will make it easier to say no the next time, and still easier the time after that. Habit can change even one's natural instincts, and either rein in the devil in us, or kick him out. Once again, good night to you, and when you want to repent, I'll ask you for your blessing too. I'm sorry about what happened to this gentleman *(pointing to* POLONIUS*),* but God wanted to punish me with this murder, and this man with me, so I'm both Heaven's executioner and its minister of justice. This is bad, but it'll get worse soon. Oh, and one other thing, madam.

GERTRUDE

What should I do?

HAMLET

Whatever you do, don't do this: let the fat king seduce you into his bed again, so he can pinch your cheek, call you his bunny, and with filthy kisses and a massage of your neck with his damned fingers, make you admit that my madness is fake, all calculated. What a great idea that would be, because why would a fair, sober, wise queen hide such things from a toad, a pig, a monster like him? Who would do that? No, no, it's *much, much* better to spill the beans right away, let the cat out of the bag, and break your neck in the process.

GERTRUDE
> Be thou assured, if words be made of breath
> And breath of life, I have no life to breathe
> What thou hast said to me.

HAMLET
> I must to England, you know that?

GERTRUDE
205 > Alack,
> I had forgot. 'Tis so concluded on.

HAMLET
> There's letters sealed, and my two schoolfellows,
> Whom I will trust as I will adders fanged,
> They bear the mandate. They must sweep my way
210 > And marshal me to knavery. Let it work,
> For 'tis the sport to have the engineer
> Hoist with his own petard. And 't shall go hard,
> But I will delve one yard below their mines,
> And blow them at the moon. Oh, 'tis most sweet
215 > When in one line two crafts directly meet.
> *(indicates* POLONIUS*)*
> This man shall set me packing.
> I'll lug the guts into the neighbor room.
> Mother, good night. Indeed this counselor
> Is now most still, most secret, and most grave
220 > Who was in life a foolish prating knave.—
> Come, sir, to draw toward an end with you.—
> Good night, mother.

> *Exeunt,* HAMLET *tugging in* POLONIUS

GERTRUDE

You can rest easy, since words are made of breath, and breathing requires that you be alive. I feel too dead to breathe a word of what you've told me.

HAMLET

I have to go to England, don't you know that?

GERTRUDE

Ah, I'd forgotten all about that! It's been decided.

HAMLET

Yes, it's a done deal, the documents are ready, and my two schoolmates, whom I trust about as much as rattlesnakes, are in charge. They're the ones who'll lead me on my march to mischief. Let it happen. It's fun to watch the engineer get blown up by his own explosives, and with any luck I'll dig a few feet below their bombs and blow them to the moon. Oh, it's nice to kill two birds with one stone. (*points to* POLONIUS) Now that I've killed this guy, I'll be off in a hurry. I'll lug his guts into the next room. Mother, have a good night. This politician who was in life a babbling idiot is now quiet and serious. Come on, sir, let's get to the end of our business. Good night, mother.

They exit, HAMLET *dragging* POLONIUS *offstage.*

ACT FOUR

SCENE 1

Enter King CLAUDIUS *and Queen* GERTRUDE, *with*
ROSENCRANTZ *and* GUILDENSTERN

CLAUDIUS

(to GERTRUDE*)* There's matter in these sighs, these profound
heaves.
You must translate. 'Tis fit we understand them.
Where is your son?

GERTRUDE

(to ROSENCRANTZ *and* GUILDENSTERN*)*
Bestow this place on us a little while.

Exeunt ROSENCRANTZ *and* GUILDENSTERN

5   Ah, my good lord, what have I seen tonight!

CLAUDIUS

What, Gertrude? How does Hamlet?

GERTRUDE

Mad as the sea and wind when both contend
Which is the mightier. In his lawless fit,
Behind the arras hearing something stir,
10   Whips out his rapier, cries, "A rat, a rat!"
And in this brainish apprehension kills
The unseen good old man.

CLAUDIUS

                  O heavy deed!
It had been so with us, had we been there.
His liberty is full of threats to all—
15   To you yourself, to us, to everyone.
Alas, how shall this bloody deed be answered?
It will be laid to us, whose providence
Should have kept short, restrained and out of haunt,
This mad young man. But so much was our love,
20   We would not understand what was most fit,

ACT FOUR
SCENE 1

CLAUDIUS *and* GERTRUDE *enter with* ROSENCRANTZ *and* GUILDENSTERN.

CLAUDIUS

(to GERTRUDE*)* These deep, heaving sighs of yours mean something. You have to tell me what. I need to know. Where's your son?

GERTRUDE

Let us speak privately awhile, please.

> ROSENCRANTZ *and* GUILDENSTERN *exit.*

Ah, my lord, you wouldn't believe what I've witnessed tonight!

CLAUDIUS

What, Gertrude? How is Hamlet?

GERTRUDE

As mad as the waves and the wind when they struggle together in a storm. In an insane rage, he hears something behind the tapestry, whips out his sword, shouts, "A rat, a rat!" and in his deranged state of mind he kills the good old man, who is still hidden.

CLAUDIUS

Oh, this is terrible! It would've happened to me if I'd been there. His wildness is a threat to all of us—to you, to me, to everyone. How will we deal with this violent deed? I'm the one who will be blamed for not restraining and confining this mad young man. But I loved him so much I didn't want to think about what I had to do.

But, like the owner of a foul disease,
To keep it from divulging, let it feed
Even on the pith of life. Where is he gone?

GERTRUDE

To draw apart the body he hath killed,
25   O'er whom his very madness, like some ore
Among a mineral of metals base,
Shows itself pure. He weeps for what is done.

CLAUDIUS

O Gertrude, come away!
The sun no sooner shall the mountains touch
30   But we will ship him hence, and this vile deed
We must, with all our majesty and skill,
Both countenance and excuse.—Ho, Guildenstern!

Enter ROSENCRANTZ *and* GUILDENSTERN

Friends both, go join you with some further aid.
Hamlet in madness hath Polonius slain,
35   And from his mother's closet hath he dragged him.
Go seek him out, speak fair, and bring the body
Into the chapel. I pray you, haste in this.
              Exeunt ROSENCRANTZ *and* GUILDENSTERN
Come, Gertrude, we'll call up our wisest friends,
And let them know both what we mean to do
40   And what's untimely done. So dreaded slander—
Whose whisper o'er the world's diameter,
As level as the cannon to his blank,
Transports the poisoned shot—may miss our name
And hit the woundless air. Oh, come away!
45   My soul is full of discord and dismay.
                                        Exeunt

So, like someone suffering from a nasty disease who refuses to divulge his condition and lets it infect him to the core, I kept Hamlet's condition secret and let it grow more and more dangerous. Where has he gone?

GERTRUDE

To remove the corpse of the man he killed. His madness allows a glimmering of morality to shine through, like a vein of gold in a chunk of coal. He weeps for what he has done.

CLAUDIUS

Oh, Gertrude, let's go. As soon as the sun sets we'll ship him off to England. It'll take all my diplomatic know-how to explain and excuse the murder he's committed. Hey, Guildenstern!

ROSENCRANTZ *and* GUILDENSTERN *enter.*

My friends, go find others to help you. Hamlet in his madness has killed Polonius and dragged him out of his mother's bedroom. Go find him and speak nicely to him, and bring the corpse into the chapel. Please hurry.

ROSENCRANTZ *and* GUILDENSTERN *exit.*

Come, Gertrude. We'll confer with our wisest friends and tell them what we're going to do, and what terrible deed has been done already. Let's hope slander—a bullet that can travel halfway around the world and still hit its exact target—spares us. Oh, we must go. I'm full of confusion and despair.

They exit.

ACT 4, SCENE 2

Enter HAMLET

HAMLET
Safely stowed.

GENTLEMEN
(from within) Hamlet! Lord Hamlet!

HAMLET
But soft, what noise? Who calls on Hamlet?
Oh, here they come.

Enter ROSENCRANTZ, GUILDENSTERN, *and others*

ROSENCRANTZ
5   What have you done, my lord, with the dead body?

HAMLET
Compounded it with dust, whereto 'tis kin.

ROSENCRANTZ
Tell us where 'tis, that we may take it thence
And bear it to the chapel.

HAMLET
Do not believe it.

ROSENCRANTZ
10   Believe what?

HAMLET
That I can keep your counsel and not mine own. Besides, to
be demanded of a sponge! What replication should be made
by the son of a king?

ROSENCRANTZ
Take you me for a sponge, my lord?

ACT 4, SCENE 2

HAMLET *enters.*

HAMLET

The body is safely hidden.

GENTLEMEN

(from offstage) Hamlet, Lord Hamlet!

HAMLET

What's that noise? Who's calling for Hamlet? Oh, here they come.

ROSENCRANTZ *and* GUILDENSTERN *enter with others.*

ROSENCRANTZ

What have you done with the corpse, my lord?

HAMLET

I've gotten it dirty—ashes to ashes, and dust to dust.

ROSENCRANTZ

But tell us where it is, so we can take it to the chapel.

HAMLET

Don't believe it.

ROSENCRANTZ

Believe what?

HAMLET

That I'd take your advice rather than keep my own secret. Besides, you're a sponge! What is the son of a king supposed to say to a sponge?

ROSENCRANTZ

You think I'm a sponge, my lord?

HAMLET

15 Ay, sir, that soaks up the king's countenance, his rewards, his authorities. But such officers do the king best service in the end. He keeps them, like an ape, in the corner of his jaw, first mouthed to be last swallowed. When he needs what you have gleaned, it is but squeezing you and, sponge, you

20 shall be dry again.

ROSENCRANTZ

I understand you not, my lord.

HAMLET

I am glad of it. A knavish speech sleeps in a foolish ear.

ROSENCRANTZ

My lord, you must tell us where the body is and go with us to the king.

HAMLET

25 The body is with the king, but the king is not with the body. The king is a thing—

GUILDENSTERN

A thing, my lord?

HAMLET

Of nothing. Bring me to him. Hide, fox, and all after.

Exeunt

HAMLET

Yes, sir, a sponge that soaks up the king's approval, his rewards, and his decisions. Officers like that give the king the best service in the end. He keeps them in his mouth like an ape. First he moves them around, then he swallows them. When he needs what you have found out, he can just squeeze you like a sponge and you'll be dry again.

ROSENCRANTZ

I don't follow, my lord.

HAMLET

I'm glad about that. Sly words are never understood by fools.

ROSENCRANTZ

My lord, you have to tell us where the body is, and then go with us to see the king.

HAMLET

The body's with the king, but the king's not with the body. The king's a thing . . .

GUILDENSTERN

A "thing," my lord?

HAMLET

A thing of no importance. Take me to him. Ready or not, here I come!

They exit.

ACT 4, SCENE 3

Enter King CLAUDIUS *and two or three attendants*

CLAUDIUS
I have sent to seek him and to find the body.
How dangerous is it that this man goes loose!
Yet must not we put the strong law on him.
He's loved of the distracted multitude,
5   Who like not in their judgment, but their eyes.
And where 'tis so, th' offender's scourge is weighed,
But never the offense. To bear all smooth and even,
This sudden sending him away must seem
Deliberate pause. Diseases desperate grown
10   By desperate appliance are relieved,
Or not at all.

Enter ROSENCRANTZ

How now, what hath befall'n?

ROSENCRANTZ
Where the dead body is bestowed, my lord,
We cannot get from him.

CLAUDIUS
But where is he?

ROSENCRANTZ
15   Without, my lord; guarded, to know your pleasure.

CLAUDIUS
Bring him before us.

ROSENCRANTZ
Ho, Guildenstern! Bring in my lord.

Enter HAMLET *and* GUILDENSTERN

CLAUDIUS
Now, Hamlet, where's Polonius?

ACT 4, SCENE 3

CLAUDIUS *enters with two or three of his attendants.*

CLAUDIUS

I've sent men to find him and retrieve the body. How dangerous to have this madman on the loose! But we can't throw him in jail. The people love him, because they judge based on appearance rather than reason. They'll pay attention to the severity of the punishment, not the severity of the crime. No, we must seem calm and fair-minded, and our sending him away must seem like a carefully considered move. But a terminal disease requires extreme treatment, or nothing at all.

ROSENCRANTZ *enters.*

So what's happened?

ROSENCRANTZ

We can't get him to tell us where he's put the body.

CLAUDIUS

But where is he?

ROSENCRANTZ

Outside, my lord, under guard, waiting for your orders.

CLAUDIUS

Bring him to me.

ROSENCRANTZ

Hey, Guildenstern! Bring in my lord.

GUILDENSTERN *enters with* HAMLET.

CLAUDIUS

Now, Hamlet, where's Polonius?

HAMLET
> At supper.

CLAUDIUS
20 > At supper where?

HAMLET
> Not where he eats, but where he is eaten. A certain convocation of politic worms are e'en at him. Your worm is your only emperor for diet. We fat all creatures else to fat us, and we fat ourselves for maggots. Your fat king and your
25 > lean beggar is but variable service—two dishes, but to one table. That's the end.

CLAUDIUS
> Alas, alas!

HAMLET
> A man may fish with the worm that hath eat of a king, and eat of the fish that hath fed of that worm.

CLAUDIUS
30 > What dost you mean by this?

HAMLET
> Nothing but to show you how a king may go a progress through the guts of a beggar.

CLAUDIUS
> Where is Polonius?

HAMLET
> In heaven. Send hither to see. If your messenger find him
35 > not there, seek him i' th' other place yourself. But if indeed you find him not within this month, you shall nose him as you go up the stairs into the lobby.

CLAUDIUS
> *(to attendants)* Go seek him there.
>
> > *Exeunt some attendants*

HAMLET
> He will stay till ye come.

HAMLET

At dinner.

CLAUDIUS

At dinner where?

HAMLET

Not where he's eating, but where he's being eaten. A certain conference of worms is chowing down on him. Worms are the emperor of all diets. We fatten up all creatures to feed ourselves, and we fatten ourselves for the worms to eat when we're dead. A fat king and a skinny beggar are just two dishes at the same meal. That's all I have to say.

Hamlet is punning on a famous event in European history, the Diet of Worms, which was a gathering convened by the Holy Roman Emperor in 1521.

CLAUDIUS

Oh no, oh no!

HAMLET

A man can fish with the worm that ate a king, and then eat the fish he catches with that worm.

CLAUDIUS

What do you mean by that?

HAMLET

Nothing much, just to demonstrate that a king can move through the bowels of a beggar.

CLAUDIUS

Where is Polonius?

HAMLET

In heaven. Send a messenger there if you want to be sure. If your messenger can't find him, you can check hell yourself. But seriously, if you don't find him within the next month, you'll be sure to smell him as you go upstairs into the main hall.

CLAUDIUS

(to attendants) Go look for him there.

Some attendants exit.

HAMLET

No need to hurry, he's not going anywhere.

CLAUDIUS
40 Hamlet, this deed, for thine especial safety—
Which we do tender as we dearly grieve
For that which thou hast done—must send thee hence
With fiery quickness. Therefore prepare thyself.
The bark is ready and the wind at help,
45 Th' associates tend, and everything is bent
For England.

HAMLET
For England?

CLAUDIUS
Ay, Hamlet.

HAMLET
Good.

CLAUDIUS
50 So is it, if thou knew'st our purposes.

HAMLET
I see a cherub that sees them. But come, for England.
Farewell, dear mother.

CLAUDIUS
Thy loving father, Hamlet.

HAMLET
My mother. Father and mother is man and wife, man and
55 wife is one flesh, and so, my mother.—Come, for England!
Exit HAMLET

CLAUDIUS
Follow him at foot. Tempt him with speed aboard.
Delay it not. I'll have him hence tonight.
Away! For everything is sealed and done
That else leans on the affair. Pray you, make haste.
Exeunt all but CLAUDIUS
60 And, England, if my love thou hold'st at aught—
As my great power thereof may give thee sense,
Since yet thy cicatrice looks raw and red
After the Danish sword and thy free awe

CLAUDIUS

Hamlet, I care for you just as much as I grieve for Polonius. For your own protection, I must send you to England at once. So get ready to leave. The ship is set to sail, the wind is favorable, your servants are waiting for you—everything is ready for you to go to England.

HAMLET

To England?

CLAUDIUS

Yes, Hamlet.

HAMLET

Good.

CLAUDIUS

Yes, you'd think so, if you knew why I was sending you.

HAMLET

I know an angel who can read your mind. But okay, off to England! Good-bye, dear mother.

CLAUDIUS

I'm your father, Hamlet—your father who loves you.

HAMLET

You're my mother. When you married my mother, the two of you became one flesh, so if you're my father you're also my mother. Come on, off to England!

HAMLET exits.

CLAUDIUS

Follow him on foot, and get him on board as quickly as possible. Don't waste any time. I want him out of here tonight. Go now; everything else is ready. Please hurry.

Everyone except CLAUDIUS exits.

And you, dear king of England, if you care about me at all—and you should, since you can still feel the damage that Denmark has done to you in the past and, so, fear and respect us—then you won't ignore my let-

Pays homage to us—thou mayst not coldly set
65   Our sovereign process, which imports at full,
By letters congruing to that effect,
The present death of Hamlet. Do it, England,
For like the hectic in my blood he rages,
And thou must cure me. Till I know 'tis done,
70   Howe'er my haps, my joys were ne'er begun.

                                                        Exit

ters instructing you to kill Hamlet immediately. Do it, English king, since he's raging like a fever in my brain, and you must cure me. Until I know it's been done, I'll never be happy, no matter how much luck I have.

He exits.

ACT 4, SCENE 4

Enter FORTINBRAS *with his army and a* CAPTAIN

FORTINBRAS
Go, Captain, from me greet the Danish king
Tell him that, by his license, Fortinbras
Craves the conveyance of a promised march
Over his kingdom. You know the rendezvous.
5   If that his majesty would aught with us,
We shall express our duty in his eye,
And let him know so.

CAPTAIN
I will do 't, my lord.

FORTINBRAS
Go softly on.

Exeunt all except the CAPTAIN
Enter HAMLET, ROSENCRANTZ, GUILDENSTERN, *and others*

HAMLET
10   Good sir, whose powers are these?

CAPTAIN
They are of Norway, sir.

HAMLET
How purposed, sir, I pray you?

CAPTAIN
Against some part of Poland.

HAMLET
Who commands them, sir?

CAPTAIN
The nephew to old Norway, Fortinbras.

HAMLET
Goes it against the main of Poland, sir,
15   Or for some frontier?

ACT 4, SCENE 4

FORTINBRAS *enters with his army and a* CAPTAIN.

FORTINBRAS

Go, Captain, and give the Danish king my greetings. Tell him that Fortinbras asks permission to move his troops across Denmark. You know the meeting place we've arranged. If His Majesty wants us to do any favor for him, tell him his wish is my command.

CAPTAIN

I'll tell him, my lord.

FORTINBRAS

Go ahead, then.

Everyone except the CAPTAIN *exits.*
HAMLET, ROSENCRANTZ, GUILDENSTERN, *and others enter.*

HAMLET

Sir, whose troops are these?

CAPTAIN

The king of Norway's, sir.

HAMLET

What are they doing here, sir?

CAPTAIN

They're on their way to invade some part of Poland.

HAMLET

Who's commanding them, sir?

CAPTAIN

The nephew of the old king of Norway, Fortinbras.

HAMLET

Is he attacking the heartland of Poland or some frontier?

CAPTAIN
> Truly to speak, and with no addition,
> We go to gain a little patch of ground
> That hath in it no profit but the name.
> To pay five ducats, five, I would not farm it.
> 20 Nor will it yield to Norway or the Pole
> A ranker rate, should it be sold in fee.

HAMLET
> Why, then the Polack never will defend it.

CAPTAIN
> Yes, it is already garrisoned.

HAMLET
> Two thousand souls and twenty thousand ducats
> 25 Will not debate the question of this straw.
> This is th' impostume of much wealth and peace,
> That inward breaks and shows no cause without
> Why the man dies.—I humbly thank you, sir.

CAPTAIN
> God be wi' you, sir.

Exit **CAPTAIN**

ROSENCRANTZ
> Will 't please you go, my lord?

HAMLET
> 30 I'll be with you straight. Go a little before.

Exeunt all except **HAMLET**

> How all occasions do inform against me,
> And spur my dull revenge! What is a man
> If his chief good and market of his time
> Be but to sleep and feed? A beast, no more.
> 35 Sure, he that made us with such large discourse,
> Looking before and after, gave us not
> That capability and godlike reason
> To fust in us unused. Now, whether it be
> Bestial oblivion, or some craven scruple

CAPTAIN

To tell the truth, we're fighting to win a little patch of ground that's not worth anything. I myself wouldn't pay five ducats for it, if someone offered it to me to farm. And it won't provide any more profits than that to either the Norwegian or the Pole.

HAMLET

So then the Poles won't be willing to defend it.

CAPTAIN

Oh, yes they will. They've already stationed troops there.

HAMLET

(*to himself*) Even two thousand men and twenty-thousand ducats are just the beginning of what it will cost to settle this pointless matter. This is what happens when countries have too much money and peace. This quarrel is like an abcess that grows inside someone until it bursts and kills them, and no one knows why. (*to the* CAPTAIN) Thank you very much for the information, sir.

CAPTAIN

Good-bye, sir.

The CAPTAIN *exits.*

ROSENCRANTZ

Will you please come now, my lord?

HAMLET

I'll be there in a minute. Start without me.

Everyone except HAMLET *exits.*

My God! Everything I see shows me how wrong I am and tells me to hurry up and get on with my revenge. What is a human being if he just eats and sleeps? Nothing more than a beast. God didn't create us with such a huge power of thought and a divine capacity for reason in order for us not to use them. Now, whether it's animal-like mindlessness, or the cowardly hesita-

40 Of thinking too precisely on th' event—
    A thought which, quartered, hath but one part wisdom
    And ever three parts coward—I do not know
    Why yet I live to say "This thing's to do,"
    Sith I have cause and will and strength and means
45 To do 't. Examples gross as earth exhort me.
    Witness this army of such mass and charge
    Led by a delicate and tender prince,
    Whose spirit with divine ambition puffed
    Makes mouths at the invisible event,
50 Exposing what is mortal and unsure
    To all that fortune, death, and danger dare,
    Even for an eggshell. Rightly to be great
    Is not to stir without great argument,
    But greatly to find quarrel in a straw
55 When honor's at the stake. How stand I then,
    That have a father killed, a mother stained,
    Excitements of my reason and my blood,
    And let all sleep—while, to my shame, I see
    The imminent death of twenty thousand men,
60 That for a fantasy and trick of fame
    Go to their graves like beds, fight for a plot
    Whereon the numbers cannot try the cause,
    Which is not tomb enough and continent
    To hide the slain? Oh, from this time forth,
65 My thoughts be bloody, or be nothing worth!

Exit

tion that comes from thinking too much (thinking thoughts that are one part wisdom, three parts cowardice), I don't know why I'm still alive to say "I have to do this deed" rather than having done it already. I have the motivation, the willpower, the ability, and the means to do it. It's as plain as the ground beneath my feet that I must do it. Look at this massive army led by a delicate and tender prince who's so puffed up with divine ambition that he puts his fragile life at risk, exposing it to danger and death, for a reason as thin as an eggshell. To be truly great doesn't mean you'd only fight for a good reason. It means you'd fight over nothing if your honor was at stake. So where does that leave me, whose father has been murdered and mother defiled, ignoring these mental and emotional provocations and letting well enough alone? Meanwhile, to my shame, I watch twenty thousand men go marching to their deaths for an illusion and a little bit of fame, fighting for a tiny piece of land not even big enough to bury them all. From now on, if my thoughts aren't violent I'll consider them worthless.

He exits.

ACT 4, SCENE 5

Enter HORATIO, GERTRUDE, *and a* GENTLEMAN

GERTRUDE
I will not speak with her.

GENTLEMAN
                                        She is importunate,
Indeed distract. Her mood will needs be pitied.

GERTRUDE
What would she have?

GENTLEMAN
She speaks much of her father, says she hears
5   There's tricks i' th' world, and hems, and beats her heart,
Spurns enviously at straws, speaks things in doubt
That carry but half sense. Her speech is nothing,
Yet the unshaped use of it doth move
The hearers to collection. They aim at it,
10   And botch the words up fit to their own thoughts,
Which, as her winks and nods and gestures yield them,
Indeed would make one think there might be thought,
Though nothing sure, yet much unhappily.

HORATIO
'Twere good she were spoken with, for she may strew
15   Dangerous conjectures in ill-breeding minds.

GERTRUDE
Let her come in.

Exit GENTLEMAN

(aside)   To my sick soul (as sin's true nature is)
Each toy seems prologue to some great amiss.
So full of artless jealousy is guilt,
It spills itself in fearing to be spilt.

Enter OPHELIA, *distracted*

ACT 4, SCENE 5

HORATIO, GERTRUDE, *and a* GENTLEMAN *enter.*

GERTRUDE

I won't speak to her.

GENTLEMAN

She's insistent. In fact, she's crazed. You can't help feeling sorry for her.

GERTRUDE

What does she want?

GENTLEMAN

She talks about her father a lot, and says she hears there are conspiracies around the world, and coughs, and beats her breast, and gets angry over tiny matters, and talks nonsense. Her words don't mean anything, but her babbling causes her listeners to draw conclusions. They hear what they want to hear. Her winks and nods and gestures do suggest that she means to convey a message, and not a happy one.

HORATIO

It's a good idea to speak to her, since she might lead those with evil intentions to dangerous conclusions.

GERTRUDE

Show her in.

The GENTLEMAN *exits.*
(to herself) To my sick soul (since sin is always a sickness), every detail looks like an omen of disaster to come. Guilt makes you so full of stupid suspicions that you give yourself away because you're trying so hard not to.

OPHELIA *enters, insane.*

OPHELIA

20   Where is the beauteous majesty of Denmark?

GERTRUDE
        How now, Ophelia?

OPHELIA
        (sings)
                How should I your true love know
                        From another one?
                By his cockle hat and staff,
25   *And his sandal shoon.*

GERTRUDE
        Alas, sweet lady, what imports this song?

OPHELIA
        Say you? Nay, pray you, mark.
        (sings)
                He is dead and gone, lady,
                        He is dead and gone,
30   *At his head a grass-green turf,*
                        At his heels a stone.
        Oh, ho!

GERTRUDE
        Nay, but, Ophelia—

OPHELIA
        Pray you, mark.
        (sings)
35   *White his shroud as the mountain snow—*

        Enter CLAUDIUS

GERTRUDE
        Alas, look here, my lord.

OPHELIA
        (sings)
                Larded all with sweet flowers,
                Which bewept to the ground did not go
                        With true-love showers.

OPHELIA

Where is the beautiful queen of Denmark?

GERTRUDE

What are you doing, Ophelia?

OPHELIA

(sings)
> *How can you tell the difference*
> > *Between your true lover and some other?*
> *Your true one wears a pilgrim's hat*
> > *And a pilgrim's sandals and staff.*

GERTRUDE

Oh heavens, what does that song mean, my dear?

OPHELIA

I'm sorry, did you say something? Please just listen.
(sings)
> *He is dead and gone, lady,*
> > *He is dead and gone.*
> *At his head is a patch of green grass,*
> > *And at his feet there is a tomb stone.*

Oh, ho!

GERTRUDE

No, Ophelia—

OPHELIA

Just listen, please.
(sings)
> *His death shroud was as white as snow—*

CLAUDIUS *enters.*

GERTRUDE

My lord, look at this poor girl.

OPHELIA

(sings)
> *Covered with sweet flowers*
> *Which did not fall to the ground*
> *In true-love showers.*

CLAUDIUS

40 How do you, pretty lady?

OPHELIA

Well, God'ield you! They say the owl was a baker's daughter. Lord, we know what we are, but know not what we may be. God be at your table.

CLAUDIUS

Conceit upon her father.

OPHELIA

45 Pray you, let's have no words of this, but when they ask you what it means, say you this:

(sings)

> Tomorrow is Saint Valentine's day,
> All in the morning betime,
> And I a maid at your window,
> 50 To be your Valentine.
> Then up he rose, and donned his clothes,
> And dupped the chamber door.
> Let in the maid that out a maid
> Never departed more.

CLAUDIUS

55 Pretty Ophelia—

OPHELIA

Indeed, without an oath I'll make an end on 't:

(sings)

> By Gis and by Saint Charity,
> Alack, and fie, for shame!
> Young men will do 't, if they come to 't.
> 60 By Cock, they are to blame.
> Quoth she, "Before you tumbled me,
> You promised me to wed."
> He answers,
> "So would I ha' done, by yonder sun,
> 65 An thou hadst not come to my bed."

CLAUDIUS

How are you doing, my pretty lady?

OPHELIA

I'm quite well, and may God give you what you deserve. They say the baker's daughter was turned into an owl for refusing Jesus' bread. My lord, we know what we are now, but not what we may become. May God be at your table.

CLAUDIUS

She's talking about her dead father.

OPHELIA

Oh, let's not talk about that, but when they ask you what it means, just say:
(sings)
> Tomorrow is St. Valentine's Day
>> And early in the morning
> I'm a girl below your window
>> Waiting to be your Valentine.
> Then he got up and put on his clothes
>> And opened the door to his room.
> He let in the girl, and when she left
>> She wasn't a virgin anymore.

CLAUDIUS

Pretty Ophelia—

OPHELIA

Hang on, I'll end it soon, I promise:
(sings)
> By the name of Jesus and Saint Charity,
>> My goodness, what a shame it is,
> Young men will do it if they get a chance:
>> By God, they're very bad.
> She said, "Before you got me into bed,
>> You promised to marry me."
> He answers:
> "I would have married you, I swear,
>> If you hadn't gone to bed with me."

CLAUDIUS

How long hath she been thus?

OPHELIA

I hope all will be well. We must be patient, but I cannot choose but weep, to think they should lay him i' th' cold ground. My brother shall know of it, and so I thank you for your good counsel. Come, my coach! Good night, ladies. Good night, sweet ladies. Good night, good night.

Exit OPHELIA

CLAUDIUS

Follow her close. Give her good watch, I pray you.

Exit HORATIO

Oh, this is the poison of deep grief. It springs
All from her father's death, and now behold!
O Gertrude, Gertrude,
When sorrows come, they come not single spies
But in battalions. First, her father slain.
Next, your son gone, and he most violent author
Of his own just remove. The people muddied,
Thick, and unwholesome in their thoughts and whispers
For good Polonius' death, and we have done but greenly
In hugger-mugger to inter him. Poor Ophelia
Divided from herself and her fair judgment,
Without the which we are pictures, or mere beasts.
Last—and as much containing as all these—
Her brother is in secret come from France,
Feeds on his wonder, keeps himself in clouds,
And wants not buzzers to infect his ear
With pestilent speeches of his father's death,
Wherein necessity, of matter beggared,
Will nothing stick our person to arraign
In ear and ear. O my dear Gertrude, this,
Like to a murdering piece, in many places
Gives me superfluous death.

CLAUDIUS

How long has she been like this?

OPHELIA

I hope everything will turn out fine. We must be patient, but I can't help crying when I think of him being laid in the cold ground. My brother will hear about this. And so I thank you for your good advice. Come, driver! Good night, ladies, good night, sweet ladies, good night, good night.

OPHELIA exits.

CLAUDIUS

Follow her. Keep an eye on her, please.

HORATIO exits.

Oh, her grief has poisoned her mind. Her father died and now look at her! Oh, Gertrude, Gertrude, when bad things happen, they don't come one at a time, like enemy spies, but all at once like an army. First her father was killed, then your son was taken away— because of his own violent actions. The people are confused and spreading nasty rumors about Polonius's death, and I was a fool to bury him in a hurry, without a proper state funeral. Poor Ophelia has been robbed of her sanity, without which we're just pictures, or animals. Last but not least, her brother has secretly returned from France and is surrounded by gossip-mongers, who fill his ears with wicked stories about his father's death. Deprived of proper evidence, he'll naturally attribute the murder to me. Oh, dear Gertrude, I feel as though I'm being murdered many times over.

A noise within

GERTRUDE

Alack, what noise is this?

CLAUDIUS

95 Where are my Switzers? Let them guard the door.

Enter a **MESSENGER**

What is the matter?

MESSENGER

Save yourself, my lord.
The ocean, overpeering of his list,
Eats not the flats with more impiteous haste
Than young Laertes, in a riotous head,
100 O'erbears your officers. The rabble call him "lord"
And—as the world were now but to begin,
Antiquity forgot, custom not known,
The ratifiers and props of every word—
They cry, "Choose we! Laertes shall be king!"
105 Caps, hands, and tongues applaud it to the clouds:
"Laertes shall be king, Laertes king!"

GERTRUDE

How cheerfully on the false trail they cry.
O, this is counter, you false Danish dogs!

Noise within

CLAUDIUS

The doors are broke.

Enter **LAERTES** *with others*

A noise offstage.

GERTRUDE

Oh, no—what's that noise?

CLAUDIUS

Listen! Where are my bodyguards? Let them guard the door.

A MESSENGER *enters.*

What is it?

MESSENGER

You must save yourself, my lord. The young Laertes, like the ocean when it floods the shore and devours the lowlands, is leading a rebellion against your government. The crowd calls him "lord" and shouts, "We want Laertes to be king!" It's as if they were starting the world from scratch right now, throwing out the traditions and ancient customs that are the support of every word we utter. They throw their caps in the air and yell, "Laertes will be king! Laertes king!"

GERTRUDE

They sound so cheerful as they hunt down the wrong prey! Oh, you're on the wrong track, you disloyal Danish dogs!

A noise offstage.

CLAUDIUS

The doors have been smashed open.

LAERTES *enters with others.*

LAERTES

110 Where is this king?—Sirs, stand you all without.

ALL

No, let's come in!

LAERTES

I pray you, give me leave.

ALL

We will, we will.

Exeunt **LAERTES' FOLLOWERS**

LAERTES

I thank you. Keep the door.—O thou vile king,

115 Give me my father!

GERTRUDE

Calmly, good Laertes.

LAERTES

That drop of blood that's calm proclaims me bastard,
Cries "Cuckold!" to my father, brands the "harlot"
Even here between the chaste unsmirchèd brow
Of my true mother.

CLAUDIUS

What is the cause, Laertes,

120 That thy rebellion looks so giant-like?—
Let him go, Gertrude. Do not fear our person.
There's such divinity doth hedge a king
That treason can but peep to what it would,
Acts little of his will.—Tell me, Laertes,

125 Why thou art thus incensed.—Let him go, Gertrude.—
Speak, man.

LAERTES

Where is my father?

CLAUDIUS

Dead.

GERTRUDE

But not by him.

CLAUDIUS

Let him demand his fill.

LAERTES

Where's this so-called king? Men, wait outside.

ALL

No, let us in!

LAERTES

Please wait.

ALL

All right, we will, we will.

LAERTES' FOLLOWERS *exit.*

LAERTES

Thank you. Guard the door. (*to* CLAUDIUS) Oh, you vile king, give me my father!

GERTRUDE

Calm down, good Laertes.

LAERTES

Laertes suggests that since he hasn't yet punished his father's murderer, he must not be his real son.

I've got exactly one calm drop of blood in my body, and it proclaims that I'm a bastard, says my father was betrayed, and stamps the label "whore" on the pure forehead of my devoted mother.

CLAUDIUS

Laertes, what makes you so rebellious? Let him go, Gertrude. Don't worry about my getting hurt. God protects the king, so traitors can't hurt him.—Tell me, Laertes, why you're so angry.—Gertrude, let him go.—Tell me, man.

LAERTES

Where's my father?

CLAUDIUS

He's dead.

GERTRUDE

But the king didn't kill him.

CLAUDIUS

Let him ask what he wants to ask.

LAERTES
How came he dead? I'll not be juggled with.
To hell, allegiance! Vows, to the blackest devil!
130   Conscience and grace, to the profoundest pit!
I dare damnation. To this point I stand
That both the worlds I give to negligence.
Let come what comes, only I'll be revenged
Most thoroughly for my father.

CLAUDIUS
135   Who shall stay you?

LAERTES
My will, not all the world.
And for my means, I'll husband them so well,
They shall go far with little.

CLAUDIUS
                                        Good Laertes,
If you desire to know the certainty
140   Of your dear father's death, is 't writ in your revenge,
That, swoopstake, you will draw both friend and foe,
Winner and loser?

LAERTES
None but his enemies.

CLAUDIUS
Will you know them then?

LAERTES
145   To his good friends thus wide I'll ope my arms
And, like the kind life-rendering pelican,
Repast them with my blood.

CLAUDIUS
                                        Why, now you speak
Like a good child and a true gentleman.
That I am guiltless of your father's death
150   And am most sensible in grief for it,
It shall as level to your judgment pierce
As day does to your eye.

LAERTES

How did he end up dead? Don't mess with me. To hell with my vows of allegiance to you! Vows can go to hell! Conscience, too! I don't care if I'm damned. I don't care what happens to me in this world or the next. Whatever happens, happens, but I'll get revenge for my father's murder.

CLAUDIUS

Who's stopping you?

LAERTES

Only my free will—nothing else. What little means I have, I'll use against you.

CLAUDIUS

My dear Laertes, in your eagerness to know the truth about your father's death, are you determined to hurt your father's friends and enemies alike?

LAERTES

No, only his enemies.

CLAUDIUS

Do you want to know who they are, then?

LAERTES

Pelicans were believed to feed their young with their own blood.

I'll open my arms wide to his true friends, and like a mother pelican with her brood, I'll even give my life for them.

CLAUDIUS

Why, now you're talking like a good son and a true gentleman. I'll prove to you as clearly as daylight that I'm innocent of your father's death, and am struck with grief over it.

Noise within: "Let her come in!"

LAERTES
How now? What noise is that?

Enter OPHELIA

155 O heat, dry up my brains! Tears seven times salt,
Burn out the sense and virtue of mine eye!
By heaven, thy madness shall be paid by weight,
Till our scale turn the beam. O rose of May,
Dear maid, kind sister, sweet Ophelia!
160 O heavens, is 't possible a young maid's wits
Should be as mortal as an old man's life?
Nature is fine in love, and where 'tis fine,
It sends some precious instance of itself
After the thing it loves.

OPHELIA
(sings)
165 *They bore him barefaced on the bier,*
Hey, non nonny, nonny, hey, nonny,
And in his grave rained many a tear.
Fare you well, my dove.

LAERTES
Hadst thou thy wits, and didst persuade revenge,
170 It could not move thus.

OPHELIA
You must sing *A-down a-down*—And you, *Call him a-down-a*—Oh, how the wheel becomes it! It is the false steward that stole his master's daughter.

LAERTES
This nothing's more than matter.

OPHELIA
175 There's rosemary, that's for remembrance. Pray you, love, remember. And there is pansies, that's for thoughts.

A voice offstage, "Let her in!"

LAERTES

What's that noise?

OPHELIA *enters.*

Oh, heat, dry up my brains! Salty tears, burn my eyes! By heaven, I'll get revenge for your madness! Oh, you springtime rose, dear maiden, kind sister, sweet Ophelia! Is it possible that a young woman's mind could fade away as easily as an old man's life? Human nature is refined and thoughtful—person graciously gives a valuable part of herself away to her beloved, as Ophelia has sent off her sanity to her dead father.

OPHELIA

(sings)
> They carried him uncovered in the coffin,
>> Hey non nonny, nonny, hey nonny.
> And tears poured down into his grave.

Good-bye, honey.

LAERTES

If you were sane and could urge me to take revenge, you couldn't be more persuasive than you are now.

OPHELIA

You're supposed to sing, "A down a-down," and you, "Call him a-down-a." Oh, how it turns around like a wheel! Like the worker who stole his boss's daughter.

LAERTES

This nonsense means more than rational speech.

OPHELIA

Look at my flowers. There's rosemary, that's for remembering. Please remember, love. And there are pansies, they're for thoughts.

LAERTES

A document in madness. Thoughts and remembrance fitted.

OPHELIA

There's fennel for you, and columbines.—There's rue for
180 you, and here's some for me. We may call it "herb of grace"
o' Sundays.—Oh, you must wear your rue with a
difference.—There's a daisy. I would give you some violets,
but they withered all when my father died. They say he
made a good end *(sings) For bonny sweet Robin is all my joy—*

LAERTES

185 Thought and affliction, passion, hell itself,
She turns to favor and to prettiness.

OPHELIA

(sings)
> *And will he not come again?*
> *And will he not come again?*
> *No, no, he is dead,*
190 > *Go to thy deathbed.*
> *He never will come again.*

> *His beard was as white as snow,*
> *All flaxen was his poll.*
> *He is gone, he is gone,*
195 > *And we cast away moan,*
> *God ha' mercy on his soul.—*
And of all Christian souls, I pray God. God be wi' ye.

Exit OPHELIA

LAERTES

Do you see this, O God?

LAERTES

A case study in madness, to connect memory and thought.

OPHELIA

(to GERTRUDE*)* Here are fennel and columbines for you—they symbolize adultery. *(to* CLAUDIUS*)* And here's rue for you—it symbolizes repentance. We can call it the merciful Sunday flower. You should wear it for a different reason. And here's a daisy, for unhappy love. I'd give you some violets, flowers of faithfulness, but they all dried up when my father died. They say he looked good when he died. *(sings) For good sweet Robin is all my joy.*

LAERTES

Sadness and torment, suffering, hell itself—she makes them almost pretty.

OPHELIA

(sings)
> *And won't he come again?*
> *And won't he come again?*
> > *No, no, he's dead.*
> > *Go to your deathbed.*
> *He'll never come again.*

> *His beard was white as snow,*
> *His hair was all white too.*
> > *He's gone, he's gone,*
> > *And we moan as we're cast away.*
> *God have mercy on his soul.*

And on the souls of all good Christians, I hope. Goodbye, God be with you.

OPHELIA exits.

LAERTES

Do you see this, oh, God?

CLAUDIUS
　　　　Laertes, I must commune with your grief,
200　　　Or you deny me right. Go but apart,
　　　　Make choice of whom your wisest friends you will.
　　　　And they shall hear and judge 'twixt you and me.
　　　　If by direct or by collateral hand
　　　　They find us touched, we will our kingdom give,
205　　　Our crown, our life, and all that we can ours,
　　　　To you in satisfaction. But if not,
　　　　Be you content to lend your patience to us,
　　　　And we shall jointly labor with your soul
　　　　To give it due content.

LAERTES
　　　　　　　　　　　　Let this be so.
210　　　His means of death, his obscure funeral—
　　　　No trophy, sword, nor hatchment o'er his bones,
　　　　No noble rite nor formal ostentation—
　　　　Cry to be heard as 'twere from heaven to earth,
　　　　That I must call 't in question.

CLAUDIUS
　　　　　　　　　　　　　So you shall.
215　　　And where the offense is, let the great ax fall.
　　　　I pray you, go with me.

　　　　　　　　　　　　　　　　　　　Exeunt

CLAUDIUS

Laertes, I have a right to share your grief. Go choose your wisest friends, and have them listen to both of us and decide which of us is right. If directly or indirectly they find me implicated in your father's murder, I'll give up my kingdom, my crown, my life, and everything I call my own to you as restitution. But if they find me innocent, then be patient and I'll work to satisfy to the fullest extent your deepest need for revenge.

LAERTES

All right, then. The way he died, his secret funeral, no funeral rites or military display, no noble rites or formal ceremony—shout out from heaven and earth that I must call the way he died into question.

CLAUDIUS

And you're right to do so. May the guilty party be punished by death. Please, come with me.

They exit.

ACT 4, SCENE 6

Enter HORATIO *and a* SERVANT

HORATIO
What are they that would speak with me?

SERVANT
Seafaring men, sir. They say they have letters for you.

HORATIO
Let them come in.

Exit SERVANT

I do not know from what part of the world
5   I should be greeted, if not from Lord Hamlet.

Enter SAILORS

SAILOR
God bless you, sir.

HORATIO
Let him bless thee too.

SAILOR
He shall, sir, an 't please Him. There's a letter for you, sir—
it comes from the ambassador that was bound for
10   England—if your name be Horatio, as I am let to know it is.
(gives HORATIO *letter)*

HORATIO
(reads)
        "Horatio,
        When thou shalt have overlooked this, give these fel-
        lows some means to the king. They have letters for
        him. Ere we were two days old at sea, a pirate of very
15   warlike appointment gave us chase. Finding ourselves
        too slow of sail, we put on a compelled valor, and in the
        grapple I boarded them. On the instant, they got clear
        of our ship, so I alone became their prisoner. They
        have dealt with me like thieves of mercy, but they
20   knew what they did; I am to do a good turn for them.
        Let the king have the letters I have sent, and repair

ACT 4, SCENE 6

HORATIO *and a* SERVANT *enter.*

HORATIO

Who are the people who want to speak with me?

SERVANT

Sailors, sir. They say they have letters for you.

HORATIO

Show them in.

SERVANT *exits.*

I don't know who else would send me a letter from abroad except Hamlet.

SAILORS *enter.*

SAILOR

Hello, sir. God bless you.

HORATIO

May He bless you, too.

SAILOR

He will, sir, if He wants to. There's a letter for you, sir. It's from the ambassador, Lord Hamlet, who was going to England—if your name's Horatio, as they told me it is. *(he hands* HORATIO *a letter)*

HORATIO

(reading the letter)
   "Horatio,
   When you've read this letter, find a way to let these guys see the king. They have letters for him. Before we were at sea for even two days, a pirate ship equipped for battle pursued us. We were too slow to escape, so we were forced to stand and fight. In the battle that followed I ended up on the pirate ship. Just then they left our ship behind, so I became the only prisoner on board. They've treated me quite mercifully for thieves, but they knew what they were doing. They want me to do a

thou to me with as much speed as thou wouldst fly
death. I have words to speak in thine ear will make
thee dumb, yet are they much too light for the bore of
the matter. These good fellows will bring thee where
25   I am. Rosencrantz and Guildenstern hold their course
for England. Of them I have much to tell thee. Farewell.

> He that thou knowest thine,
> Hamlet."

30

Come, I will give you way for these your letters,
And do 't the speedier, that you may direct me
To him from whom you brought them.

Exeunt

favor for them. Give the king the letters I've sent, and come to me as fast as you would run from death. I've got things to tell you that will make you speechless, and they aren't even half the story. These guys will take you to me. Rosencrantz and Guildenstern are on their way to England. I have a lot to tell you about them. Good-bye.

Your trusted friend,
Hamlet."

Come, men. I'll show you where to deliver these letters as quickly as possible, so that you can take me to the man who sent them.

They exit.

ACT 4, SCENE 7

Enter CLAUDIUS *and* LAERTES

CLAUDIUS

Now must your conscience my acquaintance seal,
And you must put me in your heart for friend,
Sith you have heard, and with a knowing ear,
That he which hath your noble father slain
5   Pursued my life.

LAERTES

                    It well appears. But tell me
Why you proceeded not against these feats,
So criminal and so capital in nature,
As by your safety, wisdom, all things else,
You mainly were stirred up.

CLAUDIUS

                              Oh, for two special reasons,
10   Which may to you perhaps seem much unsinewed,
But yet to me they are strong. The queen his mother
Lives almost by his looks, and for myself—
My virtue or my plague, be it either which—
She's so conjunctive to my life and soul,
15   That, as the star moves not but in his sphere,
I could not but by her. The other motive
Why to a public count I might not go,
Is the great love the general gender bear him,
Who, dipping all his faults in their affection,
20   Would, like the spring that turneth wood to stone,
Convert his gyves to graces—so that my arrows,
Too slightly timbered for so loud a wind,
Would have reverted to my bow again,
And not where I had aimed them.

ACT 4, SCENE 7

CLAUDIUS *and* LAERTES *enter.*

CLAUDIUS

Now you've got to acknowledge my innocence and believe I'm your friend, since you've heard and understood that the man who killed your father was trying to kill me.

LAERTES

It looks that way. But tell me why you didn't take immediate action against his criminal acts, when your own safety and everything else would seem to call for it.

CLAUDIUS

Oh, for two main reasons which may seem weak to you, but strong to me. The queen, his mother, is devoted to him. And (for better or worse, whichever it is) she is such a part of my life and soul that I can't live apart from her, any more than a planet can leave its orbit. The other reason why I couldn't prosecute and arrest Hamlet is that the public loves him. In their affection they overlook all his faults. Like magic, they convert them into virtues, so whatever I said against him would end up hurting me, not him.

LAERTES

25   And so have I a noble father lost,
      A sister driven into desperate terms,
      Whose worth, if praises may go back again,
      Stood challenger on mount of all the age
      For her perfections. But my revenge will come.

CLAUDIUS

30   Break not your sleeps for that. You must not think
      That we are made of stuff so flat and dull
      That we can let our beard be shook with danger
      And think it pastime. You shortly shall hear more.
      I loved your father, and we love ourself.

35   And that, I hope, will teach you to imagine—

Enter a **MESSENGER**

      How now, what news?

MESSENGER

                Letters, my lord, from Hamlet.
      This to your majesty, this to the queen. *(gives* **CLAUDIUS**
         letters)

CLAUDIUS

      From Hamlet? Who brought them?

MESSENGER

      Sailors, my lord, they say. I saw them not.

40   They were given me by Claudio. He received them
      Of him that brought them.

CLAUDIUS

      Laertes, you shall hear them.—Leave us.

                           Exit **MESSENGER**

      (reads)

         "High and mighty,
         You shall know I am set naked on your kingdom.

45   Tomorrow shall I beg leave to see your kingly eyes,
         when I shall, first asking your pardon thereunto,

LAERTES

And so I've lost my noble father, had my sister driven insane—my sister who once was (if I can praise her for what she once was, not what she is now) the most perfect girl who ever lived. But I'll get my revenge.

CLAUDIUS

Don't you worry about that. You must not think that I'm so lazy and dull that I can be severely threatened and think it's just a game. You'll hear more about my plans soon enough. I loved your father, and I love myself, which should be enough to—

A MESSENGER enters with letters.

What is it? What's the news?

MESSENGER

Letters, my lord, from Hamlet. This one's for Your Highness, this one for the queen. *(gives CLAUDIUS letters)*

CLAUDIUS

From Hamlet? Who delivered them?

MESSENGER

Sailors, my lord, or so they say. I didn't see them. Claudio gave them to me, and he got them from the one who delivered them.

CLAUDIUS

Laertes, I want you to hear what they say. Leave us alone now.

The MESSENGER exits.

(reads)

"High and Mighty one,
You know I've been set down naked, you might say, in your kingdom. Tomorrow I'll beg permission to look into your kingly eyes, at which point

> recount the occasion of my sudden and more strange
> return.
>
> > > Hamlet."

50 What should this mean? Are all the rest come back?
Or is it some abuse, and no such thing?

LAERTES
Know you the hand?

CLAUDIUS
'Tis Hamlet's character. "Naked"?
And in a postscript here, he says "alone."
Can you advise me?

LAERTES
55 I'm lost in it, my lord. But let him come.
It warms the very sickness in my heart
That I shall live and tell him to his teeth,
"Thus diddest thou."

CLAUDIUS
If it be so, Laertes—
As how should it be so? How otherwise?—
60 Will you be ruled by me?

LAERTES
Ay, my lord—
So you will not o'errule me to a peace.

CLAUDIUS
To thine own peace. If he be now returned,
As checking at his voyage, and that he means
No more to undertake it, I will work him
65 To an exploit, now ripe in my devise,
Under the which he shall not choose but fall.
And for his death no wind of blame shall breathe,
But even his mother shall uncharge the practice
And call it accident.

LAERTES
My lord, I will be ruled
70 The rather if you could devise it so
That I might be the organ.

I'll tell you the story (after first apologizing) of how I came back to Denmark so strangely and suddenly.

Hamlet."

What does this mean? Has everyone else come back too? Or is it all a lie—and no one has yet returned?

LAERTES

Do you recognize the handwriting?

CLAUDIUS

It's Hamlet's writing. "Naked," he says. And in a P.S. he adds, "alone." Can you help me out with this?

LAERTES

I have no clue, my lord. But let him come. It warms my weary heart to think I'll get the chance to look him in the eye and say, "You did this."

CLAUDIUS

If that's how you feel, Laertes—and why shouldn't you? Will you let me guide and direct you?

LAERTES

Yes, my lord, as long as you won't lead me toward peace.

CLAUDIUS

No, just toward your own peace of mind. If he's come back to Denmark without plans to continue on his trip, then I'll trick him into an undertaking, which I'm working out now, that's sure to kill him. When he dies, no one will be blamed, even his mother will call it an accident.

LAERTES

My lord, I'll let you make the decision. I only ask to be in on your plans, the agent of his death.

CLAUDIUS
                                        It falls right.
You have been talked of since your travel much—
And that in Hamlet's hearing—for a quality
Wherein, they say, you shine. Your sum of parts
75   Did not together pluck such envy from him
As did that one, and that, in my regard,
Of the unworthiest siege.

LAERTES
                                    What part is that, my lord?

CLAUDIUS
A very ribbon in the cap of youth,
Yet needful too, for youth no less becomes
80   The light and careless livery that it wears
Than settled age his sables and his weeds,
Importing health and graveness. Two months since,
Here was a gentleman of Normandy.
I've seen myself, and served against, the French,
85   And they can well on horseback. But this gallant
Had witchcraft in 't. He grew unto his seat,
And to such wondrous doing brought his horse
As he had been encorpsed and demi-natured
With the brave beast. So far he topped my thought,
90   That I, in forgery of shapes and tricks,
Come short of what he did.

LAERTES
                                        A Norman was 't?

CLAUDIUS
A Norman.

LAERTES
Upon my life, Lamond!

CLAUDIUS
                                        The very same.

LAERTES
I know him well. He is the brooch indeed
95   And gem of all the nation.

CLAUDIUS

That'll be fine. Since you left, people have been talking about—and within earshot of Hamlet—a certain quality of yours in which, they say, you shine. All your talents and gifts didn't arouse as much envy from him as this one quality did, though to me it's far from your best attribute.

LAERTES

What quality is that, my lord?

CLAUDIUS

A trivial little ribbon on the cap of youth—yet an important one, too, since casual clothes suit young people as much as serious business suits and overcoats suit the middle-aged. Two months ago I met a gentleman from Normandy. I've fought against the French and have seen how well they ride, but this man was a magician on horseback. It was as if he were part of the horse, so skillful that even having seen him, I can hardly conceive of the tricks he did.

LAERTES

Hmm, he was from Normandy, you say?

CLAUDIUS

Yes, from Normandy.

LAERTES

I bet it was Lamond.

CLAUDIUS

Yes, that's the one.

LAERTES

I know him well. He's his homeland's jewel.

CLAUDIUS

He made confession of you,
And gave you such a masterly report
For art and exercise in your defense,
And for your rapier most especially,
That he cried out 'twould be a sight indeed
100 If one could match you. The 'scrimers of their nation,
He swore, had had neither motion, guard, nor eye,
If you opposed them. Sir, this report of his
Did Hamlet so envenom with his envy
That he could nothing do but wish and beg
105 Your sudden coming o'er, to play with him.
Now, out of this—

LAERTES

What out of this, my lord?

CLAUDIUS

Laertes, was your father dear to you?
Or are you like the painting of a sorrow,
A face without a heart?

LAERTES

Why ask you this?

CLAUDIUS

110 Not that I think you did not love your father
But that I know love is begun by time,
And that I see, in passages of proof,
Time qualifies the spark and fire of it.
There lives within the very flame of love
115 A kind of wick or snuff that will abate it.
And nothing is at a like goodness still.
For goodness, growing to a pleurisy,
Dies in his own too-much. That we would do,
We should do when we would, for this "would" changes
120 And hath abatements and delays as many
As there are tongues, are hands, are accidents.
And then this "should" is like a spendthrift sigh
That hurts by easing.—But to the quick of th' ulcer:

CLAUDIUS

He mentioned you to me, giving you such high marks in fencing that he exclaimed it would be a miracle if someone could match you. French fencers wouldn't be good enough for you, he said, since they don't have the right moves or skills. Hamlet was so jealous when he heard Lamond's report that he talked about nothing else but having you come over and play against him. Now, the point is . . .

LAERTES

What's the point, my lord?

CLAUDIUS

Laertes, did you love your father? Or is your grief just an illusion—a mere painting of sorrow?

LAERTES

How could you ask?

CLAUDIUS

Not that I suspect you didn't love your father, but I've seen it happen that, as the days go by, time dampens the flame of love. The fire of love always burns itself out, and nothing stays the way it began. Even a good thing can grow too big and die from its own excess. We should do what we intend to do right when we intend it, since our intentions are subject to as many weakenings and delays as there are words in the dictionary and accidents in life. And then all our "woulds" and "shoulds" are nothing but hot air. But back to my point:

Hamlet comes back. What would you undertake
125 To show yourself in deed your father's son
More than in words?

LAERTES

To cut his throat i' th' church.

CLAUDIUS

No place, indeed, should murder sanctuarize.
Revenge should have no bounds. But, good Laertes,
Will you do this, keep close within your chamber.
130 Hamlet returned shall know you are come home.
We'll put on those shall praise your excellence
And set a double varnish on the fame
The Frenchman gave you, bring you in fine together
And wager on your heads. He, being remiss,
135 Most generous and free from all contriving,
Will not peruse the foils; so that, with ease,
Or with a little shuffling, you may choose
A sword unbated, and in a pass of practice
Requite him for your father.

LAERTES

I will do 't.
140 And for that purpose I'll anoint my sword.
I bought an unction of a mountebank,
So mortal that, but dip a knife in it,
Where it draws blood no cataplasm so rare,
Collected from all simples that have virtue
145 Under the moon, can save the thing from death
That is but scratched withal. I'll touch my point
With this contagion, that if I gall him slightly
It may be death.

CLAUDIUS

Let's further think of this,
Weigh what convenience both of time and means
150 May fit us to our shape. If this should fail,
And that our drift look through our bad performance,
'Twere better not assayed. Therefore this project

Hamlet's coming back. What proof will you offer—in action, not just words—that you're your father's son?

LAERTES

I'll cut Hamlet's throat in church.

CLAUDIUS

It's true, no place—not even a church—should offer refuge to that murderer. Revenge should have no limits. But Laertes, will you do this: stay in your room? When Hamlet comes home he'll learn you're here. I'll have people praise your excellence and put a double coat on the fame the Frenchman gave you. In short, we'll get you together and place bets on you. Hamlet's so careless, high-minded, and unsuspecting that he won't examine the swords beforehand, so you can easily choose one with a sharpened point and in one thrust avenge the death of your father.

LAERTES

I'll do it, and I'll put a little dab of something on my sword as well. From a quack doctor I bought some oil so poisonous that if you dip a knife in it, no medicine in the world can save the person who's scratched by it. If I even graze his skin slightly, he's likely to die.

CLAUDIUS

Let's think about this, and consider what time and what method will be most appropriate. If our plan were to fail, and people found out about it, it would be better never to have tried it.

155 Should have a back or second that might hold
If this should blast in proof.—Soft, let me see.—
We'll make a solemn wager on your cunnings.—
I ha 't! When in your motion you are hot and dry,
As make your bouts more violent to that end,
And that he calls for drink, I'll have prepared him
A chalice for the nonce, whereon but sipping,
160 If he by chance escape your venomed stuck,
Our purpose may hold there.—But stay, what noise?

Enter GERTRUDE

GERTRUDE
One woe doth tread upon another's heel,
So fast they follow.—Your sister's drowned, Laertes.

LAERTES
Drowned? Oh, where?

GERTRUDE
165 There is a willow grows aslant a brook
That shows his hoar leaves in the glassy stream.
There with fantastic garlands did she come
Of crowflowers, nettles, daisies, and long purples,
That liberal shepherds give a grosser name,
170 But our cold maids do "dead men's fingers" call them.
There, on the pendant boughs her coronet weeds
Clambering to hang, an envious sliver broke,
When down her weedy trophies and herself
Fell in the weeping brook. Her clothes spread wide,
175 And mermaid-like a while they bore her up,
Which time she chanted snatches of old lauds
As one incapable of her own distress,
Or like a creature native and indued
Unto that element. But long it could not be
180 Till that her garments, heavy with their drink,
Pulled the poor wretch from her melodious lay
To muddy death.

We should have a backup ready in case the first plan
doesn't work. Let me think. We'll place bets on you
and Hamlet—that's it! When the two of you have gotten all sweaty and hot—keep him jumping around a
lot for that purpose—Hamlet will ask for something
to drink. I'll have a cup ready for him. If by chance he
escapes your poisoned sword tip, the drink will kill
him. But wait, what's that sound?

GERTRUDE *enters.*

GERTRUDE

The bad news just keeps on coming, one disaster after
another. Your sister's drowned, Laertes.

LAERTES

Drowned? Oh, where?

GERTRUDE

There's a willow that leans over the brook, dangling
its white leaves over the glassy water. Ophelia made
wild wreaths out of those leaves, braiding in crowflowers, thistles, daisies, and the orchises that vulgar
shepherds have an obscene name for, but which pure-
minded girls call "dead men's fingers." Climbing into
the tree to hang the wreath of weeds on the hanging
branches, she and her flowers fell into the gurgling
brook. Her clothes spread out wide in the water, and
buoyed her up for a while as she sang bits of old
hymns, acting like someone who doesn't realize the
danger she's in, or like someone completely accus-
tomed to danger. But it was only a matter of time
before her clothes, heavy with the water they
absorbed, pulled the poor thing out of her song, down
into the mud at the bottom of the brook.

LAERTES
Alas, then she is drowned.

GERTRUDE
Drowned, drowned.

LAERTES
185 Too much of water hast thou, poor Ophelia,
And therefore I forbid my tears. But yet
It is our trick. Nature her custom holds,
Let shame say what it will. When these are gone,
The woman will be out.—Adieu, my lord.
190 I have a speech of fire that fain would blaze,
But that this folly doubts it.

Exit **LAERTES**

CLAUDIUS
Let's follow, Gertrude.
How much I had to do to calm his rage!
Now fear I this will give it start again.
Therefore let's follow.

Exeunt

LAERTES

So she is drowned.

GERTRUDE

Drowned, drowned.

LAERTES

You've had too much water already, poor Ophelia, so I won't shed watery tears for you. But crying is what humans do. We do what's in our nature, even if we're ashamed of it. After I stop crying I'll be through acting like a woman. Good-bye, my lord. I have some fiery words I could speak now, but my foolish tears are drowning them out.

LAERTES exits.

CLAUDIUS

Let's follow him, Gertrude. I worked so hard to calm him down, and now I'm worried he's getting all excited again. Let's follow him.

They exit.

ACT FIVE
SCENE 1

Enter a GRAVEDIGGER *and the* OTHER *gravedigger*

GRAVEDIGGER
Is she to be buried in Christian burial when she willfully seeks her own salvation?

OTHER
I tell thee she is. Therefore make her grave straight. The crowner hath sat on her and finds it Christian burial.

GRAVEDIGGER
How can that be, unless she drowned herself in her own defense?

OTHER
Why, 'tis found so.

GRAVEDIGGER
It must be *se offendendo*. It cannot be else. For here lies the point: if I drown myself wittingly, it argues an act. And an act hath three branches—it is to act, to do, to perform. Argal, she drowned herself wittingly.

OTHER
Nay, but hear you, Goodman Delver—

GRAVEDIGGER
Give me leave. Here lies the water. Good. Here stands the man. Good. If the man go to this water and drown himself, it is, will he nill he, he goes. Mark you that. But if the water come to him and drown him, he drowns not himself. Argal, he that is not guilty of his own death shortens not his own life.

OTHER
But is this law?

ACT FIVE
SCENE 1

*A **GRAVEDIGGER** and the **OTHER** gravedigger enter.*

GRAVEDIGGER

In Shakespeare's time, people who committed suicide were not given a Christian burial.

Are they really going to give her a Christian burial after she killed herself?

OTHER

I'm telling you, yes. So finish that grave right away. The coroner examined her case and says it should be a Christian funeral.

GRAVEDIGGER

But how, unless she drowned in self-defense?

OTHER

That's what they're saying she did.

GRAVEDIGGER

Sounds more like "self-offense," if you ask me. What I'm saying is, if she knew she was drowning herself, then that's an act. An act has three sides to it: to do, to act, and to perform. Therefore she must have known she was drowning herself.

OTHER

No, listen here, gravedigger sir—

GRAVEDIGGER

Let me finish. Here's the water, right? And here's a man, okay? If the man goes into the water and drowns himself, he's the one doing it, like it or not. But if the water comes to him and drowns him, then he doesn't drown himself. Therefore, he who is innocent of his own death does not shorten his own life.

OTHER

Is that how the law sees it?

GRAVEDIGGER
20   Ay, marry, is 't. Crowner's quest law.

OTHER
Will you ha' the truth on 't? If this had not been a
gentlewoman, she should have been buried out o' Christian
burial.

GRAVEDIGGER
Why, there thou sayst. And the more pity that great folk
25   should have countenance in this world to drown or hang
themselves more than their even Christian. Come, my
spade. There is no ancient gentleman but gardeners,
ditchers, and grave-makers. They hold up Adam's
profession.

OTHER
30   Was he a gentleman?

GRAVEDIGGER
He was the first that ever bore arms.

OTHER
Why, he had none.

GRAVEDIGGER
What, art a heathen? How dost thou understand the
Scripture? The Scripture says Adam digged. Could he dig
35   without arms? I'll put another question to thee. If thou
answerest me not to the purpose, confess thyself—

OTHER
Go to.

GRAVEDIGGER
What is he that builds stronger than either the mason, the
shipwright, or the carpenter?

OTHER
40   The gallows-maker, for that frame outlives a thousand
tenants.

GRAVEDIGGER
I like thy wit well, in good faith. The gallows does well, but
how does it well? It does well to those that do ill. Now thou

GRAVEDIGGER

It sure is. The coroner's inquest law.

OTHER

Do you want to know the truth? If this woman hadn't been rich, she wouldn't have been given a Christian burial.

GRAVEDIGGER

Well there, now you've said it. It's a pity that the rich have more freedom to hang or drown themselves than the rest of us Christians. Come on, shovel. The most ancient aristocrats in the world are gardeners, ditch-diggers, and gravediggers. They keep up Adam's profession.

OTHER

Was he an aristocrat? With a coat of arms?

GRAVEDIGGER

He was the first person who ever had arms.

OTHER

He didn't have any.

GRAVEDIGGER

What, aren't you a Christian? The Bible says Adam dug in the ground. How could he dig without arms? I'll ask you another question. If you can't answer it—

OTHER

Go ahead!

GRAVEDIGGER

What do you call a person who builds stronger things than a stonemason, a shipbuilder, or a carpenter does?

OTHER

The one who builds the gallows to hang people on, since his structure outlives a thousand inhabitants.

GRAVEDIGGER

You're funny, and I like that. The gallows do a good job. But how? It does a good job for those who do bad.

45   dost ill to say the gallows is built stronger than the church.
            Argal, the gallows may do well to thee. To 't again, come.

OTHER
            "Who builds stronger than a mason, a shipwright, or a
            carpenter?"

GRAVEDIGGER
            Ay, tell me that, and unyoke.

OTHER
            Marry, now I can tell.

GRAVEDIGGER
50   To 't.

OTHER
            Mass, I cannot tell.

            Enter HAMLET *and* HORATIO *afar off*

GRAVEDIGGER
            Cudgel thy brains no more about it, for your dull ass will
            not mend his pace with beating. And when you are asked
            this question next, say "A grave-maker." The houses that
55   he makes last till doomsday. Go, get thee in. Fetch me a
            stoup of liquor.

                                            Exit OTHER

            (digs and sings)
                In youth when I did love, did love,
                    Methought it was very sweet
                To contract–o–the time, for–a–my behove,
60   *Oh, methought, there–a–was nothing–a–meet.*

HAMLET
            Has this fellow no feeling of his business? He sings at grave-
            making.

Now, it's wrong to say that the gallows are stronger than a church. Therefore, the gallows may do *you* some good. Come on, your turn.

OTHER

Let's see, "Who builds stronger things than a stonemason, a shipbuilder, or a carpenter?"

GRAVEDIGGER

That's the question, so answer it.

OTHER

Ah, I've got it!

GRAVEDIGGER

Go ahead.

OTHER

Damn, I forgot.

HAMLET *and* HORATIO *enter in the distance.*

GRAVEDIGGER

Don't beat your brains out over it. You can't make a slow donkey run by beating it. The next time someone asks you this riddle, say "a gravedigger." The houses he makes last till Judgment Day. Now go and get me some booze.

The OTHER GRAVEDIGGER *exits.*
(the GRAVEDIGGER *digs and sings)*
  In my youth I loved, I loved,
    And I though it was very sweet
  To set—ohh—the date for—ahh—my duty
    Oh, I thought it—ahh—was not right.

HAMLET

Doesn't this guy realize what he's doing? He's singing while digging a grave.

HORATIO
Custom hath made it in him a property of easiness.

HAMLET
'Tis e'en so. The hand of little employment hath the
65 daintier sense.

GRAVEDIGGER
(sings)
> *But age with his stealing steps*
> > *Hath clawed me in his clutch,*
> *And hath shipped me into the land*
> > *As if I had never been such.*
(throws up a skull)

HAMLET
70 That skull had a tongue in it and could sing once. How the
knave jowls it to the ground, as if it were Cain's jawbone,
that did the first murder! It might be the pate of a politician,
which this ass now o'erreaches, one that would circumvent
God, might it not?

HORATIO
75 It might, my lord.

HAMLET
Or of a courtier, which could say, "Good morrow, sweet
lord!" "How dost thou, good lord?" This might be my Lord
Such-a-one that praised my Lord Such-a-one's horse when
he meant to beg it, might it not?

HORATIO
80 Ay, my lord.

HAMLET
Why, e'en so. And now my Lady Worm's, chapless and
knocked about the mazard with a sexton's spade. Here's
fine revolution, an we had the trick to see 't. Did these bones
cost no more the breeding but to play at loggets with them?
85 Mine ache to think on 't.

HORATIO

He's gotten so used to graves that they don't bother him anymore.

HAMLET

Yes, exactly. Only people who don't have to work can afford to be sensitive.

GRAVEDIGGER

(sings)

> But old age has sneaked up on me
> And grabbed me in his claws,
> And has shipped me into the ground
> As if I'd never been like that.

(he throws up a skull)

HAMLET

That skull had a tongue in it once and could sing. That jackass is throwing it around as if it belonged to Cain, who did the first murder! It might be the skull of a politician once capable of talking his way around God, right? And now this idiot is pulling rank on him.

HORATIO

Indeed, my lord.

HAMLET

Or a courtier, who could say things like, "Good night, my sweet lord! How are you doing, good lord?" This might be the skull of Lord So-and-So, who praised Lord Such-and-Such's horse when he wanted to borrow it, right?

HORATIO

Yes, my lord.

HAMLET

Exactly. And now it's the property of Lady Worm, its lower jaw knocked off and thwacked on the noggin with a shovel. That's quite a reversal of fortune, isn't it, if we could only see it? Are these bones worth nothing more than bowling pins now? It makes my bones ache to think about it.

GRAVEDIGGER
(sings)
> *A pickax and a spade, a spade,*
> > *For and a shrouding sheet,*
> *Oh, a pit of clay for to be made*
> > *For such a guest is meet.*
(throws up another skull)

HAMLET
90 There's another. Why may not that be the skull of a lawyer? Where be his quiddities now, his quillities, his cases, his tenures, and his tricks? Why does he suffer this rude knave now to knock him about the sconce with a dirty shovel and will not tell him of his action of battery? Hum! This fellow
95 might be in 's time a great buyer of land, with his statutes, his recognizances, his fines, his double vouchers, his recoveries. Is this the fine of his fines and the recovery of his recoveries, to have his fine pate full of fine dirt? Will his vouchers vouch him no more of his purchases, and double
100 ones too, than the length and breadth of a pair of indentures? The very conveyances of his lands will hardly lie in this box, and must the inheritor himself have no more, ha?

HORATIO
Not a jot more, my lord.

HAMLET
105 Is not parchment made of sheepskins?

HORATIO
Ay, my lord, and of calfskins too.

HAMLET
They are sheep and calves which seek out assurance in that. I will speak to this fellow.—Whose grave's this, sirrah?

GRAVEDIGGER
Mine, sir.

GRAVEDIGGER

> *(sings)*
>> *A pickax and a shovel, a shovel,*
>>> *And a sheet for a funeral shroud,*
>> *Oh, a pit of dirt is what we need*
>>> *For a guest like this one here.*
> *(he throws up another skull)*

HAMLET

There's another. Could that be a lawyer's skull? Where's all his razzle-dazzle legal jargon now? Why does he allow this idiot to knock him on the head with a dirty shovel, instead of suing him for assault and battery? Maybe this guy was once a great landowner, with his deeds and contracts, his tax shelters and his annuities. Is it part of his deed of ownership to have his skull filled up with dirt? Does he only get to keep as much land as a set of contracts would cover if you spread them out on the ground? The deeds to his properties would barely fit in this coffin—and the coffin's all the property he gets to keep?

HORATIO

No more than that, my lord.

HAMLET

Isn't the parchment of a legal document made of sheepskin?

HORATIO

Yes, my lord, and calfskin too.

HAMLET

Anyone who puts his trust in such documents is a sheep or a calf. I'll talk to this guy.—Excuse me, sir, whose grave is this?

GRAVEDIGGER

It's mine, sir.

(sings)
110   *Oh, a pit of clay for to be made*
    For such a guest is meet.

HAMLET
I think it be thine, indeed, for thou liest in 't.

GRAVEDIGGER
You lie out on 't, sir, and therefore it is not yours. For my part, I do not lie in 't, and yet it is mine.

HAMLET
115   Thou dost lie in 't, to be in 't and say it is thine. 'Tis for the dead, not for the quick. Therefore thou liest.

GRAVEDIGGER
'Tis a quick lie, sir. 'Twill away gain from me to you.

HAMLET
What man dost thou dig it for?

GRAVEDIGGER
For no man, sir.

HAMLET
120   What woman, then?

GRAVEDIGGER
For none, neither.

HAMLET
Who is to be buried in 't?

GRAVEDIGGER
One that was a woman, sir, but, rest her soul, she's dead.

HAMLET
How absolute the knave is! We must speak by the card, or
125   equivocation will undo us. By the Lord, Horatio, these three years I have taken a note of it. The age is grown so picked that the toe of the peasant comes so near the heel of the courtier he galls his kibe.—How long hast thou been a grave-maker?

(sings)
> *Oh, a pit of dirt is what we need*
> *For a guest like this one here.*

HAMLET

I think it really must be yours, since you're the one lying in it.

GRAVEDIGGER

And you're lying outside of it, so it's not yours. As for me, I'm not lying to you in it—it's really mine.

HAMLET

But you *are* lying in it, being in it and saying it's yours. It's for the dead, not the living. So you're lying.

GRAVEDIGGER

That's a lively lie, sir—it jumps so fast from me to you.

HAMLET

What man are you digging it for?

GRAVEDIGGER

For no man, sir.

HAMLET

What woman, then?

GRAVEDIGGER

For no woman, either.

HAMLET

Who's to be buried in it?

GRAVEDIGGER

One who used to be a woman but—bless her soul—is dead now.

HAMLET

How literal this guy is! We have to speak precisely, or he'll get the better of us with his wordplay. Lord, Horatio, I've been noticing this for a few years now. The peasants have become so clever and witty that they're nipping at the heels of noblemen.—How long have you been a gravedigger?

GRAVEDIGGER
130 Of all the days i' the year, I came to 't that day that our last King Hamlet overcame Fortinbras.

HAMLET
How long is that since?

GRAVEDIGGER
Cannot you tell that? Every fool can tell that. It was the very day that young Hamlet was born, he that is mad and sent
135 into England.

HAMLET
Ay, marry, why was he sent into England?

GRAVEDIGGER
Why, because he was mad. He shall recover his wits there, or, if he do not, it's no great matter there.

HAMLET
Why?

GRAVEDIGGER
140 'Twill not be seen in him there. There the men are as mad as he.

HAMLET
How came he mad?

GRAVEDIGGER
Very strangely, they say.

HAMLET
How "strangely"?

GRAVEDIGGER
145 Faith, e'en with losing his wits.

HAMLET
Upon what ground?

GRAVEDIGGER
Why, here in Denmark. I have been sexton here, man and boy, thirty years.

HAMLET
How long will a man lie i' the earth ere he rot?

GRAVEDIGGER

Of all the days in the year, I started the day that the late King Hamlet defeated Fortinbras.

HAMLET

How long ago was that?

GRAVEDIGGER

You don't know that? Any fool could tell you, it was the day that young Hamlet was born—the one who went crazy and got sent off to England.

HAMLET

Why was he sent to England?

GRAVEDIGGER

Because he was crazy. He'll recover his sanity there. Or if he doesn't, it won't matter in England.

HAMLET

Why not?

GRAVEDIGGER

Because nobody will notice he's crazy. Everyone there is as crazy as he is.

HAMLET

How did he go crazy?

GRAVEDIGGER

In a strange way, they say.

HAMLET

What do you mean, "in a strange way"?

GRAVEDIGGER

By losing his mind.

HAMLET

On what grounds?

GRAVEDIGGER

Right here in Denmark. I've been the church warden here for thirty years, since childhood.

HAMLET

How long will a man lie in his grave before he starts to rot?

GRAVEDIGGER

150   Faith, if he be not rotten before he die—as we have many
        pocky corses nowadays that will scarce hold the laying in—
        he will last you some eight year or nine year. A tanner will
        last you nine year.

HAMLET

        Why he more than another?

GRAVEDIGGER

155   Why, sir, his hide is so tanned with his trade that he will
        keep out water a great while, and your water is a sore
        decayer of your whoreson dead body. *(indicates a skull)*
        Here's a skull now. This skull has lain in the earth three-
        and-twenty years.

HAMLET

160   Whose was it?

GRAVEDIGGER

        A whoreson mad fellow's it was. Whose do you think it was?

HAMLET

        Nay, I know not.

GRAVEDIGGER

        A pestilence on him for a mad rogue! He poured a flagon of
        Rhenish on my head once. This same skull, sir, was Yorick's
165   skull, the king's jester.

HAMLET

        This?

GRAVEDIGGER

        E'en that.

HAMLET

        Let me see. *(takes the skull)* Alas, poor Yorick! I knew him,
        Horatio, a fellow of infinite jest, of most excellent fancy.
170   He hath borne me on his back a thousand times, and now,
        how abhorred in my imagination it is! My gorge rises at it.
        Here hung those lips that I have kissed I know not how oft.
        —Where be your gibes now? Your gambols? Your songs?

GRAVEDIGGER

Well, if he's not rotten before he dies (and there are a lot of people now who are so rotten they start falling to pieces even before you put them in the coffin), he'll last eight or nine years. A leathermaker will last nine years.

HAMLET

Why does he last longer?

GRAVEDIGGER

Because his hide is so leathery from his trade that he keeps the water off him a long time, and water is what makes your goddamn body rot more than anything. Here's a skull that's been here twenty-three years.

HAMLET

Whose was it?

GRAVEDIGGER

A crazy bastard. Who do you think?

HAMLET

I really don't know.

GRAVEDIGGER

Damn that crazy madman! He poured a pitcher of white wine on my head once. This is the skull of Yorick, the king's jester.

HAMLET

This one?

GRAVEDIGGER

Yes, that one.

HAMLET

Let me see. *(he takes the skull)* Oh, poor Yorick! I used to know him, Horatio—a very funny guy, and with an excellent imagination. He carried me on his back a thousand times, and now—how terrible—this is him. It makes my stomach turn. I don't know how many times I kissed the lips that used to be right here. Where are your jokes now? Your pranks? Your songs?

Your flashes of merriment that were wont to set the table on
175 a roar? Not one now to mock your own grinning? Quite
chapfallen? Now get you to my lady's chamber and tell her,
let her paint an inch thick, to this favor she must come.
Make her laugh at that.—Prithee, Horatio, tell me one
thing.

HORATIO
180 What's that, my lord?

HAMLET
Dost thou think Alexander looked o' this fashion i' th'
earth?

HORATIO
E'en so.

HAMLET
And smelt so? Pah! *(puts down the skull)*

HORATIO
185 E'en so, my lord.

HAMLET
To what base uses we may return, Horatio. Why may not
imagination trace the noble dust of Alexander till he find it
stopping a bunghole?

HORATIO
'Twere to consider too curiously, to consider so.

HAMLET
190 No, faith, not a jot. But to follow him thither with modesty
enough, and likelihood to lead it, as thus: Alexander died,
Alexander was buried, Alexander returneth to dust, the
dust is earth, of earth we make loam—and why of that loam,
whereto he was converted, might they not stop a beer
195 barrel?
Imperious Caesar, dead and turned to clay,
Might stop a hole to keep the wind away.
Oh, that that earth, which kept the world in awe,
Should patch a wall t' expel the winter's flaw!
200 But soft, but soft a while.

Your flashes of wit that used to set the whole table laughing? You don't make anybody smile now. Are you sad about that? You need to go to my lady's room and tell her that no matter how much makeup she slathers on, she'll end up just like you some day. That'll make her laugh. Horatio, tell me something.

HORATIO

What's that, my lord?

HAMLET

Do you think Alexander the Great looked like this when he was buried?

HORATIO

Exactly like that.

HAMLET

And smelled like that, too? Whew! *(he puts down the skull)*

HORATIO

Just as bad, my lord.

HAMLET

How low we can fall, Horatio. Isn't it possible to imagine that the noble ashes of Alexander the Great could end up plugging a hole in a barrel?

HORATIO

If you thought that you'd be thinking too much.

HAMLET

No, not at all. Just follow the logic: Alexander died, Alexander was buried, Alexander returned to dust, the dust is dirt, and dirt makes mud we use to stop up holes. So why can't someone plug a beer barrel with the dirt that used to be Alexander? The great emperor Caesar, dead and turned to clay, might plug up a hole to keep the wind away. Oh, to think that the same body that once ruled the world could now patch up a wall! But quiet, be quiet a minute.

Enter King CLAUDIUS, *Queen* GERTRUDE, LAERTES, *and a coffin, with a* PRIEST *and other lords attendant.*

                            Here comes the king,
The queen, the courtiers—who is this they follow,
And with such maimèd rites? This doth betoken
The corse they follow did with desperate hand
Fordo its own life. 'Twas of some estate.
205   Couch we a while and mark.

                   HAMLET *and* HORATIO *withdraw*

LAERTES
                        What ceremony else?

HAMLET
    That is Laertes, a very noble youth, mark.

LAERTES
    What ceremony else?

PRIEST
    Her obsequies have been as far enlarged
    As we have warranty. Her death was doubtful,
210   And, but that great command o'ersways the order,
    She should in ground unsanctified have lodged
    Till the last trumpet. For charitable prayers
    Shards, flints and pebbles should be thrown on her.
    Yet here she is allowed her virgin crants,
215   Her maiden strewments, and the bringing home
    Of bell and burial.

LAERTES
    Must there no more be done?

PRIEST
    No more be done.
    We should profane the service of the dead
220   To sing a requiem and such rest to her
    As to peace-parted souls.

LAERTES
                  Lay her i' th' earth,
    And from her fair and unpolluted flesh

CLAUDIUS *enters with* GERTRUDE, LAERTES, *and a coffin, with a* PRIEST *and other lords attendant.*

Here comes the king, the queen, and the noblemen of court. Who are they following? And with such a plain and scrawny ceremony? It means the corpse they're following took its own life. Must have been from a wealthy family. Let's stay and watch a while.

HAMLET *and* HORATIO *step aside.*

LAERTES

What other rites are you going to give her?

HAMLET

That's Laertes, a very noble young man. Listen.

LAERTES

What other rites are you going to give her?

PRIEST

I've performed as many rites as I'm permitted. Her death was suspicious, and were it not for the fact that the king gave orders to bury her here, she'd have been buried outside the church graveyard. She deserves to have rocks and stones thrown on her body. But she has had prayers read for her and is dressed up like a pure virgin, with flowers tossed on her grave and the bell tolling for her.

LAERTES

Isn't there any other rite you can perform?

PRIEST

No, nothing. We would profane the other dead souls here if we sang the same requiem for her that we sang for them.

LAERTES

Lay her in the ground, and let violets bloom from her lovely and pure flesh!

             May violets spring! I tell thee, churlish priest,
             A ministering angel shall my sister be
225   When thou liest howling.

HAMLET
        (to HORATIO*)* What, the fair Ophelia?

GERTRUDE
        Sweets to the sweet. Farewell! *(scatters flowers)*
        I hoped thou shouldst have been my Hamlet's wife.
        I thought thy bride-bed to have decked, sweet maid,
230   And not have strewed thy grave.

LAERTES
                            Oh, treble woe
        Fall ten times treble on that cursèd head,
        Whose wicked deed thy most ingenious sense
        Deprived thee of! Hold off the earth awhile
        Till I have caught her once more in mine arms.
        (leaps into the grave)
235   Now pile your dust upon the quick and dead,
        Till of this flat a mountain you have made,
        T' o'ertop old Pelion or the skyish head
        Of blue Olympus.

HAMLET
        (comes forward)   What is he whose grief
        Bears such an emphasis, whose phrase of sorrow
240   Conjures the wandering stars, and makes them stand
        Like wonder-wounded hearers? This is I,
        Hamlet the Dane. *(leaps into the grave)*

LAERTES
        The devil take thy soul!

        HAMLET *and* LAERTES *grapple*

HAMLET
        Thou pray'st not well.
245   I prithee, take thy fingers from my throat,
        For though I am not splenitive and rash,

I'm telling you, you jerk priest, my sister will be an angel in heaven while you're howling in hell.

HAMLET

(to HORATIO*)* What, the beautiful Ophelia?

QUEEN

Sweet flowers for a sweet girl. Goodbye! *(she scatters flowers)* I once hoped you'd be my Hamlet's wife. I thought I'd be tossing flowers on your wedding bed, my sweet girl, not on your grave.

LAERTES

Oh, damn three times, damn ten times the evil man whose wicked deed deprived you of your ingenious mind. Hold off burying her until I've caught her in my arms once more.

(he jumps into the grave)

Now pile the dirt onto the living and the dead alike, till you've made a mountain higher than Mount Pelion or Mount Olympus.

In Greek myth, Mt. Olympus is home to the gods, and giants piled Mt. Ossa on top of Mt. Pelion to climb to heaven.

HAMLET

(coming forward) Who is the one whose grief is so loud and clear, whose words of sadness make the planets stand still in the heavens as if they've been hurt by what they've heard? It's me, Hamlet the Dane. *(he jumps into the grave)*

LAERTES

To hell with your soul!

HAMLET *and* LAERTES *wrestle with each other.*

HAMLET

That's no way to pray. *(they fight)* Please take your hands off my throat. I may not be rash and quick to

Yet have I something in me dangerous,
Which let thy wisdom fear. Hold off thy hand.

CLAUDIUS
Pluck them asunder.

GERTRUDE
Hamlet, Hamlet!

ALL
250 Gentlemen—

HORATIO
(to HAMLET*)* Good my lord, be quiet.

Attendants separate HAMLET *and* LAERTES

HAMLET
Why, I will fight with him upon this theme
Until my eyelids will no longer wag.

GERTRUDE
O my son, what theme?

HAMLET
255 I loved Ophelia. Forty thousand brothers
Could not with all their quantity of love
Make up my sum. What wilt thou do for her?

CLAUDIUS
O, he is mad, Laertes.

GERTRUDE
For love of God, forbear him.

HAMLET
260 'Swounds, show me what thou'lt do.
Woo't weep? Woo't fight? Woo't fast? Woo't tear thyself?
Woo't drink up eisel, eat a crocodile?
I'll do 't. Dost thou come here to whine,
To outface me with leaping in her grave?
265 Be buried quick with her?—and so will I.
And if thou prate of mountains let them throw
Millions of acres on us, till our ground,
Singeing his pate against the burning zone,

anger, but I have something dangerous in me which you should beware of. Take your hands off.

CLAUDIUS

Pull them apart.

GERTRUDE

Hamlet! Hamlet!

ALL

Gentlemen!

HORATIO

(to HAMLET*)* Please, my lord, calm down.

Attendants separate HAMLET *and* LAERTES.

HAMLET

I'll fight him over this issue till I don't have the strength to blink.

GERTRUDE

Oh, my son, what issue is that?

HAMLET

I loved Ophelia. Forty thousand brothers, if you added all their love together, couldn't match mine. What are you going to do for her?

CLAUDIUS

Oh, he's crazy, Laertes!

GERTRUDE

For the love of God, be patient with him.

HAMLET

Damn it, show me what you're going to do for her. Will you cry? Fight? Stop eating? Cut yourself? Drink vinegar? Eat a crocodile? I'll do all that. Did you come here to whine? To outdo me by jumping into her grave so theatrically? To be buried alive with her? So will I. And if you rattle on about mountains, then let them throw millions of acres over us. It will be so high a peak that it scrapes against heaven and

Make Ossa like a wart! Nay, an thou'lt mouth,
270 I'll rant as well as thou.

GERTRUDE
       This is mere madness.
And thus a while the fit will work on him.
Anon, as patient as the female dove
When that her golden couplets are disclosed,
His silence will sit drooping.

HAMLET
         Hear you, sir.
275 What is the reason that you use me thus?
I loved you ever. But it is no matter.
Let Hercules himself do what he may,
The cat will mew and dog will have his day.

           Exit HAMLET

CLAUDIUS
I pray thee, good Horatio, wait upon him.

           Exit HORATIO
280 *(to* LAERTES*)* Strengthen your patience in our last night's
   speech.
We'll put the matter to the present push.—
Good Gertrude, set some watch over your son.—
This grave shall have a living monument.
An hour of quiet shortly shall we see.
285 Till then in patience our proceeding be.

            Exeunt

makes Mount Ossa look like a wart. See? I can talk crazy as well as you.

GERTRUDE

This is pure insanity. He'll be like this for a little while. Then he'll be as calm and quiet as a dove waiting for her eggs to hatch.

HAMLET

Listen, sir, why do you treat me like this? I always loved you. But it doesn't matter. Even a hero like Hercules can't keep cats from acting like cats, and dogs like dogs.

HAMLET exits.

CLAUDIUS

Please, Horatio, go with him.

HORATIO exits.

(to LAERTES) Don't forget our talk last night, and try to be patient. We'll take care of this problem soon. —Gertrude, have the guards keep an eye on your son. A monument shall be built for Ophelia that will last forever, I promise. We'll have the quiet we need soon. In the meantime, let's proceed patiently.

They exit.

ACT 5, SCENE 2

Enter HAMLET *and* HORATIO

HAMLET
So much for this, sir. Now shall you see the other.
You do remember all the circumstance?

HORATIO
Remember it, my lord?

HAMLET
Sir, in my heart there was a kind of fighting
5   That would not let me sleep. Methought I lay
Worse than the mutines in the bilboes. Rashly—
And praised be rashness for it: let us know
Our indiscretion sometimes serves us well
When our deep plots do pall, and that should teach us
10   There's a divinity that shapes our ends,
Rough-hew them how we will—

HORATIO
That is most certain.

HAMLET
Up from my cabin,
My sea-gown scarfed about me, in the dark
15   Groped I to find out them, had my desire,
Fingered their packet, and in fine withdrew
To mine own room again, making so bold
(My fears forgetting manners) to unseal
Their grand commission, where I found, Horatio—
20   O royal knavery!—an exact command,
Larded with many several sorts of reasons
Importing Denmark's health, and England's too,
With—ho!—such bugs and goblins in my life
That, on the supervise (no leisure bated,
25   No, not to stay the grinding of the ax)
My head should be struck off.

ACT 5, SCENE 2

HAMLET *and* HORATIO *enter.*

HAMLET

That's enough about that. Now I'll tell you the other story about my journey. Do you remember the circumstances?

HORATIO

How could I forget, my lord!

HAMLET

There was a kind of war in my brain that wouldn't let me sleep. It was worse than being a captive in chains. Sometimes it's good to be rash—sometimes it works out well to act impulsively when our careful plans lose steam. This should show us that there's a God in heaven who's always guiding us in the right direction, however often we screw up—

HORATIO

Well, of course.

HAMLET

So I came up from my cabin with my robe tied around me, groped in the dark to find what I was looking for, found it, looked through their packet of papers, and returned to my cabin again. I was bold enough (I guess my fears made me forget my manners) to open the document containing the king's instructions. And there I found, Horatio, such royal mischief—a precisely worded order, sugared with lots of talk about Denmark's well-being and England's too, to cut off my head, without even waiting to sharpen the ax.

HORATIO

Is 't possible?

HAMLET

(shows HORATIO *a document)*
Here's the commission. Read it at more leisure.
But wilt thou hear me how I did proceed?

HORATIO

I beseech you.

HAMLET

30 Being thus benetted round with villainies—
Ere I could make a prologue to my brains,
They had begun the play—I sat me down,
Devised a new commission, wrote it fair.
I once did hold it, as our statists do,

35 A baseness to write fair, and labored much
How to forget that learning, but, sir, now
It did me yeoman's service. Wilt thou know
Th' effect of what I wrote?

HORATIO

Ay, good my lord.

HAMLET

40 An earnest conjuration from the king,
As England was his faithful tributary,
As love between them like the palm might flourish,
As peace should stiff her wheaten garland wear
And stand a comma 'tween their amities,

45 And many suchlike "as's" of great charge,
That, on the view and knowing of these contents,
Without debatement further, more or less,
He should the bearers put to sudden death,
Not shriving time allowed.

HORATIO

50 How was this sealed?

HORATIO

Is it possible?

HAMLET

(he shows HORATIO *a document)* Here's the document. Read it in your free time. But do you want to hear what I did then?

HORATIO

Yes, please tell me.

HAMLET

So there I was, caught in their evil net. Before I could even start processing the situation, they had started the ball rolling. I sat down and wrote out a new official document with new instructions. I wrote it in a bureaucrat's neat handwriting. I used to think having nice handwriting was for servants, just like our politicians think, and I had to work hard to overcome that prejudice—but it sure came in handy then. Do you want to know what I wrote?

HORATIO

Yes, my lord.

HAMLET

A sincere plea from the king, who commands the respect of England, and who hopes that the love between the two countries can flourish, and that peace can join them in friendship—and other fancy mumbo jumbo like that—saying that, once they read this document, without any debate, the ones delivering the letter should be put to death immediately, without giving them time to confess to a priest.

HORATIO

But how could you put an official seal on it?

HAMLET

Why, even in that was heaven ordinant.
I had my father's signet in my purse,
Which was the model of that Danish seal.
Folded the writ up in form of th' other,
Subscribed it, gave 't th' impression, placed it safely,
55 The changeling never known. Now, the next day
Was our sea fight, and what to this was sequent
Thou know'st already.

HORATIO

So Guildenstern and Rosencrantz go to 't.

HAMLET

60 Why, man, they did make love to this employment.
They are not near my conscience. Their defeat
Does by their own insinuation grow.
'Tis dangerous when the baser nature comes
Between the pass and fell incensèd points
65 Of mighty opposites.

HORATIO

Why, what a king is this!

HAMLET

Does it not, think thee, stand me now upon—
He that hath killed my king and whored my mother,
Popped in between th' election and my hopes,
70 Thrown out his angle for my proper life
(And with such cozenage!)—is 't not perfect conscience
To quit him with this arm? And is 't not to be damned
To let this canker of our nature come
In further evil?

HORATIO

75 It must be shortly known to him from England
What is the issue of the business there.

HAMLET

Heaven helped me out with that too. I had my father's
signet ring in my pocket, with the royal seal of Denmark on it. I folded up the new document, signed it,
sealed it, and put it safely back so that no one noticed
any difference. The next day we had our fight at sea,
and you know what happened after that.

HORATIO

So Rosencrantz and Guildenstern are in for it.

HAMLET

Man, they were asking for it. I don't feel guilty about
them at all. They got what they deserved. It's always
dangerous when little people get caught in the cross-
fire of mighty opponents.

HORATIO

What a king Claudius is!

HAMLET

Don't you think it's my duty now to kill him with this
weapon? This man who killed my king, made my
mother a whore, took the throne that I hoped for, and
set a trap to kill me. Isn't it completely moral to kill
him now with this sword—and an easy conscience?
And wouldn't I be damned if I let this monster live to
do more harm?

HORATIO

He'll find out soon what happened in England.

HAMLET
> It will be short. The interim's mine.
> And a man's life's no more than to say "one."
> But I am very sorry, good Horatio,
> That to Laertes I forgot myself,
> For by the image of my cause I see
> The portraiture of his. I'll court his favors.
> But sure the bravery of his grief did put me
> Into a towering passion.

HORATIO
> Peace.—Who comes here?

Enter young OSRIC, *a courtier, hat in hand*

OSRIC
> Your lordship is right welcome back to Denmark.

HAMLET
> I humbly thank you, sir. *(aside to* HORATIO*)* Dost know this water-fly?

HORATIO
> *(aside to* HAMLET*)* No, my good lord.

HAMLET
> *(aside to* HORATIO*)* Thy state is the more gracious, for 'tis a vice to know him. He hath much land, and fertile. Let a beast be lord of beasts and his crib shall stand at the king's mess. 'Tis a chough, but, as I say, spacious in the possession of dirt.

OSRIC
> Sweet lord, if your lordship were at leisure, I should impart a thing to you from His Majesty.

HAMLET
> I will receive it, sir, with all diligence of spirit. Put your bonnet to his right use. 'Tis for the head.

OSRIC
> I thank your lordship. It is very hot.

HAMLET

Soon enough. But I have the meantime. A human life is hardly long enough to count to one in. But I really feel bad, Horatio, about losing control of myself with Laertes. His situation is very much like my own. I'll be nice to him. It was just that the showiness of his grief sent me into a fury.

HORATIO

Hang on a minute—who are you?

OSRIC, *a young courtier, enters with his hat in his hand.*

OSRIC

Welcome back to Denmark, my lord.

HAMLET

Thank you kindly, sir. *(speaking so that only* HORATIO *can hear)* Do you know this insect?

HORATIO

(speaking so that only HAMLET *can hear)* No, my lord.

HAMLET

(speaking so that only HORATIO *can hear)* You're lucky, since knowing him is most unpleasant. He owns a lot of good land. Give an animal a lot of money, and he'll be welcome at the king's table. He's a jerk, but he owns a whole lot of dirt, so he's treated well.

OSRIC

My lord, if you have a free moment, I have a message from His Majesty.

HAMLET

I'll hang on every word you say. Put your hat back on, where it belongs: it's for your head, not for your hands to hold.

OSRIC

No thank you, my lord. It's very hot.

HAMLET

100   No, believe me, 'tis very cold. The wind is northerly.

OSRIC

It is indifferent cold, my lord, indeed.

HAMLET

But yet methinks it is very sultry and hot for my complexion.

OSRIC

Exceedingly, my lord. It is very sultry—as 'twere—I cannot
105   tell how. My lord, his majesty bade me signify to you that
he has laid a great wager on your head. Sir, this is the
matter—

HAMLET

I beseech you, remember—*(indicates that* OSRIC *should put
on his hat)*

OSRIC

Nay, good my lord, for mine ease, in good faith. Sir, here is
110   newly come to court Laertes, believe me, an absolute
gentleman, full of most excellent differences, of very soft
society and great showing. Indeed, to speak feelingly of
him, he is the card or calendar of gentry, for you shall find
in him the continent of what part a gentleman would see.

HAMLET

115   Sir, his definement suffers no perdition in you, though I
know to divide him inventorially would dizzy th'
arithmetic of memory, and yet but yaw neither, in respect of
his quick sail.

HAMLET

No, I'm telling you, it's very cold, with a northerly wind.

OSRIC

It is rather cold, indeed, my lord.

HAMLET

And yet I feel it's very hot and humid, which is bad for my complexion.

OSRIC

Yes indeed it is, sir. Very humid, I can't tell you how humid it is. My lord, His Majesty wanted me to tell you that he's placed a large bet on you. This is what it's all about—

HAMLET

Please, I beg you—*(he points to* OSRIC*'s hat)*

OSRIC

Osric's language is vague and blustery, and Hamlet's is too when he mimics Osric. Together they sometimes make almost no sense.

No, my lord, I'm comfortable like this, thank you. Sir, there's someone named Laertes who's recently come to the court. He's an absolute gentleman, totally outstanding in so many respects, very easy in society, and displaying all his excellent qualities. If I were to expose my true feelings about him, I'd have to say he's like a business card for the upper classes—he's that wonderful. You'll find that he's the sum total of what a perfect gentleman should be.

HAMLET

Sir, your description of him doesn't detract from his good qualities, though I know that trying to list them all would make your head spin, and even so you wouldn't be able to keep up with him.

But in the verity of extolment, I take him to be a soul of great
120   article, and his infusion of such dearth and rareness as, to
make true diction of him, his semblable is his mirror. And
who else would trace him? His umbrage, nothing more.

OSRIC
Your lordship speaks most infallibly of him.

HAMLET
The concernancy, sir? Why do we wrap the gentleman in
125   our more rawer breath?

OSRIC
Sir?

HORATIO
(aside to HAMLET*)* Is 't not possible to understand in another
tongue? You will do 't, sir, really.

HAMLET
What imports the nomination of this gentleman?

OSRIC
130   Of Laertes?

HORATIO
(aside to HAMLET*)* His purse is empty already. All 's golden
words are spent.

HAMLET
Of him, sir.

OSRIC
I know you are not ignorant—

HAMLET
135   I would you did, sir. Yet in faith, if you did, it would not
much approve me. Well, sir?

OSRIC
You are not ignorant of what excellence Laertes is—

Speaking the very truth of high praise, I can honestly say that I find him to possess a soul of such great importance, and so rare and unique in every respect, that—to speak the absolute truth—he can find an equal only when he gazes into a mirror. Anyone else is just a pale copy of him.

OSRIC

You speak absolutely correctly, sir.

HAMLET

And what's the point, sir? Why are we talking about him like this?

OSRIC

Sorry, sir?

HORATIO

(speaking so that only HAMLET can hear) Can't you talk to him in a different way?

HAMLET

(to OSRIC) What is the significance of referring to this individual?

OSRIC

Laertes, you mean?

HORATIO

(speaking so that only HAMLET can hear) All his fancy language has run out finally; his pockets are empty.

HAMLET

Yes, Laertes, sir.

OSRIC

I know you know something—

HAMLET

Thanks for the compliment, I'm happy you know that. But in fact it doesn't say much. I'm sorry, you were saying?

OSRIC

I know you know something about how excellent Laertes is—

HAMLET
> I dare not confess that lest I should compare with him in excellence, but to know a man well were to know himself.

OSRIC
140 > I mean, sir, for his weapon. But in the imputation laid on him by them, in his meed he's unfellowed.

HAMLET
> What's his weapon?

OSRIC
> Rapier and dagger.

HAMLET
> That's two of his weapons. But well.

OSRIC
145 > The king, sir, hath wagered with him six Barbary horses, against the which he has impawned, as I take it, six French rapiers and poniards with their assigns—as girdle, hangers, and so. Three of the carriages, in faith, are very dear to fancy, very responsive to the hilts, most delicate carriages,
150 > and of very liberal conceit.

HAMLET
> What call you the carriages?

HORATIO
> (aside to **HAMLET**) I knew you must be edified by the margin ere you had done.

OSRIC
> The carriages, sir, are the hangers.

HAMLET
155 > The phrase would be more germane to the matter if we could carry cannon by our sides. I would it might be hangers till then. But, on: six Barbary horses against six French swords, their assigns, and three liberal-conceited carriages—that's the French bet against the Danish. Why is
160 > this "impawned," as you call it?

HAMLET

I can't admit that, since you'd have to compare his excellence to mine. But knowing a person well is a bit like knowing oneself.

OSRIC

Excellent in fencing, I mean, sir. His reputation in fencing is unrivaled.

HAMLET

What kind of weapon does he use?

OSRIC

The rapier and the dagger.

HAMLET

Those are only two of his weapons. But, go on.

OSRIC

The king has bet six Barbary horses, and he has prepared six French rapiers and daggers with all their accessories. Three of the carriages are very imaginatively designed, and they match the fencing accessories.

HAMLET

What do you mean by "carriages"?

HORATIO

(speaking so that only HAMLET can hear) I knew you'd have to look something up in the dictionary before we were finished.

OSRIC

The carriages, sir, are the hangers—where the swords hang.

HAMLET

"Carriage" makes it sound like it's pulling around a cannon. I prefer to call it a "hanger." But anyway. Six Barbary horses, six French swords with accessories, and three imaginatively designed carriages—sounds like a French bet against the Danish. Why has all this been put on the table?

OSRIC
>The king, sir, hath laid that in a dozen passes between yourself and him, he shall not exceed you three hits. He hath laid on twelve for nine, and it would come to immediate trial if your lordship would vouchsafe the answer.

HAMLET
165
>How if I answer "No"?

OSRIC
>I mean, my lord, the opposition of your person in trial.

HAMLET
>Sir, I will walk here in the hall. If it please His Majesty, 'tis the breathing time of day with me. Let the foils be brought, the gentleman willing, and the king hold his purpose. I will
170
>win for him an I can. If not, I will gain nothing but my shame and the odd hits.

OSRIC
>Shall I redeliver you e'en so?

HAMLET
>To this effect, sir, after what flourish your nature will.

OSRIC
>I commend my duty to your lordship.

HAMLET
175
>Yours, yours.

Exit OSRIC

>He does well to commend it himself. There are no tongues else for 's turn.

HORATIO
>This lapwing runs away with the shell on his head.

HAMLET
>He did comply, sir, with his dug before he sucked it. Thus has
180
>he—and many more of the same bevy that I know the drossy age dotes on—only got the tune of the time and outward habit of encounter, a kind of yeasty collection, which carries them through and through the most fond and winnowed opinions; and do but blow them to their trial, the bubbles are out.

OSRIC

The king, sir, has bet that in a dozen rounds between you and Laertes, he won't beat you by more than three hits. You could get started immediately if you'll give me your answer.

HAMLET

But what if my answer's no?

OSRIC

I mean, if you'd agree to play against Laertes, sir.

HAMLET

Sir, I'm going to go for a walk in the hall here whether the king likes it or not. It's my exercise time. Bring in the swords, if the king still wants to go through with it and if Laertes is still willing. I'll have the king win his bet if I can. If not, I'll only have suffered some embarrassment and a few sword hits.

OSRIC

Shall I quote you in those exact words, sir?

HAMLET

Just get the point across, however flowery you want to be.

OSRIC

My services are at your command.

HAMLET

Thank you.

OSRIC exits.

It's a good thing he's here to recommend himself. No one else would.

HORATIO

That crazy bird's only half-hatched.

HAMLET

He used to praise his mother's nipple before he sucked it. He's like so many successful people in these trashy times—he's patched together enough fancy phrases and trendy opinions to carry him along. But blow a little on this bubbly talk, and it'll burst. There's no substance here.

Enter a LORD

LORD
185 My lord, his majesty commended him to you by young
Osric, who brings back to him that you attend him in the
hall. He sends to know if your pleasure hold to play with
Laertes, or that you will take longer time.

HAMLET
I am constant to my purpose. They follow the king's
190 pleasure. If his fitness speaks, mine is ready, now or
whensoever, provided I be so able as now.

LORD
The king and queen and all are coming down.

HAMLET
In happy time.

LORD
The queen desires you to use some gentle entertainment to
195 Laertes before you fall to play.

Exit LORD

HAMLET
She well instructs me.

HORATIO
You will lose this wager, my lord.

HAMLET
I do not think so. Since he went into France, I have been in
continual practice. I shall win at the odds. But thou wouldst
200 not think how ill all's here about my heart. But it is no
matter.

HORATIO
Nay, good my lord—

A LORD *enters.*

LORD

My lord, Osric has told the king about your agreeing to the fencing match. The king wishes to know if you want to play against him right away, or wait awhile.

HAMLET

I'll do whatever the king wants. If he's ready now, so am I. Otherwise, I'll do it anytime, as long as I'm able.

LORD

The king and queen are coming down with everyone else.

HAMLET

Right on cue.

LORD

The queen wants you to chat with Laertes—politely—before you begin your match.

The LORD *exits.*

HAMLET

She's full of good advice.

HORATIO

You're going to lose this bet, my lord.

HAMLET

I don't think so. I've been practicing fencing constantly since he went off to France. With the handicap they've given me, I think I'll win. But I have a sinking feeling anyway. Oh well.

HORATIO

Wait, my lord—

HAMLET

> It is but foolery, but it is such a kind of gain-giving as would
> perhaps trouble a woman.

HORATIO

205
> If your mind dislike anything, obey it. I will forestall their
> repair hither and say you are not fit.

HAMLET

> Not a whit. We defy augury. There's a special providence in
> the fall of a sparrow. If it be now, 'tis not to come. If it be not
> to come, it will be now. If it be not now, yet it will come—
210
> the readiness is all. Since no man of aught he leaves knows,
> what is 't to leave betimes? Let be.

Enter King CLAUDIUS, *Queen* GERTRUDE, LAERTES, OSRIC,
*lords, and other attendants with trumpets, drums, foils, a
table, and flagons of wine*

CLAUDIUS

> Come, Hamlet, come, and take this hand from me. *(puts*
> LAERTES' *hand into* HAMLET'S*)*

HAMLET

> Give me your pardon, sir. I've done you wrong.
> But pardon 't, as you are a gentleman.
215
> This presence knows,
> And you must needs have heard, how I am punished
> With sore distraction. What I have done,
> That might your nature, honor, and exception
> Roughly awake, I here proclaim was madness.
220
> Was 't Hamlet wronged Laertes? Never Hamlet.
> If Hamlet from himself be ta'en away,
> And when he's not himself does wrong Laertes,
> Then Hamlet does it not. Hamlet denies it.
> Who does it, then? His madness. If 't be so,

HAMLET

I know I'm being foolish, but I have the kind of vague misgiving women often get.

HORATIO

If something is telling you not to play, listen to it. I'll say you're not feeling well.

HAMLET

You'll do no such thing. I thumb my nose at superstitions. God controls everything—even something as trivial as a sparrow's death. Everything will work out as it is destined. If something is supposed to happen now, it will. If it's supposed to happen later, it won't happen now. What's important is to be prepared. Since nobody knows anything about what he leaves behind, then what does it mean to leave early? Let it be.

CLAUDIUS *enters with* GERTRUDE, LAERTES, OSRIC, *lords, and other attendants with trumpets, drums, fencing swords, a table, and pitchers of wine.*

CLAUDIUS

Come shake hands with Laertes, Hamlet. (CLAUDIUS *places* LAERTES' *and* HAMLET'S *hands together*)

HAMLET

(to LAERTES*)* I beg your pardon, sir. I've done you wrong. Forgive me as a gentleman. Everyone here knows—and I'm sure you've heard—that I'm suffering from a serious mental illness. When I insulted you it was due to insanity. Was Hamlet the one who insulted Laertes? No, not Hamlet. If Hamlet is robbed of his own mind, and insults Laertes when he's not really himself, then Hamlet's not guilty of the offense. Who is guilty, then? Hamlet's mental illness is.

225 Hamlet is of the faction that is wronged.
His madness is poor Hamlet's enemy.
Sir, in this audience,
Let my disclaiming from a purposed evil
Free me so far in your most generous thoughts
230 That I have shot mine arrow o'er the house
And hurt my brother.

LAERTES
                              I am satisfied in nature,
Whose motive in this case should stir me most
To my revenge. But in my terms of honor
I stand aloof, and will no reconcilement
235 Till by some elder masters, of known honor,
I have a voice and precedent of peace
To keep my name ungored. But till that time
I do receive your offered love like love
And will not wrong it.

HAMLET
                              I embrace it freely,
240 And will this brother's wager frankly play.—
Give us the foils. Come on.

LAERTES
                              Come, one for me.

HAMLET
I'll be your foil, Laertes. In mine ignorance
Your skill shall, like a star i' th' darkest night,
Stick fiery off indeed.

LAERTES
245 You mock me, sir.

HAMLET
No, by this hand.

CLAUDIUS
Give them the foils, young Osric.—Cousin Hamlet,
You know the wager?

And if that's true, then Hamlet is the victim of his own illness—his illness is his enemy. Sir, with this audience as witness, let me declare that I'm as innocent of premeditated evil against you as I would be if I had happened to shoot an arrow over my house and accidentally hit my brother.

LAERTES

My feelings are satisfied—even though what you have done to my father and sister should drive me to revenge. Yet when it comes to my honor, I can't forgive you so fast. I will accept no apology until experts in matters of honor show me how to make peace with you without staining my own reputation in doing so. Until then I will accept your love as love.

HAMLET

I'm grateful for your love. Come on, give us the swords, and we will play this friendly fencing match enthusiastically.

LAERTES

Yes, hand me one too.

HAMLET

I'm going to make you look sharp, Laertes. I'm so bad at the game that your skill will shine like the brightest star in the darkest night.

LAERTES

You're making fun of me.

HAMLET

No, I swear I'm not.

CLAUDIUS

Give them the swords, Osric. Hamlet, you know the bet?

HAMLET

                    Very well, my lord.
Your grace hath laid the odds o' th' weaker side.

CLAUDIUS

250   I do not fear it. I have seen you both.
But since he is better we have therefore odds.

LAERTES

(tests a rapier) This is too heavy. Let me see another.

HAMLET

(tests a rapier) This likes me well. These foils have all a length?

OSRIC

Ay, my good lord.

HAMLET *and* **LAERTES** *prepare to play*

CLAUDIUS

255   Set me the stoups of wine upon that table.
If Hamlet give the first or second hit
Or quit in answer of the third exchange,
Let all the battlements their ordnance fire!
The king shall drink to Hamlet's better breath,
260   And in the cup an union shall he throw
Richer than that which four successive kings
In Denmark's crown have worn. Give me the cups.
And let the kettle to the trumpet speak,
The trumpet to the cannoneer without,
265   The cannons to the heavens, the heavens to earth,
"Now the king dunks to Hamlet." Come, begin.—
And you, the judges, bear a wary eye.

Trumpets

HAMLET

Come on, sir.

HAMLET

Yes, my lord, quite well. You've bet on the weaker fencer.

CLAUDIUS

I'm not worried. I've seen both of you fence. But since Laertes is better, we've given him a handicap. He's got to outdo you by three hits to win.

LAERTES

This sword's too heavy. Show me another one.

HAMLET

I like this one. Are they all the same length?

OSRIC

Yes, my lord.

HAMLET and LAERTES get ready to fence.

CLAUDIUS

Put the goblets of wine on that table. If Hamlet makes the first or second hit, or gets back at Laertes by making the third hit, then let my soldiers give him a military salute. I'll drink to Hamlet's health, and into his goblet I'll drop a pearl even more costly than those in the crowns of the last four Danish kings. Give me the goblets. And now let the drum and the trumpet play, and the trumpet signal the cannon outside to fire, and let the cannon tell the heavens, and the heavens tell all the earth that the king is drinking now to Hamlet's health. Come on, let's begin. Judges, pay close attention.

Trumpets play.

HAMLET

Come on, sir.

LAERTES
>Come, my lord.

>**HAMLET** *and* **LAERTES** *play*

HAMLET
270 >One.

LAERTES
>No.

HAMLET
>Judgment?

OSRIC
>A hit, a very palpable hit.

LAERTES
>Well, again.

CLAUDIUS
275 >Stay, give me drink.—Hamlet, this pearl is thine.
>Here's to thy health.

>*Drums, trumpets sound, shot goes off*
>**CLAUDIUS** *drops pearl into cup*

>Give him the cup.

HAMLET
>I'll play this bout first. Set it by a while.
>Come.

>**HAMLET** *and* **LAERTES** *play*

>Another hit. What say you?

LAERTES
280 >A touch, a touch, I do confess 't.

CLAUDIUS
>Our son shall win.

GERTRUDE
>He's fat, and scant of breath.—
>Here, Hamlet, take my napkin, rub thy brows.

LAERTES

Come on, my lord.

HAMLET and LAERTES fence.

HAMLET

That was one hit.

LAERTES

No, it wasn't.

HAMLET

Referee!

OSRIC

It was obviously a hit.

LAERTES

Well, let's go on.

CLAUDIUS

Give me a goblet.—Hamlet, this pearl's yours. Here's to your health.

Drums and trumpets play, and a gun is fired. CLAUDIUS drops a pearl into a cup.

Give him the goblet.

HAMLET

Let me just finish this round. Set it down awhile. Let's play.

HAMLET and LAERTES fence.

Another hit. What do you say?

LAERTES

You got me, I admit it.

CLAUDIUS

My son will win.

GERTRUDE

He's flabby and out of breath.—Here, Hamlet, take my handkerchief and wipe your forehead.

The queen carouses to thy fortune, Hamlet.
(picks up the cup with the pearl)

HAMLET
285 Good madam.

CLAUDIUS
                    Gertrude, do not drink.

GERTRUDE
I will, my lord. I pray you, pardon me. *(drinks)*

CLAUDIUS
(aside) It is the poisoned cup. It is too late.

HAMLET
I dare not drink yet, madam. By and by.

GERTRUDE
290 Come, let me wipe thy face.

LAERTES
(aside to CLAUDIUS*)* My lord, I'll hit him now.

CLAUDIUS
I do not think 't.

LAERTES
(aside) And yet it is almost 'gainst my conscience.

HAMLET
Come, for the third, Laertes. You do but dally.
300 I pray you, pass with your best violence.
I am afeard you make a wanton of me.

LAERTES
Say you so? Come on.

                    HAMLET *and* LAERTES *play*

OSRIC
                                        Nothing, neither way.

LAERTES
Have at you now!

                    LAERTES *wounds* HAMLET
                    In scuffling, they change rapiers. HAMLET *wounds* LAERTES

The queen drinks to your good luck and happiness, Hamlet. *(she lifts the cup with the pearl)*

HAMLET

Thank you, madam.

CLAUDIUS

Gertrude, don't drink that.

GERTRUDE

Excuse me. I'll drink it if I like. *(she drinks)*

CLAUDIUS

(to himself) That was the poisoned drink. It's too late.

HAMLET

I'd better not drink now. I'll drink later.

GERTRUDE

Come on, let me wipe your face.

LAERTES

(to CLAUDIUS*)* I'll get him now.

CLAUDIUS

I doubt it.

LAERTES

(to himself) But I almost feel guilty.

HAMLET

Get ready for the third hit, Laertes. You're just playing around. Come on, give me your best shot. I sense you're treating me like a child.

LAERTES

You think so? Come on.

HAMLET *and* LAERTES *fence.*

OSRIC

They're neck and neck.

LAERTES

Take this!

LAERTES *wounds* HAMLET. *Then in a scuffle they end up with each other's swords, and* HAMLET *wounds* LAERTES.

CLAUDIUS
Part them! They are incensed.

HAMLET
305   Nay, come, again.

GERTRUDE *falls*

OSRIC
Look to the queen there, ho!

HORATIO
They bleed on both sides.—How is it, my lord?

OSRIC
How is 't, Laertes?

LAERTES
Why, as a woodcock to mine own springe, Osric. I am justly
killed with mine own treachery. *(falls)*

HAMLET
310   How does the queen?

CLAUDIUS
She swoons to see them bleed.

GERTRUDE
No, no, the drink, the drink!—O my dear Hamlet!
The drink, the drink! I am poisoned. *(dies)*

HAMLET
O villainy! Ho, let the door be locked.

Exit OSRIC

Treachery! Seek it out.

LAERTES
315   It is here, Hamlet. Hamlet, thou art slain.
No medicine in the world can do thee good.
In thee there is not half an hour of life.
The treacherous instrument is in thy hand,
Unbated and envenomed. The foul practice
320   Hath turned itself on me. Lo, here I lie,
Never to rise again. Thy mother's poisoned.
I can no more. The king, the king's to blame.

CLAUDIUS

Separate them. They're overdoing it.

HAMLET

No, come on, one more time.

GERTRUDE *collapses.*

OSRIC

Take care of the queen!

HORATIO

Both fencers are bleeding—how do you feel, my lord?

OSRIC

How do you feel, Laertes?

LAERTES

Like a mouse caught in my own trap, Osric. *(he collapses)* I've been killed by my own evil tricks.

HAMLET

How's the queen?

CLAUDIUS

She fainted at the sight of them bleeding.

GERTRUDE

No, no, the drink, the drink! Oh, my dear Hamlet! The drink, the drink! I've been poisoned. *(she dies)*

HAMLET

Oh, what evil! Lock the door.

OSRIC *exits.*

We've been betrayed! Find out who did it!

LAERTES

I'm the one, Hamlet. Hamlet, you're dead. No medicine in the world can cure you. You don't have more than half an hour to live. The treacherous weapon is right in your hand, sharp and dipped in poison. The foul plan backfired on me. Here I lie and will never get up again. Your mother's been poisoned. I can't speak anymore. The king, the king's to blame.

HAMLET

The point envenomed too!—Then, venom, to thy work.

HAMLET *hurts* CLAUDIUS

ALL

Treason! Treason!

CLAUDIUS

325   O, yet defend me, friends. I am but hurt.

HAMLET

Here, thou incestuous, murderous, damnèd Dane,
Drink off this potion. Is thy union here?
Follow my mother.

HAMLET *forces* CLAUDIUS *to drink*
CLAUDIUS *dies*

LAERTES

He is justly served.
It is a poison tempered by himself.
330   Exchange forgiveness with me, noble Hamlet.
Mine and my father's death come not upon thee,
Nor thine on me. *(dies)*

HAMLET

Heaven make thee free of it. I follow thee.—
I am dead, Horatio.—Wretched queen, adieu!—
335   You that look pale and tremble at this chance,
That are but mutes or audience to this act,
Had I but time (as this fell sergeant, Death,
Is strict in his arrest), O, I could tell you—
But let it be.—Horatio, I am dead.
340   Thou livest. Report me and my cause aright
To the unsatisfied.

HORATIO

Never believe it.
I am more an antique Roman than a Dane.
Here's yet some liquor left.
(lifts the poisoned cup)

HAMLET

The blade poisoned! Then get to work, poison!

HAMLET *wounds* CLAUDIUS.

ALL

Treason! Treason!

CLAUDIUS

Protect me, my friends. I've only been hurt, not killed.

HAMLET

Here, you goddamn incest-breeding Danish murderer, drink this. Is your little pearl in there? Follow my mother.

HAMLET *forces* CLAUDIUS *to drink.* CLAUDIUS *dies.*

LAERTES

He got what he deserved. He mixed that poison himself. Please forgive me as I forgive you, Hamlet. You're not responsible for my death and my father's, and I'm not responsible for yours. *(he dies)*

HAMLET

God will free you from blame. I'll follow you to heaven in a minute.—I'm dying, Horatio.—Goodbye, miserable queen.—And all you people watching, pale and trembling, speechless spectators of these acts, I could tell you a thing or two if I had the time (though this cruel officer, Death, doesn't allow much free time). Let it be.—Horatio, I'm dying. You're alive. Tell everyone what happened; set the story straight.

HORATIO

Not for a second. I'm more like an ancient Roman than a corrupt modern Dane. Some of this liquor's still left in the goblet. *(he picks up the poisoned cup to drink)*

HAMLET

As thou'rt a man,
Give me the cup. Let go! By heaven, I'll have 't.
(takes cup from HORATIO*)*
O God, Horatio, what a wounded name,
Things standing thus unknown, shall live behind me!
If thou didst ever hold me in thy heart
Absent thee from felicity a while,
And in this harsh world draw thy breath in pain
To tell my story.

March afar off and shout within

What warlike noise is this?

Enter OSRIC

OSRIC

Young Fortinbras, with conquest come from Poland,
To th' ambassadors of England gives
This warlike volley.

HAMLET

O, I die, Horatio.
The potent poison quite o'ercrows my spirit.
I cannot live to hear the news from England.
But I do prophesy the election lights
On Fortinbras. He has my dying voice.
So tell him, with th' occurrents, more and less,
Which have solicited. The rest is silence.
O, O, O, O. *(dies)*

HORATIO

Now cracks a noble heart.—Good night, sweet prince,
And flights of angels sing thee to thy rest!—
Why does the drum come hither?

HAMLET

> Please, give me that goblet, if you love me. Let go of it! I'll get it from you, I swear. Oh God, Horatio, what a damaged reputation I'm leaving behind me, as no one knows the truth. If you ever loved me, then please postpone the sweet relief of death awhile, and stay in this harsh world long enough to tell my story.

> *A military march is heard from offstage, and a cannon fires.*

> What are these warlike noises?

> osric *enters.*

OSRIC

> Young Fortinbras, returning in triumph from Poland, is firing his guns to greet the English ambassadors.

HAMLET

> Oh, I'm dying, Horatio! This strong poison's over-powering me. I will not live to hear the news from England. But I bet Fortinbras will win the election to the Danish crown. He's got my vote as I die. So tell him that, given the recent events here—oh, the rest is silence. Oh, oh, oh, oh. *(he dies)*

HORATIO

> Now a noble heart is breaking. Good night, sweet prince. May hosts of angels sing you to sleep.—Why are those drums approaching?

Enter FORTINBRAS *and the English* AMBASSADOR,
with drummer and attendants

FORTINBRAS

365   Where is this sight?

HORATIO

What is it ye would see?
If aught of woe or wonder, cease your search.

FORTINBRAS

This quarry cries on havoc. O proud death,
What feast is toward in thine eternal cell,
370   That thou so many princes at a shot
So bloodily hast struck?

AMBASSADOR

The sight is dismal,
And our affairs from England come too late.
The ears are senseless that should give us hearing,
To tell him his commandment is fulfilled,
375   That Rosencrantz and Guildenstern are dead.
Where should we have our thanks?

HORATIO

(indicates CLAUDIUS*)*   Not from his mouth,
Had it th' ability of life to thank you.
He never gave commandment for their death.
But since so jump upon this bloody question,
380   You from the Polack wars, and you from England,
Are here arrived, give order that these bodies
High on a stage be placèd to the view,
And let me speak to th' yet-unknowing world
How these things came about. So shall you hear
385   Of carnal, bloody, and unnatural acts,
Of accidental judgments, casual slaughters,
Of deaths put on by cunning and forced cause,
And, in this upshot, purposes mistook
Fall'n on th' inventors' heads. All this can I
390   Truly deliver.

FORTINBRAS *and the English* AMBASSADOR
enter with a drummer and attendants.

FORTINBRAS

What do I see here?

HORATIO

What would you like to see? If it's a tragedy, you've come to the right place.

FORTINBRAS

These corpses suggest mayhem. Oh, proud Death, what banquet are you preparing that you've needed to knock off so many princes at one stroke?

AMBASSADOR

This is a horrible sight. Our news arrives from England too late, since the people that should have heard it are dead. We meant to tell the king that his orders have been carried out, and Rosencrantz and Guildenstern are dead. Who will thank us now?

HORATIO

(indicates CLAUDIUS*)* Not the king, even if he were still alive to thank you. He never ordered their deaths. But since you've come so soon after this bloodbath, you from battles in Poland and you from England, then give your men orders to display these corpses on a high platform, and let me tell the world how all this happened. You'll hear of violent and unnatural acts, terrible accidents, casual murders, deaths caused by trickery and by threat, and finally murderous plans that backfired on their perpetrators. All this I can explain.

FORTINBRAS

                Let us haste to hear it,
And call the noblest to the audience.
For me, with sorrow I embrace my fortune.
I have some rights of memory in this kingdom,
Which now to claim my vantage doth invite me.

HORATIO

395   Of that I shall have also cause to speak,
And from his mouth whose voice will draw on more.
But let this same be presently performed,
Even while men's minds are wild, lest more mischance
On plots and errors happen.

FORTINBRAS

400   Let four captains
Bear Hamlet like a soldier to the stage,
For he was likely, had he been put on,
To have proved most royally. And, for his passage,
The soldiers' music and the rites of war
405   Speak loudly for him.
Take up the bodies. Such a sight as this
Becomes the field, but here shows much amiss.
Go, bid the soldiers shoot.

Exeunt marching, carrying the bodies,
after the which a peal of ordnance are shot off

FORTINBRAS

> Let's hear about it right away and invite all the noblemen to listen. As for me, I welcome my good luck with sadness. I have some rights to claim this kingdom, and by arriving at this moment I have an opportunity to put them into effect.

HORATIO

> I also have a few things to say about that, which Hamlet just told me. But let's get down to business—even though people are in a frenzy of grief—to avoid any further plots and mishaps.

FORTINBRAS

> Let four captains carry Hamlet like a soldier onto the stage. He would have been a great king if he had had the chance to prove himself. Military music and military rites will speak for his heroic qualities. Pick up the corpses. A sight like this suits a battlefield, but here at court it shows that much went wrong. Go outside and tell the soldiers to fire their guns in honor of Hamlet.

> *They exit marching, carrying the bodies. Cannons are fired.*

Notes

Notes

SPARKNOTES LITERATURE GUIDES

1984
The Adventures of Huckleberry Finn
The Adventures of Tom Sawyer
The Aeneid
All Quiet on the Western Front
And Then There Were None
Angela's Ashes
Animal Farm
Anna Karenina
Anne of Green Gables
Anthem
Antony and Cleopatra
Aristotle's Ethics
As I Lay Dying
As You Like It
Atlas Shrugged
The Autobiography of Malcolm X
The Awakening
The Bean Trees
The Bell Jar
Beloved
Beowulf
Billy Budd
Black Boy
Bless Me, Ultima
The Bluest Eye
Brave New World
The Brothers Karamazov
The Call of the Wild
Candide
The Canterbury Tales
Catch-22
The Catcher in the Rye
The Chocolate War
The Chosen
Cold Mountain
Cold Sassy Tree
The Color Purple
The Count of Monte Cristo
Crime and Punishment
The Crucible
Cry, the Beloved Country
Cyrano de Bergerac

David Copperfield
Death of a Salesman
The Death of Socrates
The Diary of a Young Girl
A Doll's House
Don Quixote
Dr. Faustus
Dr. Jekyll and Mr. Hyde
Dracula
Dune
Edith Hamilton's Mythology
Emma
Ethan Frome
Fahrenheit 451
Fallen Angels
A Farewell to Arms
Farewell to Manzanar
Flowers for Algernon
For Whom the Bell Tolls
The Fountainhead
Frankenstein
The Giver
The Glass Menagerie
Gone With the Wind
The Good Earth
The Grapes of Wrath
Great Expectations
The Great Gatsby
Grendel
Gulliver's Travels
Hamlet
The Handmaid's Tale
Hard Times
Harry Potter and the Sorcerer's Stone
Heart of Darkness
Henry IV, Part I
Henry V
Hiroshima
The Hobbit
The House of Seven Gables
I Know Why the Caged Bird Sings
The Iliad
Inferno
Inherit the Wind
Invisible Man

Jane Eyre
Johnny Tremain
The Joy Luck Club
Julius Caesar
The Jungle
The Killer Angels
King Lear
The Last of the Mohicans
Les Miserables
A Lesson Before Dying
The Little Prince
Little Women
Lord of the Flies
The Lord of the Rings
Macbeth
Madame Bovary
A Man for All Seasons
The Mayor of Casterbridge
The Merchant of Venice
A Midsummer Night's Dream
Moby Dick
Much Ado About Nothing
My Antonia
Narrative of the Life of Frederick Douglass
Native Son
The New Testament
Night
Notes from Underground
The Odyssey
The Oedipus Plays
Of Mice and Men
The Old Man and the Sea
The Old Testament
Oliver Twist
The Once and Future King
One Day in the Life of Ivan Denisovich
One Flew Over the Cuckoo's Nest
One Hundred Years of Solitude
Othello
Our Town
The Outsiders
Paradise Lost

A Passage to India
The Pearl
The Picture of Dorian Gray
Poe's Short Stories
A Portrait of the Artist as a Young Man
Pride and Prejudice
The Prince
A Raisin in the Sun
The Red Badge of Courage
The Republic
Richard III
Robinson Crusoe
Romeo and Juliet
The Scarlet Letter
A Separate Peace
Silas Marner
Sir Gawain and the Green Knight
Slaughterhouse-Five
Snow Falling on Cedars
Song of Solomon
The Sound and the Fury
Steppenwolf
The Stranger
Streetcar Named Desire
The Sun Also Rises
A Tale of Two Cities
The Taming of the Shrew
The Tempest
Tess of the d'Ubervilles
The Things They Carried
Their Eyes Were Watching God
Things Fall Apart
To Kill a Mockingbird
To the Lighthouse
Treasure Island
Twelfth Night
Ulysses
Uncle Tom's Cabin
Walden
War and Peace
Wuthering Heights
A Yellow Raft in Blue Water